A wall ...... ......ting tracers illuminated like a deadly fireworks display directly in front of us. . . .

"Yeah, there's a lot of AAA up there," I said, trying not to let my voice crack.

My God, I thought, it looks solid, impenetrable, as if every gun were lined up abreast and firing continuously. How the hell were we going to get through it? I felt doubt, serious doubt, and for the first time real fear, not the fear that I would fuck it up, but the fear that I would die.

"Can't turn around, 13 miles. Twelve miles, a lot of fucking AAA everywhere."

Rivers didn't respond to my halfhearted request for reassurance—he was doing his job with his head in the boot, searching for the target, trusting I would keep him alive. I pushed the nose over violently, jammed the throttles to the stops, and let the radar altimeter warning deedle for a second as we raced past 400 feet. . . . Now in the thick of it I could see that there was a certain depth to it; it was not a solid wall, but layers upon layers of indiyid・・l ......ons. I snapped the wings from left to 3- to 4-G turns to avoid the growing hail of bullets. . . .

# ANGLES OF ATTACK

## An A-6 Intruder Pilot's War

**Peter Hunt**

BALLANTINE BOOKS • NEW YORK

A Ballantine Book
Published by The Ballantine Publishing Group
Copyright © 2002 by Peter Hunt

All rights reserved under International and Pan-American Copyright Conventions. Published in the United States by The Ballantine Publishing Group, a division of Random House, Inc., New York, and simultaneously in Canada by Random House of Canada Limited, Toronto.

Ballantine and colophon are registered trademarks of Random House, Inc.

www.ballantinebooks.com

ISBN 0-345-45114-7

Manufactured in the United States of America

First Edition: September 2002

OPM  10  9  8  7  6  5  4  3  2  1

Angle of attack: Measures the angle between the longitudinal axis of the aircraft and the relative wind.

*—The A-6 Naval Air Training and Operating Procedures Standardization (NATOPS) Manual*

The mission of the aircraft carrier is to put ordnance on target. Everything else is support for the Attack mission. . . . You win war by killing the bastards by the thousands, not one at a time at twenty thousand feet. . . . Finally, Attack aviators understand the most fundamental law of wartime negotiations: you negotiate with the enemy with your knee in his chest and your knife in his throat.

—From *The Mission—Attack*; author unknown

# Contents

# Contents

# Acknowledgments

Many people encouraged me in writing this book. I would like to give special thanks to my parents, Bruce and Marcia, and siblings, Sarah, Eliza, and Chris, for their help and support. The suggestions of two of my friends, Quiver and Snax, also were invaluable in improving the first draft.

Mac Talley (who obtained the manuscript with the help of Lisa Senz) took an initial interest in the book and put me in touch with my agent, Sam Fleishman. Thank you, Lisa and Mac.

Sam Fleishman offered a wealth of detailed, pertinent, and sage advice. His comprehensive vision and diplomatic manner steered the reorganization of the manuscript in a more cogent direction. Sam, you made the book far better; thank you.

Finally, two people were indispensable to my seeing this through. Rivers, the last of the great B/Ns, thanks for sitting next to me and keeping me alive. Laurie, my wonderful wife, thanks for your patience and for putting up with all that I do.

Written for Emily and Jared.

# Introduction

This is a true story. I have used my daily journal, notes, strike debriefs, logbooks, videos, mission recordings, letters, and photographs to provide accurate detail, and to portray my feelings and sentiments as they were when the events described occurred. Not all of the circumstances as I understood them at the time, however, were complete or factual. Instead of rewriting what I was thinking during *Ranger*'s 1990–1991 cruise, I have included footnotes to highlight the inaccuracies from the comfort of hindsight and history. I also have added explanatory notes to better fill in the details of events that I was not necessarily privy to at the time of the Gulf War.

The sources used other than my own varied from *Jane's*, to newspapers and magazines, to the Internet. I would like to credit three books that were used for researching the majority of the region's general history: *Babylonia & Assyria* (H.W.F. Saggs), *Guardians of the Gulf* (Michael A. Palmer), and *Desert Victory* (Norman Friedman).

The timing of several minor circumstances and brief portions of re-created dialogue have been altered slightly to provide a smoother flow. Only those personally involved would ever know the difference (assuming their memory served them this well).

Finally, I am not attempting to speak for anyone but myself when I express opinions; I don't doubt that there are naval aviators who might take issue with some of my observations and conclusions.

# Chapter One

# And the rockets' red glare . . .

The Persian Gulf, 0150 Hours, 17 January 1991

The ready room went stone silent as the ship's 1MC public address system became audible, and Captain Ernest E. Christensen Jr., the commanding officer of USS *Ranger*, began to speak:

> *In August last year Iraq invaded and dismantled a country, Kuwait. That country has virtually ceased to exist. Iraq's armed forces occupy Kuwait—approximately 530,000 men in 41 divisions. They man the KTO.*
>
> *In October, the United Nations resolved that if Iraq did not withdraw from Kuwait by 15 January force would be authorized. The time for Iraq to withdraw has passed. United Nations coalition forces are now authorized to use force. On 16 January the National Command Authority declared DEFCON Two.*
>
> *A few minutes ago I was informed by our operational commander, Rear Admiral Zlatoper, that the president has ordered the U.S. Central Command to engage Iraq in hostilities.*
>
> *Few Americans are as privileged to stand up and be counted. . . . We have been given the honor of representing our country in combat. We are here in this moment in history.*

1

*We volunteered for this duty. We are trained for this day. We are ready for this day.*

Ranger *will launch . . . Air Wing Two will strike . . . targets within Iraq this morning. We shall make our presence felt. This ship . . . this air wing . . . these staffs . . . will make in history a measurable difference on this day, and on the days to follow.*

*The wing will fly tonight and tomorrow and in the days that follow. . . .*

*From those of us who cannot go . . . we wish you good luck. For those of us who steam, fuel, feed, arm, and launch the aircraft on this ship . . . we are greatly counted upon, for what we do here in the near future will guarantee what this nation does in the far future.*

*To the air wing . . . Godspeed, good hunting . . . keep your powder dry and your knots up.*

*For the rest of us . . . let's go get 'em!*[1]

The aviator-filled room projected an aura of unease at the solemn tone and content of Captain Christensen's speech. This was definitely not the routine rendition of the ship's progress through cruise that the flight crews were used to digesting. The Attack Squadron 155 (call sign "Jakals") commanding officer continued with his strike briefing to the packed ready room, standing room only as those not actually involved in the strike filled in the back to listen to the plan. Sixty minutes had passed since we had first sat down, and the Jakal CO was reaching the end point of his brief.

"Last words, let's make sure that our flight suits are sanitized." He tore the Velcro-backed name tag with "CO" written on it off of his flight suit, the last step in ensuring a minimum of information to any potential Iraqi captors. The sound of tearing Velcro reverberated throughout the ready room.

---

1. Thanks to *Ranger*'s 1991 cruisebook for jogging my memory of the exact wording of the speech Captain Christensen gave to the ship on 17 January.

The brief had been quick and concise—virtually everyone flying the mission had been intimately involved in the planning and had flown the practice strike three days earlier. The briefing was more of a final review and update for any late-changing information. The individual mission components of bombers, fighters, radar jammers, high-speed antiradiation missile (HARM) shooters, and tankers broke off into separate groups to discuss their plans in greater detail. The room emptied until only the six Intruder bomber crews remained, and even this final face-to-face went exceedingly quickly. We all knew what to do; there was simply nothing left but to get on with it.

Rivers and I made the long walk forward to our ready room in silence, absorbing the strange stares of the sailors in the passageway. They knew that we were preparing for a flight quite different from what *Ranger* had grown accustomed to launching. I opened the bright green door, barely glancing at the finely painted logo—"VA-145 Swordsmen"—and walked directly toward the schedule board behind the squadron duty officer's desk. Next to our names was the side number of our Intruder for the mission, 502, with the ordnance load out in bright red. All five of the A-6's bomb stations were filled—two with six rockeye cluster bombs apiece, one with a HARM missile, and one with an ALQ-126 jamming pod to confuse the SA-6 surface-to-air missile (SAM) radar. The SA-6 was a particularly lethal SAM. The last station held a center drop tank to carry an additional 2,700 pounds of fuel. No surprises here. Rivers and I wrote down the appropriate weights for 502 and her load for the catapult shot, gave it to the duty officer, and sat down for a final redundant review of the briefing checklist. It took all of five minutes.

"Had enough, Rivs?" I had. The standing around was too much.

"Let's get geared up; I'd rather wait on deck." I followed Rivers down the passage to the pararigger shop, where we joined our fellow Swordsmen crews.

Nobody said a word as they suited up. The parariggers stood by, ready to assist in any way they could, mildly out of place not wearing flight gear, with a look of concern in their eyes. The TV was tuned to CNN, with the volume turned all the way down. It was absolutely quiet while the aviators got dressed. Outside in the passageway, I could barely discern that the ship's 1MC loudspeaker was alive; Admiral Zlatoper was speaking, but none of us could make out the words. Snax walked into the room with his camera hanging around his neck.

"Snax, did you catch that on the 1MC?" I figured that whatever the battle group admiral had to say, it was probably more important than calling away "sweepers" for the ship's nightly cleaning.

"The battle group launched Tomahawks a couple of hours ago. We're officially attacking Iraq."

Oh, shit. It seemed less likely by the second that our mission would be scrubbed in a last-minute peace deal. I just nodded my head, uncharacteristically at a loss for a smart-ass retort.

The audience, half clad in their bulky flight gear, cumulatively switched their attention back to the TV, where the backdrop was Baghdad. Everyone in the room froze. Snax reached to turn up the volume, and the reporter's voice became audible.

"There are explosions in Baghdad; I repeat, there are explosions in Baghdad. Hostilities have commenced." We had known about it for the past ten seconds. CNN finally scooped by the navy.

The noise of the TV blended into the background clutter, and the four Attack Squadron 145 Swordsmen crews completed their silent routine of dressing and getting psyched up for the hop. Rivers and I were in the fourth bomber slated to cross the beach; Fang and Beef were in the fifth. Our sister A-6 squadron, radio call sign "Jakals," preceded us in the one-through-three positions. Both of the dedicated HARM missile shooter A-6s were Swordsmen. Each carried a load out of four of the radar homing missiles. The pararigger shop emptied slowly, each pair of aviators maintaining crew integrity and not straying off, sticking together as if they were already strapped next to one another in their red-lit cockpits. It was human nature to grasp out for the known and familiar, the close proximity of a comrade, and the snug fit of the flight gear.

The feelings of patriotism and political calculation that had been steadily growing for the past weeks were thrust to the back of my consciousness, all considerations pushed aside except for those necessary to get bombs on target. Rivers and I filed out last, deliberate in our movements and slow in their execution. We were striving to reach that meditative state of self-assurance where you were untouchable, completely in control of your emotions, utterly in command of your faculties. You were the person in charge, you were taking the action that others would have to react to. Nobody could hurt you; they might kill you, but they could not hurt you because you would not allow yourself to be bothered with the hurt. It was all part of the preparation process, building a frame of mind conducive to action and the exclusion of second-guessing and hesitation. The time for that was past, the plan was made, the groundwork complete, for better or worse it was all real time and operational from here on out. Time to go to work.

We took one last swing through the ready room to check out our pistols. Rivers picked up one of the squadron 45s, and I took my personal 9mm from home out of the safe. I holstered the handgun, and opened the large front pocket in my SV-2 survival vest to make room for two extra ammunition clips. I pushed the shot kits with their anti–nerve agent atropine and accelerator slightly to the side, and squeezed the bullet magazines next to my folded "blood chit." The blood chit was a survival parchment that explained in Arabic and Farsi who I was if I was found after an ejection and how a

reward would be given to anyone who would assist in my evasion. This represented a real act of desperation if it came
down to the blood chit saving our asses, but you never knew.
Rivers and I took the long walk across the ready room with a
great attempt at nonchalance, doing our best not to look
around but to maintain our focus on the next few hours. A few
"good lucks" were shouted out, but the serious tones and lack
of true spontaneity belied any comfort they might provide.
The ready room door hit me in the ass on the way out.

Rivers and I faced each other on the moving escalator as
we were carried up the three levels, each of us at a compete
loss for anything to say. Rivers had a big, dumb grin on his
face, and who knows what idiotic expression I had on mine.
The closer we got to our jet the easier it became; as with everything on the ship, the waiting was the worst. What we needed
to do was strap in and get going. We reached the top of the
escalator, and the lights turned to night-vision-adapting red
for the short walk to the hatch that led out onto the catwalk
adjacent to catapult one. We stopped to put on our skullcaps
and helmets, screwed the red lenses onto our flashlights, and
stepped outside.

The salt spray in the air mixed naturally with the odor of jet
fuel and the exhaust from the yellow gear tow tractors. I
pressed the button on my flashlight and trained the red beam
on the tails of the A-6s lined up on the catapult until I found
the number 502; we struck out for it. The ordnancemen were
just finishing up when we reached the boarding ladders. A
group of six "ordies" were on the port side of the jet, wres-
tling with the "hernia" bar attached to a 500-pound rockeye.
They manhandled the cluster weapon into position on the multiple ejector rack where the other five bombs were already secured. A second contingent was hoisting the 900-pound HARM
onto station four with a motorized winch that sounded like a
chain saw in the stiff breeze. More waiting. I put my flight
boot on the boarding ladder and stretched my calf out, working the knots out of my legs, as if the coach were about to put

me in the big game. The ordies finished their work and hurried off en masse to their next assignment. I looked up at the stars in the clear, dark sky and climbed up the ladder.

Good. Dark meant it would be difficult to see our Intruder from the ground. Clear meant that we would be able to see the tracers and missiles that would be fired up at us. Clear also indicated that the forward-looking infrared TV should be a player in the target acquisition game. The forward-looking infrared (flir) sensed contrasts in relative heat to produce a black-and-white image. The flir could not look through fog. I strapped in and pressed the light button on my watch: 0345, there was still 36 minutes until our turn at the cat; it would be a while before it was time to start engines. Rivers motioned to close the canopy, and I gave him a thumbs-up. Seconds later we were wrapped in our protective cocoon, temporarily shielded from the wind and noise. I set up my kneeboard and triple-checked that the cards were in the order I desired. Meanwhile, Rivs set up his side of the cockpit to the right of me, typing into the computer the coordinates for our route of flight to the target. We sat and waited.

The yellow-shirted sailor in front of us perked up as if raw energy had been pumped into him from his radio headset; he turned to 502 and whipped his fingers in the engine-turn-up signal. The waiting was over; events were set in motion. The engines had barely reached idle when the yellow shirt gave us the break-down signal. Out of the corner of my eye I saw several dark forms scurry under our jet and remove the chocks and chains holding us in place. The yellow shirt checked the extension of our tailhook and began to taxi us forward. My eyes were glued to the yellow wands, trusting our taxiing jet completely to their direction until my eyes grew more accustomed to the darkness. The catapult began its rhythmic firing. First to go was the E-2, with its early-warning radar dish, then the tankers and their Tomcat fighter and Prowler radar jamming customers. Finally our turn, wings down, flaps down, a rapid check of the flight controls, taxi forward into the catapult track. Our Intruder pointed toward the desolation of the night waters, and time seemed to stand still. We waited for the ordies to unpin the safety latch on the forward-firing HARM hanging under our wing. Then the handoff to the catapult officer, and suddenly we felt the familiar out-of-control vibration of the A-6 at full power in tension, shaking and rattling its old bones against the small metal hold-back fitting, the only thing between us and the water's edge.

I scanned the fuzzy red of the engine instruments as the cockpit quaked and shuddered. It all looked good, everything normal as I keyed the cockpit intercommunication button.

"Ready?" Rivers gave me a decisive thumbs-up. I extended my left thumb, and flicked the external lights master switch to the up position. I dug my head back into the ejection seat and waited.

The staccato of the catapult racing down the cat track slammed to a halt, and the Intruder rocketed off the bow of USS *Ranger* at 155 knots. The extra weight and drag of our weapons load required a greater-than-normal catapult acceleration, increasing my disorientation. I shook my head like a cuffed dog in an attempt to recage my eyeballs and get them to focus back onto the instruments. Sixty feet off of the water and climbing: landing gear up. It became quiet. We were flying.

Seven miles from the ship I reefed back on the stick and pulled the jet into a 4-G climb toward the inertial navigation steering on my attitude direction indicator TV screen. The steering pathway began to center up on the ADI.

"That the rendezvous point?"

"Yeah, steering's good. Let's start the combat checklist in the climb," Rivers answered.

"Roger." The Intruder continued upward to our assigned altitude of 15,000 feet. "ALQ-126?"

"Stand by." Rivers reached down to his side console to warm up our ancient onboard radar jammer.

"ALR-67?"

"On and bit checks." Missile alerts flashed on our circular warning screen with the depression of the built-in test button. The list continued for several minutes as we verified the function of all of the items that we could not check on the carrier deck: the chaff dispenser, terrain clearance ground mapping radar, flir, and the proper functioning of all of the components of the armament panel. If a critical item was inoperable, there still was time to launch the spare A-6 that was manned, loaded, and ready onboard *Ranger*.

"Missile test passed, all CBs checked in." Rivers reviewed the final items, the interface of the missile computer and the HARM's seeker head, and the big "gotcha"—the multiple panels of circuit breakers that lined the cockpit. A single "popped" circuit breaker could void our entire mission.

"Roger that, we're at the rendezvous." Technically there was not going to be any rendezvous, but we used the term for lack of a better description. I could see the lights of the other A-6 bombers, Jakals one through three below us, and Fang and Beef 1,000 feet above us in Rustler 503. The Jakal commanding officer's voice came over the tactical frequency we had dialed into our number one radio.

"Iron, check in." Tonight we would not use our respective A-6 squadron call signs of Rustler or Jakal. We would utilize the Air Wing 2 call sign "Iron" for all radio transmissions while the strike was under way. Normally, hearing "Rustler" or "Jakal" would clearly and immediately indicate which A-6 was from which squadron. Tonight, for the bombers, it did not matter—we were all in this together.

"Two, three, four, five" was transmitted by each bomber in rapid succession. The gang was all here.

"Iron flight, rolex 5, rolex 5. Acknowledge." The Jakal CO transmitted, and his four wingmen answered with their respective numbers once again.

"Shit, what's that all about?" I asked Rivers. Rolex 5 was the code for a delay of 5 minutes to the strike package's master timeline.

"I think I heard one of the fighters having some trouble getting his gas; we're probably just waiting for him." No big deal, I thought. We had a fifteen-minute window to hit our target. After that there would be no guaranteed deconfliction with the other friendly forces going "feet dry" on additional strikes. "Feet dry" meant leaving the safety of the ocean beneath you and flying over enemy territory. "Feet wet" meant the reverse. The prospect of "blue on blue" remained a nagging concern—nothing could be worse than getting shot down by your own guys.

The radios stayed fairly quiet for the next ten minutes, and at exactly 0453 and 50 seconds it was time for our Intruder, Iron 4, to push toward our first checkpoint. I eased off the throttles and started a descent to 5,000 feet above the water, keeping our jet on a gradual downward slope just below enemy radar coverage. We approached the coast of Kuwait. Eighteen minutes later we reached the first waypoint, and it was time to get down in the weeds.

"Winds are coming down, good Radalt." Rivers checked for excessive drift in the inertial navigation system, and verified to me that he had heard the radar altimeter tone go off when it became unmasked and began to indicate our exact height above the water below.

"Five thousand feet, just about 10 seconds slow, I don't see lead." I reset the Radalt warning bug to 400 feet and peered into the darkness, looking for the lights of the Jakal Intruders ahead of us. The radar altimeter tone would now go off if we descended below 400 feet.

"I think I've got the Jakals there in front of us. It's either that or a flare on the water," said Rivers.

We were still far enough away from shore that we had our lights on as a safety precaution to keep us from running into one another while we worked on the spacing we would need to maintain until we were over the target.

"Okay. Showing us a couple of seconds behind still." I clicked back on the stick trim button to slow our rate of descent into the darkness. "Twelve miles to the turn point. Terrain clearance is coming on, okay?"

"Roger." Rivers was ready for his radar screen to narrow its field of view when I punched on the terrain clearance (TC) radar display.

"Okay, Radalt's at 400. Looks like no display so far on one." I had selected the lowest setting for our terrain clearance, button one, and the smooth waters of the Persian Gulf were not reflecting a solid enough radar return to build a display on my attitude direction indicator. My ADI showed nothing but water underneath us—no problem, for now.

"King's clean." The E-2, high and miles behind us, reported over the strike common radio frequency that he had no radar contact with enemy fighters.

"Yep, I see Jakal lead and two in front of us. Jakal lead is just about over the oil platform right now." Our position slightly higher than the three Jakals strung out 7 miles ahead of us enabled Rivers to pick out their aircraft on his radar as they overflew the designated split point for the bombers.

"We've got intermittent TC here. Looks like the radar is blanking out, we've got good Radalt information," I said.

I knew that the terrain clearance might be erratic over the water, but the display had been holding up quite well on previous flights over the ocean during the past week. I throttled back to a fuel-conserving 360-knot ground speed to stay on our timeline. The extra gas would translate into options when we pulled off target after our bombing run.

"Okay, he's making his turn, he's going right over this platform that I'm on, so . . ." Rivers trailed off and concentrated on updating his radar on the oil platform that the lead Jakal was flying over.

"Okay, leveling off at 500." I pulled gently back on the stick and took a glance outside—pitch black.

"Okay, outbound up to our initial point [IP] is going to be 325." Rivers dialed the heading bug on our compass card to 325 degrees as a reminder to cross-check the system's next programmed heading to the IP, our final checkpoint before reaching the target.

"Looks like TC is not going to be a player." I had not seen such an absence of terrain clearance radar information on the ADI over the ocean thus far on this cruise, not even an occasional upward spike of video, like flying over water was supposed to do. Without TC I would not have a display of what terrain was in front of us. The radar altimeter could only show us what was directly below us.

"Is it intermittent?"

"Yep, Radalt's 300. Okay, 325, we're twenty seconds outbound I show." Not really intermittent, just blank, but Rivers didn't need to know that just yet. I let him continue to fine-tune his radar. We approached the oil platform where the two Swordsmen A-6s would take our cut away from the Jakal's course inbound to the target. "Okay, I show us on." Good start—over the split point exactly on time.

"Okay, sixty miles to the IP," said Rivers, hunched over, intently scrutinizing his radar. Only 60 miles left until the initial point and then one last course adjustment for the remaining 30 miles to the Umm Qasr naval facility. Less than fifteen minutes to the target.

"Roger. VTR is on?" I asked about our antique radar and flir imaging recorder.

"VTR is in standby." Once I stepped the computer into attack the VTR would begin to record.

"Okay, we have the 126 in standby?" If the SA-2 surface-to-air-missile radar painted us, the ALQ-126 would come alive in a confusing array of false radar images; otherwise it would remain silent, so as not to highlight our position.

"Stand by."

"IFF is off, lights are off, CBs are checked in, check your panel again." I read, and turned off our Intruder's lights and the radar highlighting "Identification: Friend or Foe" transponder.

"All right." Rivers forced his head out of the light-blocking rubber radar boot momentarily and checked his circuit breakers for the third time since we had been catapulted from the flight deck.

"Okay, I've got us exactly six miles from lead now, when he splits—" Rivers interrupted me as I read the mileage distance to the Jakal CO off our TACAN air-to-air mode. The Tactical Air Navigation (TACAN) was a navigation instrument that would provide bearing and distance information to the aircraft carrier. It also could provide distance to another aircraft with a compatible channel selected.

"I can see him out ahead; he's about 6 miles ahead, he's way to the left of us."

"He should be to the left of us," I came back.

"Yep." Rivers was downright disinterested . . . a bombardier/navigator (B/N) with his radar, like a kid with his toy.

I took a scan of our missile warning display. "Okay, all I've got is an A-6 radar out here." The only radars that were emitting energy at the moment were from our Intruders.

"Okay. Checking the ACU, all set to go," Rivers said. I took my eyes off the ADI and the radar altimeter for a second to cross-check that all of the switches looked correct on the armament control unit for the HARM missile shot.

"Still have station select to go." I wanted to make certain we did not forget that; no station selected, no missile fired.

"Station select and master arm to go." Just so you know, Rivers, I mused.

"If you see any terrain, let me know, because I don't have TC." We were still a ways out from coast in, but I knew that there were oil platforms in the area, possibly with high-reaching antennae. I kept us flying steady and relaxed at 360 knots and 400 feet above the water.

"You just need to let me avoid any platforms or if the terrain's coming up, let me know if you've got something coming up. . . ."

"King's clean." No enemy fighters were airborne.

"Flir's coming out." Rivers flipped the switch and I felt the

A-6 nose yaw slightly as the forward-looking infrared ball rolled out of stow and exposed the flir's heat-sensing glass portal.

"Forty-one miles to the IP. Running just a little bit behind on the time, but we'll make some of that up on one of the turn points."

"Yeah, can you come out of TC for just a second? Let me see if I can get an update, get a nav checkpoint out of here, hopefully." Rivers kept his head deep in the radar boot, searching for the navigation update point. "Oh, shit . . . it's just hard to break out here, there's two of them, it's supposed to be on the southern one, it's up near the northern one."

"Okay" was about all I could say. I had no idea what he was looking for. I took a few seconds while we were nice and stable and looked out the window. "No lights anywhere. Actually, I see lights off to the right; that might be Al Faw. Back to TC?"

"Hold on here. Is that heading way off there? Okay, I can see the beach here, now. Bring it up right about there. . . ." Rivers gently slewed his radar cursors.

I flipped the toggle switch to give us hydraulic pressure to the tailhook and pushed the hook retract button. "Deisolating the hook." The target ranging laser would not fire if the hook was out of the stowed position. The laser was designed with a safety interlock to prevent it from inadvertently being turned on while landing on the ship, where it could possibly blind a sailor.

"Roger that," Rivers answered.

"Twenty-four miles. Did you just update?" I asked. The steering on my ADI screen had jumped to the left a few degrees.

"No," Rivers replied. "I moved the cursors over a little bit."

"Okay. There, we're back. Back to TC?"

"Roger." I pushed the terrain clearance select button again, willing the display to come alive with some meaningful terrain clearance symbology.

"There we go. Looking at an A-6 radar to the right, 10 miles to the accel point."

"Roger, VTR is recording." We had 30 minutes of tape before the recording system went dead.

"Roger, 19 miles from the IP. Running about 10 seconds early. Five miles . . . I'm going to accelerate now." I pushed the throttles up to the stops, and 502 surged forward. I reset the power to maintain 450 knots over the ground.

"Downtown's clear," droned the E-2. No enemy fighters circling over the target.

"No lights except over to the left over Iraq, Kuwait. Can probably see some city lights there." In fact, I looked closer and it appeared that Kuwait City was completely lit up. So much for a blackout. "Coming right." We were still a bit early. I bunted the stick off course to eat up some time.

"Looks like some buoys or something down the middle of this passage, channel." We were splitting the difference between Būbiyān Island to the west and the Al Faw peninsula to the north, attempting to stay out over the narrow channel and away from land for as long as possible.

"Roger. Ten miles, we're getting back on time, let's set up for the HARM shot." I eased us back to steering.

"Okay." Rivers reached up to the armament panel.

"Station select and master arm," I said out loud.

"Master arm is on. Got a reselect, dammit. Wait; got a ready light now."

"Got a ready light and no reselect?" We couldn't shoot with a reselect light, our indication that the armament switches were incorrectly placed; the computer wouldn't let us.

"No reselect, master arm is on." Rivers must have momentarily selected one switch out of order. Good to go now, it didn't pay to rush things; one switch out of place would make this entire evolution a very dangerous waste of time.

"Eight miles from the IP. I see some AAA from the target area," I said, and scanned the horizon furtively for antiaircraft artillery. Eight miles from our final turn toward the target.

"Downtown little bit of AAA over there." So that was what it looked like. From a distance the smattering of brightly lit tracers in the sky looked spaced far apart and not too difficult to avoid.

"There's a boat here about our right one o'clock. A couple of them." Rivers stared intently at his radar screen.

"About a minute out. Still some AAA coming up from the island of Būbiyān. I see some AAA off our nose a little bit." Where the hell was this stuff coming from?

"Roger that. Boats out there, we'll avoid them." Rivers worked the radar cursors to the left, just enough to give us some space around the boats ahead of us, but not too close to the shore at Būbiyān where the Jakals were stirring up the pot.

"You can cycle IP to target if you want." I was ready to turn farther away from the growing light show of bullets coming up from the water ahead of us. I heard an erratic "beep beep" in my headset and looked down at my threat display, where the number "2" was imaged. An SA-2 radar was tracking us, but he did not have a lock and probably had not fired a missile yet.

"That's the target; should be a 292 heading." My steering jumped 40 degrees to the left.

"Yes. Okay, 34 miles," I said, pressing myself into the seat. I kept my head in constant motion among the growing lights of the Iraqi tracers outside, the ADI, and our threat display.

"You can come back to the right a little bit, we're kind of—" Rivers' voice was drowned out by a garbled voice transmitting an unintelligible contact over the tactical frequency.

"Come back to the right more?" This was the B/N's domain, steering the pilot with his cursors and voice commands to fly the least threatening track he could determine from the radar contacts.

"Yeah, come back to the right a little more or we're going to end up over the beach too soon."

"Okay, 5 miles to the shot." We seemed to be out of range of the AAA from the boats in the center of the channel, but every once in a while I saw a corkscrewing glow come upward—

shoulder-fired heat-seeker missiles. Just trying to distract us, there was virtually no chance they could get a good lock on our jet without first acquiring us visually. I was increasingly thankful for the darkness.

"Master arm's coming on." Rivers' head came out of the boot for a second; he flipped the toggle, and then went right back to heads down to ensure that the system was indeed on the coordinates of the SA-2 site.

"Are we in attack?" I didn't dare look down; I stared in the distance at the telltale orange glow of several SA-2s being launched. Still nothing but an acquisition radar on the threat display; were they waiting for the missiles to get closer before they tried to get a radar lock, or was the Prowler jamming just screwing them up?

"Yeah, we're in attack."

# Chapter Two

# . . . the bombs bursting in air . . .

The Attack

Our radar warning gear suddenly went to "high warble," the aural indication that a missile was guiding on our jet. Then, just as abruptly, it resumed its random acquisition radar beeping. The jamming was working.

"We're in range. I'm going to shoot it." The horizontal bar of the "hammer" came into view on the right side of my ADI display, indicating that the HARM was within range of the target. Our HARM was for the SA-2, the SA-2 was clearly active, let's get the hell rid of our HARM then.

"Okay, we're in range, all right." With the okay from Rivers I squeezed the commit trigger and allowed the computer to fire the missile.

WHOOSH.

Neither of us had shot a HARM before, and the noise and light show were more than we had expected, but we were not totally unprepared. I closed my right eye, and Rivers ensured that his face was covered in the rubber radar boot before I squeezed the commit trigger. Even so, the white flash was singularly impressive as the 900-pound missile accelerated away from our 450-knot Intruder as if it were standing still. I tore my gaze away from the HARM's climbing brilliance and scanned quickly for any fire that might be drawn to us by the missile's bright launch.

Not only was this Carrier Air Wing 2's first shot of the war, but it was also the first HARM to be launched by an A-6 in combat.

"Master arm's off, HARM away." I flipped the toggle switch down. "Coming back to the target, I'm heads down." I looked at the steering pathway on my ADI as Rivers cycled his navigational reference to Umm Qasr. The steering symbol jumped slightly. Rivers was going through the thirteen steps required to make our armament panel ready for our rockeye delivery, and his movements were unrushed, deliberate, and methodical.

"Logic reselect, that's for the tape, coming in, there you go." Rivers kept me apprised with a running commentary of his actions. The final step of selecting the correct bomb stations and deselecting the now empty HARM pylon extinguished the nightmarish reselect, the tiny amber light that, if illuminated, would make an on-target drop nearly impossible.

"Twenty-three miles." Our threat display made an occasional beep for each new enemy radar sweep detected, but so far none of the three airborne SA-2s had gotten a lock on us. Timing was right on, 450 knots over the ground. I kept the stick in constant motion and the Intruder made small, erratic course changes, continuously bracketing the correct heading to the target 400 feet above the water; it was the bullet you did not see that would get you.

"We're a good deal away from the beach," Rivers said, refocusing his attention back to our bombing run.

Our A-6 sped down the center of the channel to where it would soon turn and meander, requiring that we fly over heavily defended land for the final 15 miles of our attack run. Tracers started to fill the skyline, but they looked surreal and transparent in the distance ahead of us. The boats in the channel were behind us, the SA-2s were not tracking, and we had not yet reached the bulk of the Umm Qasr defenses. We were temporarily afforded the luxury of taking in the panorama visually to mentally plot out where the mass of the antiaircraft artillery might be.

"Eighteen miles." I read off the distance to the target so Rivers could maintain perspective on how much time he had remaining before he would have to commit to a specific aim point.

"Should be up to the north side here a little more." Rivers dragged his radar cursors slightly to the right.

"Looks like more AAA. Pretty far away, it looks like 16 miles." On time, the lead Jakal should almost be at bomb release.

"I can see the basin there." Rivers' cursors were on the naval facility. The first bombs were about to go off, and any element of surprise that remained was about to vanish.

My eyes widened and I felt the blood rush to my head, a wall of sparkling flashes and jetting tracers illuminated like a deadly fireworks display directly in front of us.

"Yeah, there's a lot of AAA up there. A lot of fucking AAA," I said, trying not to let my voice crack.

My God, I thought, it looks solid, impenetrable, as if every gun were lined up abreast and firing continuously. How the hell were we going to get through it? I felt doubt, serious doubt, and for the first time real fear, not the fear that I would fuck it up, but the fear that I would die.

"Can't turn around, 13 miles. Twelve miles, a lot of fucking AAA everywhere."

Rivers didn't respond to my halfhearted request for reassurance—he was doing his job with his head in the boot, searching for the target, trusting I would keep him alive. I pushed the nose over violently, jammed the throttles to the stops, and let the radar altimeter warning deedle for a second as we raced past 400 feet. I pulled our Intruder back level at 300 feet, reset the radar altimeter warning bug to just below 200, and increased the intensity of each turn to avoid the flying molten metal. Now in the thick of it I could see that there was a certain depth to it, it was not a solid wall, but layers upon layers of individual emplacements. I snapped the wings from left to right in 3- to 4-G turns to avoid the growing hail of bullets.

"Eleven miles," I said as methodically as I could, trying not to let the strain escape past my windpipe.

Red ropes of heavy machine-gun fire shot upward in concentrated arcs to heights of greater than 10,000 feet. Smaller predictable patterns emerged as well, some slowly circumscribing the skyline, others frantically racing back and forth, as if a madman were aimlessly ramming his weapon from side to side in its gun mount. Random shots went past the canopy on both sides, with no discernible rhyme or reason to their flight path. Oh, shit, I thought, this was just the stuff I could see. I wondered how much of this barrage of antiaircraft artillery was unlit; all I was seeing were the tracers. The bullets seemed to meet in the sky more frequently the higher they went; I kept our jet pressed down at 300 feet, where I could better identify pathways under the arcs of AAA.

"Still looking . . ." Rivers let me know that he was still awake.

"Ten miles." I thought about the surface-to-air missiles and the possibility of radar-guided AAA and double tapped the chaff-dispensing button on the starboard throttle. I heard the click in my headset, indicating the radar-fooling metal confetti had shot out the tail of our jet.

"See anything yet?" I slammed the stick to the right to avoid a red rope arcing its way toward us like a serpent.

"Well, I see the basin on radar." I pulled the A-6 back to the left, and the sidetone in my headset keyed twice as more bundles of chaff left the jet. The radar warning beeped continuously for a few seconds and then stopped. I had no idea what all this maneuvering was doing to our timing solution, but I couldn't steal my eyes to the time window and crosscheck it to my watch. My head was on a swivel: inside to the ADI as I corrected for our Intruder's balloon to 350 feet and pressed our belly back down to 250 feet above the gun mounts, then rapidly outside to judge the next highest threat. Back to the Radalt and steering. What was the SA-6 doing?

The radios were silent, but I knew that HARMs were raining down into the target area, shot from our Swordsmen A-6s, and the Prowlers from their perches high above and 30 miles behind us. The radio discipline of conducting the strike in as near silence as possible was supposed to preserve the element of surprise. Now I was not certain that we had ever enjoyed any advantage of surprise; it seemed that the gunners had been waiting for the correct moment to open up, that they knew exactly from which direction we were coming and when we were getting there.

"Eight miles," I said, and threw the stick to the right in a 4-G turn to arc us around what appeared to be the center of some of the random fire. Once past the thickest concentration I alternated the direction of the Intruder's wing dips, holding us a fraction of a second longer in the left turns to work our way back to target steering.

"Expanded." Rivers' voice was oblivious to the turmoil outside his world of the radar and forward-looking infrared. His radar image contracted to the box video of the expanded display for refining the aim point on the target. Here's where a B/N earned his money. Interpreting the difference between ground features and a man-made structure 7 miles away was not easy on a 1960s-vintage radar screen. Doing it from 300 feet high at 470 knots (560 miles per hour) did not make it any easier.

"Get the program." Rivers heard my command and reached down with his right hand to the bombardier/navigator's side console and activated the automatic chaff-dispensing program without taking his head out of the boot. I might be too busy for the next minute to remember to keep pumping out the chaff, and the program would ensure that a steady, but random, stream would shoot out our tail and hopefully frustrate the radar of any ground gunners or SAM operators.

"Seven miles."

The last 7 miles, time to start settling down the heading gyrations of our A-6 and give Rivers a chance to stabilize his radar cursors on the target. I traded my attention among the radar altimeter, the steering symbol, and the light show outside, getting our 470-knot jet to within five degrees of steering so I could make a play for the exact course in the final few miles before we dropped our rockeyes. With less room to maneuver, and the AAA increasing in density, I slapped the jet back and forth in a near-constant 3-G turn to avoid the greatest concentrations of the airborne lead.

"Can't see—" Rivers' voice was drowned out by the cycling of the radar altimeter warning tone going off the air with each turn past 60 degrees angle of bank. "The basin's fogged in; can't see anything on the flir."

"Uuuhuh! Uuuhuh!" We both grunted against the G's, fighting to maintain focus on staying alive and getting to the target.

"Five miles." My voice raised in pitch just a touch.

"Shit. I don't see any boats." Not what I wanted to hear.

"We'll get what we can. Three miles." I pulled back on the stick to get us to our planned release altitude of 400 feet, made a rapid wing dip to the left, and we were on steering. Suddenly the jet seemed motionless, flying forward at more than 560 miles per hour but in steady-state, 1-G flight. I never felt so vulnerable in my life; the extra 100 feet of altitude made me feel like we were sitting on a flagpole in the middle of a field. Only with people shooting at us.

"Two miles, got a hammer, I'm committing." I froze my eyes inside to the ADI, trying to stay rock solid on steering as the weapons release hammer marched down the right side of the display, slowly at first, and then with the momentum of a catapult as it accelerated to the bottom of the ADI and hesitated. The Intruder shuddered and the twelve rockeyes came off their bomb racks, alternating one of the 500-pound cluster weapons from each side until the hammer disappeared off the bottom of the ADI and our A-6 was 6,000 pounds lighter.

It felt like an eternity, but it had taken less than a second to release the twelve bombs. I felt the stick come alive with newfound agility now that the weight and drag of the big canisters were gone. Instantly I slammed the stick to the right and put us into an 85-degree angle of bank to get us the hell out of the target area. This was the most dangerous portion of any strike, the immediate flight off target and back to the safety of feet wet. All of the enemy defenses were alerted, and there was a tendency for the bomber crew to momentarily let their guard down now that their primary mission of bombs on target was complete. All that remained was to return to the carrier. Alive.

"Pull right! Uuuhuh! Two hundred feet, pull up!" Rivers was completely with me now. His job immediately shifted to providing another set of eyes outside for threat avoidance and to keep me from running into the ground.

The G meter clicked over to 5, and I eased out the angle of bank. I saw 200 feet on the barometric altimeter. "We're good, we're good, uuuhuh!" Intuitively I knew that we had gone through more than 90 degrees of turn and were no longer on a predictable track for the Umm Qasr gunners. I crisply moved the stick to wings level and pushed forward to unload the G and keep us accelerating away from the bombs exploding behind us.

"Passing 075 for a 125-degree—" Rivers stopped as the Radalt chimed in, signaling we had dipped back down below 200 feet. I pulled up on the stick. "Get back down there, 200 feet. . . ." The radar altimeter toned again and I leveled us off a hair above the alarm bug.

"We're good, I'm on the Radalt, I got it." I pumped the chaff button. "What's our heading?" I had started up the random oscillations again, waiting for Rivers to cycle steering to our preplanned egress point out over the marshes.

"One twenty-five." I rolled us back to the right in a 3-G turn until the heading centered on 125 degrees.

"I got some AAA, uuuhuh." I tightened up the turn to avoid some tracers ahead and clicked the chaff button.

"That's not tracking, barrage, uuuhuh!" Rivers said, indicating that the AAA was not working its way over to us but was making a random arc in the sky. The sounds of G-grunts, the radar altimeter tone cycling, and the static in our headsets as I dispensed the chaff were constant and unnerving.

"One twenty-five, coming up on it, keep your head out there." I was blind in this much of a right-hand turn and was dependent on Rivers to keep us from running into a wall of metal.

"We're clear right here, just keep coming, uuuhuh!" I pulled the Intruder back beyond a 60-degree angle of bank turn, and the Radalt deedled again.

"What's your heading?" Rivers was quickly taking over the navigation plan.

"One-thirty," I replied.

"If we come a little bit more left we'll stay away from the island."

"So how's that?" I eased us back to a 100-degree heading.

"Come back right." Evidently too far.

"Is that good? There's more AAA. Back to steering?" I took my time looking at the AAA slightly to the right coming up over Būbiyān Island.

"Yeah, back to steering." Rivers sounded bad. No boats.

The radar altimeter tone went off, and I shot my eyes over to it—descending through 200 feet.

"Pulling up! Pulling up!" I snapped in a frenzy.

"Roger," Rivers replied, and went back to the radar boot.

"Got something outside, over there." I pointed to the right into the darkness at some sporadic fire in the distance.

"Okay, we're over, over the channel." We were heading in the opposite direction from our course inbound to the target. Only 5 minutes before, we had been in this same piece of sky, having just fired the HARM, and readying ourselves for the fun. Rivers continued, "Okay, but there're boats out there.

Just keep it going this way here for a while. Let's go 10 degrees right."

"Coming right 10. Seven point seven, we look okay on gas. All the engine instruments are looking good." Seventy-seven hundred pounds was enough fuel to make it to the ship, and there were no obvious indications of battle damage. We dipped back below 200 feet, and I eased up just as the Radalt went off. I felt absolutely naked any higher than 200 feet, but I needed to watch out—running into the ground was a gift to the Iraqis.

"There's a boat, chaff, or something out here. Okay, now come back left to steering." Rivers tried to differentiate between a target on the water and possibly the remnants of one of the striker's chaff clouds.

"Did you see any flashes from ours?" Our hard right turn off target put any view of the bomb impacts on Rivers' side of the A-6.

"Yes."

"They blew up?" I pressed.

"Yes."

"Anything out in front of us?"

"Nothing in front of us." I started to relax a little. Rivers continued, "There's a boat off to the left, there, come about 5 degrees to the right. We're still over the little beach part there."

"The boats are on the display, then? I got an A-6 radar off out to the right." I looked at the indication of an Intruder's radar on my warning screen.

"Iron 1 feet wet, feet wet." There was a brief pause and then, "Iron 2 feet wet, feet wet." The first two Jakals had made it back out over the Persian Gulf.

"King copies 1 and 2." I could visualize the E-2 controller in the back of the Hawkeye making two checkmarks next to the first pair of Jakal A-6s.

The E-2 was the middleman and would be responsible for relaying any information on casualties and the battle damage assessment (BDA) to the brass waiting eagerly on board *Ranger*. The E-2 followed up with "Downtown clean." The Iraqi fighters had chosen not to come out and play.

"How's this heading?" I hunched my shoulders forward for the first time in 45 minutes and felt the strain go out of my muscles as my joints cracked.

"This is a good heading; it'll get us there." Rivers was unusually quiet, I knew because we had not hit our primary target, but the boats weren't there. What the hell were we supposed to do, shit boats?

"Have we passed Būbiyān yet?" I had no intention of pulling the throttles back off of where they had been planted at the stops of full military-rated thrust for the last 5 minutes, not until we were well away from the beach and out over the Persian Gulf.

"Not yet, just about past it." Rivers was still studying the radar, not about to let us fly into a deceivingly quiet threat zone after we had survived the worst of it.

But that wasn't all of it. For a bombardier/navigator to literally live a target for days and then not have it appear on radar or a forward-looking infrared screen was unbalancing to say the least, and I thought that it was having a pretty harsh impact on Rivers' state of mind just about now. Me? I was still so shook up from the low-level acrobatics that I was plain old happy to be alive. But those were the primary priorities assigned to a pilot and B/N; the pilot needed to keep the jet flying so the B/N could get bombs on target. I felt a certain degree of satisfaction interspersed with relief; Rivers was feeling strictly frustration and letdown.

"That was just a fucking barrel of laughs, wasn't it, Rivs, old buddy?" I said too loudly and with bravado, partially to rouse Rivers out of his funk, but also to begin the mental preparation that might be required to minimize the apparent dangers of the low-level strike—we might have to do it again.

"Yeah" was all that I could get out of my B/N.

"Jesus Christ, I can't believe we got through that AAA. Should I stay on this heading?"

"You can go ahead and come a little to the right."

"Throttling back just a little bit, are we clear of Būbiyān?" I gently worked the engines back about 3 percent RPM of their max thrust to give them a break.

"Yeah, we're clear." That was it, the worst was over. "Iron 3 feet wet, feet wet."

"Copy 3," replied the Hawkeye.

"Iron 4 is feet wet."

"Yes!" I let out emotionally. Fang and Beef had made it.

"All I know is that I was on some building. A big fucking building, too." Feeling was coming back into Rivers' voice with the recognition that the bombs weren't wasted off target, but had most likely destroyed major parts of the port facility.

"It doesn't fucking matter," I said, knowing full well that it mattered a hell of a lot. "You didn't see any boats?"

"I couldn't see anything along the quay wall and I couldn't see any boats on the flir. I don't know where the flir was looking." The Radalt gave off a last tone as we dipped below its alarm setting of 200 feet for the final time that evening.

"How far, how far out are we?" I had better start paying closer attention to our fuel state, I thought.

"We're past the IP." The initial point for our attack fell behind us.

"I'm throttling back a little bit for gas. Do you wanna put Dorra in, or are you going to put in O'Malley directly?" On our route back to the ship we needed to adhere to a strict profile if we were to avoid getting shot down by the battle group's Aegis-class missile cruiser standing guard as the picket ship to the south of us. Aegis-class cruisers were particularly deadly defenders against air attacks. Dorra and O'Malley were theater code words for geographic fixes that the "Red Crown" cruiser could expect us to fly through on the way home to *Ranger*.

"That's Dorra." Rivers cycled steering.

"O'Malley's 29 north, 49 east." I had the latitude and longitude coordinates prominently displayed on my kneeboard card just in case Rivers became incapacitated during the attack, and I was required to reach over and punch them into the computer myself.

"Let's get the squawks here." Rivers reached down with his left hand to the transponder panel on the center console and flipped on the toggles to highlight our jet to our fighters and Red Crown.

"You got the squawks. We show feet wet. The 167 and 126, you got those off?" Now that we were out of the surface-to-air missile threat there was no point in keeping our meager on-board jammers operating, giving the enemy SAMs an opportunity to study their characteristics.

"Yeah," responded Rivers.

"Okay. Did you pass BDA? Let's get in the climb first." The bigwigs would be eager for battle damage assessment.

"Yeah." Rivers was still focused on the radar and our position, and his brevity was becoming a bit annoying.

"We're going to have to climb for gas. Tell me when you think we can."

"Aw, shoot, I think we can probably climb now," Rivers said in a reversion to a South Carolina drawl lost years ago.

"How far are we from the target?"

"Forty-five miles."

"How far past the IP, about 10 miles?" I kept the questions coming.

"Yep." I began to get the feeling that Rivers was humoring me.

"We're climbing. Squawks on, right?" Blue on blue was still a very real possibility. Getting shot down by our own guys would not be good.

"Yes," replied Rivers. I pulled back on the stick and advanced the throttles once again to get us to a fuel-saving altitude more quickly.

"Our bombs didn't dud; at least it doesn't look like it to me, anyway. I know that fuckin' HARM went." We blew something up, I thought, and pushed the throttles forward to the stops and transitioned to a 300-knot climb.

"Iron 1 standing by to copy BDA." The Jakal CO was eager to consolidate whatever data we had on our hits so he could pass the abbreviated information to the E-2, who would in turn relay it to the heavies on board *Ranger*.

"Did Iron 5 call feet wet?" broke in the E-2 Hawkeye as he attempted to account for all of the strike's players.

Rivers turned to my direction and keyed his intercommunication system. "Five turned around, didn't he?"

"Yes," I replied.

"I think Iron 5 was an abort; Iron 4 is feet wet. Everybody should be off," Beef piped up over the strike common frequency. We had caught bits and pieces of the status of the fifth bomber early on during the attack, but all I could put together was that his Intruder's radar had failed and that they were breaking off their profile to the target.

"King copies."

Deep in the confines of the carrier was a multitude of people impatiently awaiting word on our battle damage assessment and possible aircraft losses—the admiral, the air wing commander, the *Ranger* CO, and our squadronmates. Linked up instantaneously by radio, it was easy to forget that the Intruder crews were still catching their breath as they were attempting to ascertain what damage they had inflicted on the target. The transition from dodging bullets to crunching administrative numbers for radio transmission was separated by only a few minutes and several dozen miles.

"Iron 1 standing by to copy BDA," the Jakal CO repeated into his mike.

"Iron 2, twelve rockeyes, unknown, radar." The second Jakal gave his honest assessment—they had dropped all twelve weapons using the radar only due to the fog, and they did not have any visual confirmation of where their weapons had impacted.

"Skybolt, one HARM, unknown, no damage," the Prowler overhead broke in with his report.

"Iron 3, one HARM, twelve rocks, radar, unknown, no damage." Rivers picked up the cadence of the strikers calling in proper order.

"Iron 2's unknown, no damage," interjected the second Jakal, realizing he had omitted an aircraft damage report in his initial transmission.

"Rustler 1's four HARM, radar, unknown, no damage." Our squadronmates transmitted, back to using our tactical call sign. The effectiveness of the HARM shooters was even more nebulous than that of the bombers—their targeted surface-to-air-missile site was dozens of miles away and could be confirmed a kill only by the loss of a radar signal coincidental with the planned missile impact. The fact that the strikers all made it through the SAM defenses did indicate, however, that the missile's radar was more than likely down for a time. Whether this was due to the soft kill of the Iraqi operators shutting down the radar, or the hard kill of a direct impact, was more difficult to determine.

"Never saw an SA-6 on there at all." Rivers made reference to our radar warning detection system.

"No, all that we had was a 2," I confirmed. The SA-2 was painting us for most of the ingress, but the more dangerous "6" never illuminated on our warning screen.

"Iron 4, twelve rocks, flir delivery. I believe we scored nine o'clock, secondary fires left burning, and no aircraft damage." Beef had been the only one to find a hole in the fog to see through with his forward-looking infrared, but as the final Intruder of the strike he was in the unique position to determine the general damage inflicted on the facility. The fact that our collective bombs had caused various things on the ground to blow up in secondary explosions was a good sign—we still did not know what we had destroyed, but it had been on a naval installation, and it went "boom" when lit.

The radio chatter became more cluttered as various aircraft, now safely out of the target area and on their return to the fleet, coordinated join-ups for a more extensive visual check-out for possible battle damage. Rivers and I were climbing to 27,500 feet en route to our funnel point back to the ship. Beef and Fang were somewhere close behind us, flying a similar profile. The sun was starting to break the horizon, and we could see that we would be flying in clear air between the clouds above and below us. Rivers directed me on some minor course corrections, but for the first time in weeks we had little to do but fly straight ahead.

A deep feeling of dread sat heavily in my gut; I wondered if this was the way it was going to be on all of the strikes. The sheer intensity of the AAA had gotten my attention in a way I had not been even close to expecting. Those sons of bitches were actually trying to kill me! I'm a nice guy. Why are they doing their damnedest to end my life? And, of course, for the first time it really settled in, not in the periphery of my con-sciousness, but in the deepest recesses of my soul—I am trying to kill them, and they are trying to kill me. Flying off the carrier, up until now, had evoked consistent emotions separated by the finest of lines: excitement, fear, fun. There was nothing fun about any of this now. This high-tech game was serious shit. And again for the first time in my short naval career I felt an unfamiliar emotion: doubt. Could I keep doing this, or was this just too intense? I began to realize that I had limits, and that they might have just been staring back at me from the precipice.

"We've got 6 point 2 in fuel now, that should be all right." I felt the need to say something, the need to shake off the lin-gering doubt before it got a handhold in a fissure of my psyche.

"Well, nothing like a little fuckin' AAA to make you feel a lot more comfortable doing 5-G turns at 200 feet. And on in-struments, oh, my God. Ha! I hope this is a quick fuckin' war, ha!" To say that my laughter was a bit strained would be an understatement.

"We're at 27 now." Rivers brought me back to the moment at hand.

"Going to 27 point 5." I began to level off our A-6 at 27,500 feet. "Want to turn Red Crown on in the back?"

Rivers gave off a little laugh of his own. I wasn't sure what he thought I said, but he did reach back and tune the radio to the Aegis missile cruiser's frequency.

Iron 1 finally managed to cut through the radio clutter and pass the strike's battle damage assessment to the orbiting E-2: "Iron 1 estimate 25 percent, estimate 25 to 50 percent, opposition heavy AAA, SA-2, twenty-eight Mark 20 rockeyes, ten HARM. Low state unknown, 405's state 6 point 8."

And that was it. The weeks of planning and minutes of flying through the devastatingly hostile environment of Umm Qasr were reduced to one disjointed sentence, which boiled down to "We think we may have destroyed 25 to 50 percent of the target."

Our intel would later confirm that the SA-2 radar did shut down at approximately the planned impact time of the HARM missile fired from our Intruder, but even that was paper thin in its substance. I suppose this is the way war really is, I thought; there is no training range debrief to tell you what you had destroyed and who you had killed. It is an endless balancing act of a guessing game between what you would like to believe and what information you actually possessed.

"Still gotta get ahold of Red Crown, Rivers." The flight was not over until we were on the ship, eating breakfast.

"Red Crown, Rustler 21. Red Crown, Rustler 21." Rivers reverted back to our squadron call sign.

"Rustler 21, Red Crown" came the reply from the robocruiser.

"Rustler 21, inbound to O'Malley angels 2 7 point 5, state 5 point 8." We had passed through the final wicket on our first strike.

"One down, anyway," I said to myself as much as to Rivers.

"Yep" was all I could drag out of him.

The sun was distinctly over the Iranian landmass to the east of us when we entered the marshal orbit 20 miles behind the ship. Our fuel state was dipping below 4,000 pounds. Ordinarily this would have raised my pucker factor while still so far away from the safety of the carrier deck, but this morning my normal fears and concerns had been supplanted by the visual image of lights filling the night sky all around our speeding low-level bomber. Although I could not reconcile in my mind how we made it through that blizzard of flying metal unscathed, I was thankful that the vast majority of the AAA consisted of tracers, visible on the dark horizon. Why had the Iraqis used tracers, which were of no use to a gunner unable to see his target, but were the difference between life and death to us as we wove a path between the visible red ropes and patches of sporadic fire? I was no more able to answer that question than I was able to figure out why Kuwait City and its outlying areas were not in blackout conditions. Maybe the Iraqis were stupid or diabolically clever, but regardless, it appeared that their utilization of tracers worked to our benefit, at least on this night.

During our short wait in marshal the sun had risen high enough to turn it into a daylight recovery. The guys in Air Operations were on the ball. They held the rest of the strike's players overhead the ship, while they vectored the low-fuel Intruder bombers down the final approach course one at a time and into the break as the ship steered west, away from the rising sun. Rivers and I strained our necks one last time for a look under our wings to positively verify that all of our ordnance had come off, and we entered the break with just a shade over 3,000 pounds of fuel left in our tanks.

The turn to final approach was second nature, and I felt the relaxed poise I had come to associate with total confidence, the kind of state achieved only through a near epiphany of total concentration or a complete "You can't hurt me because I don't give a damn" attitude. I was used to the defensive mechanism of the latter, and the testing of my calm focus behind the familiar carrier deck came as a bit of a shock to me. My clarity of thought was transformed into action through precise, effortless motions. What ordinarily came with great difficulty now flowed easily from a trancelike calm. The residue of the intensity left over from the Umm Qasr target area was alive enough to buy me a near-perfect grade of "okay" for my landing on the carrier that morning.

# Chapter Three

# On the shore dimly seen

I maintained focus until our Intruder was chocked and chained to the deck and our engines were shut down. I took a deep breath and thought about what had just happened. The A-6 Intruder was the only all-weather, day or night attack aircraft in the navy inventory. It was designed to evade enemy radar missile defenses by flying below their line-of-sight coverage, utilizing surrounding valleys, mountains, and whatever terrain features could be put between the straight-line beam of a radar pulse and the A-6. If the radar could not "see" you, then it could not guide its missile to your aircraft. But low-altitude tactics did absolutely nothing to protect against AAA.

An enemy surface-to-air missile radar could not see through dirt, and neither could the A-6's radar. Radar was the defining attribute of the Intruder. The radar, and the terrain-hugging displays it supported, enabled the pilot to keep the aircraft flying fast and low without slamming into the ground. It also gave the bombardier/navigator a precise method of finding and bombing a pinpoint target in any weather, day or night. But the target had to be there. Boats were easily moved.

The final hurdle of the morning was over; we had gotten back aboard *Ranger* and were home, safe. Getting aboard the carrier. To an aviator it meant snagging an arresting wire with the tailhook in the screeching deceleration of a "trap" a few dozen feet from the deck edge of the ship. To everyone else it meant walking up the gangway to the ship's brow, hump-backed with duffels of clothes and supplies for a six-month deployment. Thirty-nine days ago, when we left port in San Diego, we all had the opportunity to walk aboard the ship, a singularly uncomfortable experience for an aviator.

Normally an aircraft carrier's air wing would fly their jets onboard the ship after she had left port and was in the open ocean. On December 7, 1990, the final Air Wing 2 aircraft had been hoisted aboard USS *Ranger* by the huge dockside crane at Naval Air Station North Island—no chance would be taken that one of the vital war-fighting machines might break while flying out to *Ranger*. Each jet was too valuable. The probability of war with Iraq was too close.

Walking aboard the ship was unnatural for us. It was one of the many things that told us this six-month cruise would be different.

## San Diego Bay, Southern California, 8 December 1990

The *William Tell* Overture thundered through every passageway and across the flight deck of USS *Ranger* as her lines were cast off at precisely 0930. I grew up watching the *Lone Ranger*, so it made sense to me, but I had to wonder how many generations after mine would make any correlation between Rossini and a black-and-white cowboy. *Ranger*'s theme song was played every time the ship docked or left port, and during all major shipboard events. It was indelibly branded in my psyche in a confused array of emotions. The balance of those feelings would get more confused with each rendition, and with the passing of time, but the individual sentiments remained—pride, unease, fear, and excitement. Superimposed over all was the rush of adrenaline caused by the subconscious memory of the out-of-control ecstasy of catapults and night traps. This cruise portended to extend those emotions in height and breath.

The ship's loudspeaker system was designed for verbal announcements via a microphone, not the gritty blaring of an old album into a keyed mike. The *William Tell* Overture lost any subtleties it possessed piped through the jury-rigged 1MC sound system, but the ripping momentum and pure energy of the piece were lost on no one. In spite of themselves, even the most jaded salts on board *Ranger* found themselves standing a bit straighter, a new glint of determination in their eyes with the mounting power of each building stanza. This was *Ranger*, it was the carrier navy; so many times we had collectively honed our skills, sweat, bled, and occasionally died during training and deployment, building a daily intensity until something had to give. And like the song, so many times it ended where it started—in silence—leaving nothing but the raw emotions of a time past left to ponder. The roller coaster of preparedness and absolute commitment never reached release, but would slowly dissipate when the carrier turned homeward from its assigned station for the long transit Stateside. This was the routine we were accustomed to, and with the heated curiosity of an explorer and the trepidation of a trespasser, we were about to break.

Rugged-looking oceangoing tugboats gripped *Ranger*'s side, finding purchase with their fendered rails and lines made secure to the carrier. Slowly, *Ranger*'s 1,071 feet and 81,000 tons of displacement inched away from the North Island carrier pier toward the center of the port of San Diego. Officers and sailors in their dress blue uniforms lined the rails as was customary for a naval ship leaving the final review of her civilian masters ashore. The last visions of the mass of crying mothers, silent children, and news cameras faded from view, and *Ranger* moved under her own steam, past Point Loma, and out into the open Pacific Ocean. "Haze gray and under way"—the sailor's lamentation and fascination, the bittersweet slogan for weeks of boredom pondering the possibilities of the unknown and the known, the ports to be revisited, the exotic places to see. Some new challenges, most old, perhaps the fulfilling of an obligation made years ago in boot camp. The double-edged sword of dull, repetitious routine, and pure, unadulterated uncertainty: waking up each morning not knowing what the day would bring. The conflicting emotions remained shelved in the silence of each sailor's only corner of privacy, his mind, while he set to work at the rote treadmill of a carrier's workday.

*Ranger* had barely reached thirty miles offshore when her catapults began their rhythmic propelling of aircraft. Each firing of a cat was accompanied by the crescendo rumbling of the catapult's shuttle down its track embedded in the carrier's deck as it dragged its load of wing and screaming engines to the edge of the ship. The roar of jet engines and the mechanical racing of the shuttle escalated in intensity until it hurt the ears of those walking below the steel deck plates. The frenzied cacophony could not be maintained, and it ceased even more quickly than it had started when the shuttle slammed into its stops and thrust its cargo into the air at 150 knots—cargo in the guise of a jet aircraft that, only 2 seconds before, had been completely motionless. The acceleration was so great that initially the body's equilibrium could not be maintained by the inner ear—the pilot flew via reference to his instruments and more than a little faith that the cat shot "felt right."

A soft cat shot, one that produced enough energy to shoot the jet off the deck, but not enough to get the aircraft to flying airspeed, was every naval aviator's nightmare. The jet's pitot-static instruments, those gauges that measured the airflow over the aircraft and translated it to airspeed and rate of climb or sink, lagged behind in the force of the catapult. By the time the gauges caught up with the cat shot, and reference could be made as to whether the airspeed existed to fly, the jet may very well have already transited the 60 feet from the carrier deck to the ocean below. Too late to eject, unable to fly, there weren't any good options for the flight crew if they waited this long—they would be run over by the ship. The only uncertainty was whether the flight crew would be inside their aircraft when it happened. A naval aviator's only reference off the cat was the attitude of the jet through his ADI, where he could ensure that the wings were initially level for maximum lift, and put his faith in his seat-of-the-pants intuition that a cat shot was "good." The only way to develop that seat-of-the-pants feel, for what it was worth, was through experience. The most danger lay with the new pilots, or "nuggets," who might either not recognize a deteriorating situation, or might falsely find one and eject needlessly. There was no book—nor could one be written—thick enough to provide a solution for every situation. Sometimes experience was the only teacher.

Now twenty-eight years old, I had been in the navy for five years and felt as if I had lived on the carrier most of my life. I suppose that was what the ship did to you—sucked you into its routine until you filled the small niche assigned that made carrier operations work. There were five thousand such niches, one for each man—there were no women—to fill. Some were critical; all were important.

This would be my second cruise, and while no longer a "nugget," civilian life was still fresh enough in my mind to remember college in Rhode Island, growing up in New York, and for six years living in Athens, Greece. For the most part I had spent my childhood on Main Street. Literally. 504 Main Street, Northport, New York. I recited the address in my mind with the same cadence that my mother had taught it to me when I was four years old. The navy was my first "real" job, if you could call flying onto a boat a "real" job. During summers I worked in a scuba diving shop and on a charter boat, looked after mentally and physically handicapped adults in a halfway house, and did a little home remodeling. After graduating from college I spent six months driving a delivery truck in New York City for a construction company. I took my part-time work somewhat seriously, but the navy was my first experience with absolute accountability and responsibility. I liked it.

I had no inflexible ties to shore: no children, I did not own a home. My fiancée, Laurie, and I had been engaged for less than a year, and no wedding date had been set. If I had seriously considered it I might have determined that my reluctance to pick a date was due to the uncertainty of this cruise. I was rarely serious, however, and suspect that it was more likely a case of dragging my cold feet.

USS *Ranger (CV-61)* was hardly a "nugget" herself. This would be her twentieth deployment—including eight Vietnam combat cruises—since her keel was laid on 2 August 1954 in Newport News, Virginia. She was the eighth U.S. Navy warship to bear the name *Ranger* proudly on her fantail, and was the third Forrestal-class aircraft carrier to be built. It had been thirty-four years since *Ranger* was first outfitted for sea to join the fleet in 1957. But it was the crew that made a carrier work, and *Ranger* "worked" as well as any of the newer nuclear carriers. In fact, if you asked her crew, most would say better.

I had some time before my flight brief on this first day of our six-month cruise. I left the confines of my small living space for the hub of squadron activity—the ready room.

I stopped my stride along the passageway and reached down for the doorknob in front of me. I walked into the ready room and looked immediately to the grease board next to the desk of the squadron duty officer (SDO). Not too bloody yet; the schedule had encountered only minor changes. Then again, it was only 1030. I saw that I was still scheduled for two flights, both with Rivers.

Rivers and I were designated a regular crew, and it was normal for squadron operations to schedule us together. To be truly effective, you had to know your crew member as well as you knew your jet. The squadron tried to maintain distinct sets of crews throughout deployment.

Rivers, a distinguished-looking southern gentleman, was

turning prematurely gray at thirty-six. I don't know how he did it, probably because his wife, Barb, was a saint, but he had the sort of family most people idolized. Four great kids who actually listened to him (most of the time), a "home," not just a house, barbecues, skiing, church—a family. As I mentioned, he also had a lot of gray hair.

Although I was the pilot, Rivers was a lieutenant commander and outranked me. I was a lieutenant, the equivalent of a "captain" in the other armed services. Assuming that his decision did not conflict with a safety issue, he was the overall mission commander for the flight. This was almost always a moot point, since we were friends and had a similar thought process in regard to the A-6 mission. It was second nature, and made for good crew coordination, to always keep the other crew member in the decision-making loop. Two heads were better than one only if they were both used.

The pilot's and bombardier/navigator's jobs were well defined. There was only one set of flight controls in the side-by-side seating arrangement of the A-6, and B/Ns received no formal instruction or practice in how to fly the jet. If the pilot became incapacitated, a B/N could reach over to the control stick to stave off immediate disaster, but it would be virtually impossible to stretch across a pilot's bulky flight gear to get to the throttles. To attempt to do so would require that a B/N unstrap from his ejection seat, which would eliminate what in the end was the B/N's only valid option—ejection.

Both of our flights, or "sorties," today would be for carrier-landing qualifications (CQ). The ship could make only marginal headway west during CQ while it continuously searched for the course to launch and recover aircraft into the prevailing winds. But as much as *Ranger* needed to begin its westward trek, the air wing needed to have all of its pilots carrier-"qual'ed" before leaving the proximity of a divert field ashore. These conflicting goals wreaked havoc on the flight schedule these first days at sea.

There were eight squadrons in Carrier Air Wing 2, and all

except the single helicopter squadron would need to carrier-qualify. Two A-6 squadrons, two F-14, one EA-6B, one S-3, and one E-2—more than a hundred pilots had to get airborne, both during the day and at night, and exhibit sufficient skill in landing so as not to scare the landing signal officers (LSOs) or get sent to the beach for low fuel. "Flexibility" was the officially sanctioned buzzword. "Goat rope" was the more accurate description in the vernacular.

Our squadron was the VA-145 Swordsmen. The "V" stood for "fixed wing" versus the rotary wing of a helicopter. The "A" stood for "Attack." The command had been flying the A-6 with Carrier Air Wing 2 on *Ranger* with few exceptions for every deployment of the past twenty years. The Swordsmen had a long history before graduating to the A-6 in 1968. The Intruder was the fourth aircraft that VA-145 had flown since its origins as a Reservist squadron in Dallas in 1949, and the Swordsmen had seen extensive combat in Korea and Vietnam.

We were all well aware of the importance of living up to the combat tradition of Swordsmen of generations past.

I turned my attention away from the squadron duty desk. The ready room was a multifunction space and served as the officers' meeting room, flight briefing room, mail room, squadron duty office, coffee room, movie room, and in a host of other capacities. Immediately upon walking through the door it was obvious that the ready room had a distinct personality. The space was dominated by thirty-five heavily cushioned metal chairs, replete with clanky pull-out drawers at their bases, fold-up writing tops on one side, and ashtrays from a bygone era on the opposite armrests. A Naugahyde flap in the squadron color of green draped the headrest and provided the Velcro for the chair's "owner" to attach his name. Ready-room chairs were the aviator's desk and storage area while out of his stateroom. Each of the thirty squadron aviators and four of the five "ground pounders"—those officers who directed aircraft maintenance—had his own chair. The most junior ground pounder, our ordnance officer or "gunner," also happened to be the most junior officer in the Command. When the chairs ran out he was the one left standing. No matter to him, Gunner much preferred to spend his time in the company of his fellow "ordies," an exclusive clique of troops whose duty was to load bombs and missiles on the Intruders.

All chairs faced forward, where a grease board provided the tool for a Magic Marker–toting aviator to brief or debrief his comrades. Across from the entranceway in the corner was the desk for the SDO. One of the Command's junior officer aviators was responsible for a 24-hour shift one to two times a month as the SDO. He was the single point of contact responsible for running the flight schedule and providing the continuity from hour to hour to ensure that the plan of the day was conducted smoothly. Others shuffled in and out of the ready room, went flying, worked out, slept, or did paperwork in their spaces. The SDO sat behind his metal classroom desk from 0700 until the last plane was on deck, which might not be until after midnight. After that, he was on call until 0700 the next morning for any official business that required the attention of VA-145. It was not difficult work, but it was a strain considering that it was above and beyond any duties that might be required that day by the squadron duty officer's ground job.

Above the SDO desk was the icon of carrier aviation—the "Greenie Board." Here, for all to witness, was a qualitative representation of an individual's performance behind the ship "flying the ball." The landing signal officers graded every landing, or pass, at the boat, and each squadron posted the result on a 3-by-5-foot board in their ready room. An LSO's grade of green meant that the pass was "okay," or pretty damn good. Only "soft" comments: A little too high here, a little too fast there, but overall very good. A yellow indicated that while the landing was well within the parameters of safety, there was a "normal" degree of deviation from elusive perfection. This degree of proficiency in a pass was termed "fair," and in theory represented the fleet average. Bolters were the special exemption grade. By definition, the jet missed the wires and did not stop if it boltered; therefore it was very difficult at first glance to see what could be positive about it. Things could be worse, however. You could find yourself wrapped around the steel plates of the fantail in a ramp strike. That would mean that you were either dead or floating in the ocean after an ejection, neither a very appealing prospect.

The grade assigned to a bolter was not as good as a fair, but it was better than a "no-grade." A no-grade was awarded when the landing signal officers determined that while the pass was generally safe, it was only marginally so. The classic example of when a bolter was safer than a no-grade was a pass where the landing aircraft was too high to catch a wire crossing the fantail, but the pilot resisted making a wild play to get his jet on deck. Instead, he "took his bolter like a man" and went around to try again. The grade rewarded a certain maturity of the pilot in not trying to do something stupid by attempting to get his aircraft to trap when it was clearly not safe to do so.

Just below a no-grade in the hierarchy of landing grades was the wave-off. The landing signal officers had the responsibility of waving off any aircraft that, in their estimation, was making an unsafe final approach to the carrier. Perpetually clenched in the controlling LSO's hand was the "pickle," a portable joystick that operated the flashing red wave-off lights that surrounded the ball. As soon as it became evident that a jet's approach was becoming erratic or outside stable parameters for a safe approach, the LSO would squeeze the pickle trigger while simultaneously transmitting "wave-off" over the radio. The aural and visual signals were designed to be impossible to ignore, and the approaching pilot was required to immediately go to full power, retract his speed brakes, and maintain an on-speed condition of flight, while the addition of energy translated into a climb. Wave-offs were not uncommon for various situations outside the control of the landing pilot. The deck might be "fouled" by the preceding aircraft that was not yet out of the landing area, or the arresting wire that had been dragged out moments earlier might not yet be retracted and put back taut into battery. Because of the incredibly short interval between each landing aircraft, it was quite normal for the timing to occasionally get out of synch, forcing a jet to "go around" while the landing area was being properly prepared, and pilots were not penalized for it. The "technique," or purely pilot-induced, wave-off was another matter. When the pilot of a landing aircraft put his jet in a dangerous situation the landing signal officers were required to wave him off.

On the LSO grading scale a wave-off counted as a 1, and a green "okay" topped the normal scale out at a 4. There were extremes outside the normal deviations of the 1-to-4 grading system. If a pass was truly flawless, where the LSO could not detect that the incoming jet was a foot or a knot off of perfect for the full three-quarters of a mile of final approach, then an "okay"—underlined—was earned. If one of these highest of grades were awarded to any single aviator in the air wing during a 6-month deployment, it would be a lot. It was extremely unlikely for any pilot to be able to conform to the strictest parameters of perfection that an okay demanded.

At the other end of the spectrum—and hopefully, but not usually, as rare—was the "cut pass." A cut pass indicated that the pilot had come perilously close to losing his multimillion-dollar aircraft and perhaps his life. If a pilot did not advance the throttles to full power at touchdown, but instead relied on blind faith that his tailhook would engage a wire and stop him, it was a cut pass. This was due to the simple fact that if the tailhook did not catch a wire, the engines would not have enough time to spool up to full power, and the jet would dribble off of the angle deck into the water rushing by 60 feet below. If the pilot did not respond to a call from the landing signal officer to wave off, but attempted to land instead, it would be a cut pass. If the pilot flew his aircraft so low that the jet's tailhook "slapped" the rounded fantail, the "round-down," as it crossed the stern of the ship, it would be a cut pass. If the jet hit any aircraft outside of the landing area or any part of the ship through his error, it was a cut pass. A cut was worth zero points, but if an ego-bruised aviator received the grade, at least he had the consolation of being alive. He might even learn something. One thing he would certainly learn was how to get to the captain of the ship's office, because he would most certainly be sent there for a little one-on-one counseling with the head honcho.

The Greenie Board was the focus of every ready room. It was the visible representation of the one skill that transcended all individual warfare specialties among the various squadrons—landing at the ship. It was the first thing the aviator's eyes searched for as he opened the ready-room door, sometimes boldly and directly, but usually with side glances, as if it didn't really matter how the rest of the air wing was doing. Competition among aviators permeated the air wing, but landing grades were the only quantifiable arena where every pilot could be measured side by side, regardless of aircraft type, seniority, age, or experience. Perhaps the Greenie Board held more sway than it should have, but then again, landing was the most dangerous activity that the air wing was engaged in every day, in peace or war.

There was a highly publicized experiment during the Vietnam War involving stress and combat. Pilots were wired to monitors to check for stress levels during an entire mission, from the catapult to getting shot at by the enemy, and then for their return to the ship and arrested landing. The results were surprising in that the most stressful period of each sortie was not while the pilot was flying in combat but rather while on approach for a night carrier landing. The experiment was legendary in naval aviation, and I had often wondered just how much truth there was to it. My questions were put to rest early on in the deployment by the assurances that the testing had indeed been conducted: The principal subject for the experiment had been an A-6 pilot and was none other than the *Ranger* battle group's overall commander, Admiral Zlatoper.

The rest of the ready-room walls were filled with a variety of useful-to-entertaining hangings. A 4-by-6-foot grease board on the back wall depicted the daily flight schedule, listing crews, aircraft numbers, launch and recovery times, and the mission of the day. The squadron duty officer dutifully marked all changes to the oversized companion to the computer-generated flight schedule in red. This drew the commanding officer's eyes immediately to those portions that were different from what he had approved in the early hours of the morning, when the schedule was brought to his stateroom for his signature. A quick glance would reveal how smoothly the flight schedule was going. If the board was bloodred with changes, it was not a good day for the SDO. Bulletin boards, aviation pictures, calendars, and a huge set of wooden pilot and B/N wings adorned the remaining space.

Adjacent to the squadron duty officer's desk was a safe for secret material to be checked out by aircrews on their way to their jets, and next to the entry door was the elaborate and expensive part task missile trainer (PTT). During most of the workups the PTT had been referred to as the "part task coffee table." Now that our entry into hostilities seemed imminent, it was curiously busy on that side of the ready room as aviators practiced simulations of "switchology" and correct procedure for firing the new weapons that our latest aircraft upgrade had brought with it.

The first of more than five hundred A-6s was delivered to the navy by the Grumman Corporation in 1963, but most advances of technology had been incorporated into her airframe over the years. The PTT was supposed to help us train to the latest change.

Over the years computers and radars were replaced. The forward-looking infrared (flir) was added to provide a heat-sensing TV display for more accurate bomb deliveries. The flir referenced the angle to the target in conjunction with the A-6's height above the ground to determine the distance to the target for the bomb release computation. A laser also had been installed, to fine-tune the ranging capability of the flir and to enable the Intruder to drop laser-guided weapons.

The subsonic A-6 was the first truly all-weather attack aircraft in the world, and even in 1990 her capabilities were husbanded closely by the United States. The Intruder was never exported, and perhaps because of her homely, bulbous nose and prominent refueling probe, she was never utilized by the air force. The U.S. Navy and Marine Corps had relied on the Intruder since Vietnam for precision munitions delivery, and to fill the gap between "light" and air force "heavy" bombers: the A-6 was the official "medium" attack aircraft of the U.S. Navy.

Across from the part task missile trainer, slotted mailboxes covered most of one ready-room wall, intermediate resting spots for pieces of hot paperwork that the senior aviators foisted on the junior, and the ground pounders foisted on all. Next to the mailboxes was the lubricant that kept the squadron running, the coffeepot. After the Greenie Board the coffee corner was the ready room's busiest hub.

My mailbox was already starting to fill—rough drafts of sailor evaluations and myriad enlisted qualifications requiring the signature of my boss, the maintenance officer. "Never let your box stay full for more than a day," Rivers had advised me. "Fix it, pass it up, or throw it out, but don't let it stack up or you'll never catch up. Keep it moving." I had decided that it was wise to pay particular attention to that advice due to Rivers' sage years and bountiful experience. Besides, he was my boss. Rivers ran the maintenance department for the squadron, and I ran the aircraft division within that department. Most of my duties were administrative—the ground pounders and the squadron chief petty officers ran the production side of things. They were the full-time professionals who knew which end of a wrench to hold. Officers, on the other hand, were almost universally college graduates and dealt with the paperwork and personnel issues such as training and job assignments. The stack of folders and paperclip-attached packets took the wind out of my sails for a moment as I sifted through the navy-speak and sorted them into piles of varying importance. I stuck the rearranged bundle under my arm and set off for a quick tour of the aircraft division squadron spaces.

The six work centers in the aircraft division were scattered throughout *Ranger*'s decks and passageways. It was a constant fight for space on the ship, and you took what you could get, wherever that might be. If the shop had good ducting to the air conditioning a lot of other faults could be overlooked. It took me half an hour to take a quick peek in each space, show my face, and make sure that the chaos was gradually subsiding. The first class petty officers in charge of each work center had the whips out, and the boxes were getting unpacked with surprising speed. It didn't take long to realize that my presence was distracting and slowing the process. Time to head back to the ready room and prepare for my hop.

# Chapter Four

# What so proudly we hailed . . .

Off the Coast of Southern California,
8 December 1990

Rivs and I were scheduled to "hot-seat/hot-pump" into the Intruder that VA-145's commanding officer, Commander Denby Starling, and Snax were flying for their day carrier landing qualification (CQ). This meant that after the CO and Snax completed their required refresher traps, their jet would be chained down with the engines still running. Rivers and I would dodge propellers and jet exhaust on the flight deck, make our way to their A-6, and climb in after they had gotten out. We would then close the canopy to offer some protection in the event of a fire, and the deck crew would begin to pump fuel into the Intruder's fuselage. After we had gotten airborne and completed our day CQ the routine would presumably be repeated with another aircrew. In this manner the maximum number of pilots could get qualified as quickly as possible with the fewest aircraft taking up precious deck space. The other six tailhook squadrons were doing the exact same thing, and it all worked great on paper until airplanes began to break, the weather turned, or somebody had trouble getting aboard. In other words, it usually looked great but it rarely turned out great. CQ would be completed prior to any other flying; this was assured regardless of how painful or how long it might take. Carrier qualifications were generally an evolution that was endured, not enjoyed.

Having satisfied the anxiety that I was missing some vital change to the flight schedule, I moved over to the coffeepot and looked for my cup. My trademark coffee mug was not very macho or navylike: it boasted an image of asparagus stalks and the word "Asparagus." I wasn't particularly fond of asparagus, but nobody ever confused my cup with theirs, and I thought it added a touch of levity to an occasionally strained environment. Evidently the executive officer (XO) did not agree with me. Commander Rick Cassara was second in command of VA-145. The XO was traditionally in charge of the squadron "heads and beds." He had the unsavory collateral duty of cracking the whip to ensure that all the squadron spaces were clean, boots were shined, and the other assorted mundane, but crucial, elements of discipline were enforced. Uniformity of coffee cups apparently was a new one for me to add to the list. I found all of the aviators' mugs that did not have the squadron emblem on them stuffed in a drawer, leaving a mere three auspiciously hanging from the coffee peg board—CO, XO, and VIP. At least I had plenty of company. I filled up with coffee and made a mental note to stow my cup in the drawer in my ready room chair—the last thing I wanted to do was antagonize the XO. He was a great guy and a super XO, which meant that most of the time his position did not allow him to show that he was a great guy. It is the little things that prey on the tired mind; I let it go and refilled my asparagus cup.

I sipped coffee and watched Rivers arrive through the side entrance to the ready room. The door led to the ordnance staging area, a rare open alcove off the main passageway on the starboard side of the ship. Ordnance was prepositioned here, midway between the permanent storage far belowdecks and the flight deck four levels above. Most of the ship's larger spaces had a minimum of two exits on opposite sides for quick evacuation in the event that one hatchway was blocked by fire. We still had about 20 minutes to our designated brief time, so I continued to take in my surroundings and adjust to the operational tempo of the morning.

The effectiveness with which the air wing managed the flight schedule for its seventysome aircraft was critical in determining how long *Ranger* was required to maintain steerage into the wind. Every second that *Ranger* pointed into the wind she was a slave to a predictable course for her enemies to track. It was essential, therefore, that launches and recoveries be conducted in as expeditious a manner as possible, while simultaneously allowing for the inevitable problems that would arise. Each mission required a certain number of aircraft, and spare jets needed to be available on the flight deck as fill-ins on a moment's notice. The limited amount of space on the carrier deck required special coordination of the air wing flight schedule to accommodate the necessary aircraft for a specific mission.

The most logical solution was in cyclic flight operations. While one wave of aircraft was catapulted into the air, the previous series of flying machines would circle overhead the carrier, anxiously watching their fuel tanks empty as they waited for the signal to drop their tailhooks and begin their approach to the ship. In this manner twenty to thirty aircraft could be kept airborne at any one time, while the additional space freed up on the flight deck could be used to move, or "respot," aircraft to make ready for the next launch. The huge flight deck elevators could transfer aircraft back and forth to the hangar bay as the flight schedule or maintenance issues dictated during these gaps in carrier deck flight operations.

The continuous cycle of launch and immediate recovery reduced the time that the carrier steamed into the wind, and gave the flight deck time and space to ready itself for the next cycle. *Ranger*'s four catapults could launch twenty aircraft in about 10 minutes, and theoretically she could recover twenty jets to her single angled deck in as little as 15 minutes. A total of 25 minutes cruising a predictable courseline into the wind to complete a cycle of twenty aircraft was ideal, but a few minutes over that could be achieved with regularity once the air wing and carrier interface began to click. Paring down the time required for launches and recoveries was a constant chore, and demanded the continual vigilance of every pilot and sailor working the flight deck.

When the final cycle was completed for the night, the ultimate balancing act began. Whereas only twenty aircraft had been maneuvering on the flight deck, soon there would be forty parked for the night. The trick was to "spot" each aircraft, to utilize the least amount of space, while freeing a path to at least one catapult for the first launch in the morning. This meant that jets would park mere inches from one another immediately upon clearing the ship's landing area, in a painstakingly contrived pattern. Wheels came within inches of the deck edge, and each aircraft's folding wings lined up at the hinges with a like-configured jet next to it. The Air Department ran the show from Flight Deck Control, where a tabletop representation of the carrier deck reflected every aircraft's real-time position, as updated by radio. A slip in the rush hour of aircraft movement could mean gridlock, a fouled landing area, and an airborne jet that had to wave off his approach and burn more precious fuel as the mess on the flight deck was sorted out.

The routine exception to cyclic flight operations was during carrier qualifications. CQ required multiple traps, catapults, and touch-and-gos for each pilot, and it was more practical to come up with a launch and recovery plan with greater flexibility than cyclic operations. For this situation there was "flex deck." As soon as an aircraft was catapulted airborne, it might be directed to turn back toward the ship to land, or it might be instructed to hold high over the ship while the flight deck gradually cleared itself of airplanes. Regardless, once a pilot started his approach to the ship he would either be told to go hook up for a touch-and-go, or hook down for an arrested landing. Traps translated into experience in the carrier environment, and an aviator's trap count was a source of pride and accomplishment. Tailhook pilots hated touch-and-gos—why go through all of the work, fly a nice pass, and then not even attempt to stop? Why practice bleeding? Besides, nobody made flight jacket patches depicting the number of touch-and-gos a pilot may have achieved. Patches were reserved for arrested landing milestones.

During flex deck at least one of two bow catapults was constantly firing, while the two waist catapults in the landing area remained clear so a steady succession of aircraft could touch down. The moment an aircraft trapped it would be pulled back slightly with the retraction of the arresting cable, and then the pilot would be told to raise his hook via hand signals when enough slack existed in the wire to work the tailhook free. The jet's wings would be folding up even as the Intruder began taxiing forward. It was critical for the landing area to be cleared as quickly as possible; another aircraft could be expected to touch down 45 short seconds after the preceding one trapped. A fast taxi later and the jet's wings would be spread, the aircraft hooked up to the catapult, and then launched into the air scant minutes after it had landed. This evolution was repeated day and night, interrupted only by hot refueling and hot seating, until all of a squadron's pilots had accomplished the necessary number of landings to achieve currency. The flight deck was a buzz of activity during carrier qualifications, even more so than during cyclic operations.

Brief time for our flight was fast approaching, so I took my navigation bag out of my seat drawer and walked up to Rivers, seated at the front of the ready room. He was wading through a stack of folders and loose papers a foot thick, reading and signing certain forms, and putting aside others that required closer scrutiny. Once the flight briefing began, all unrelated paperwork was supposed to halt until the flight was over and the debriefing concluded. This was a valid plan in theory, and would assist an aircrew in maintaining their focus during a mission. The constant battle of the pen encouraged a bit of cheating, though, and this rule was often broken. Because

Rivers and I flew together regularly as a crew, many of the briefing items were redundant and had been covered many times before. This did not mean that we would not brief them again, only that the full hour allotted for our face-to-face could effectively be whittled down to fifteen minutes.

Standard flight briefings began 2 hours prior to he scheduled launch of the cycle. This gave an aircrew enough time to discuss the flight as it pertained to the various aircraft participating in the particular exercise, and still left time for the pilot and B/N to brief with one another. I sat down alongside Rivers and watched the clock click over to 1100. The TV screen in the front corner of the ready room lit up with the hourly weather and general ship's orientation broadcast. Ordinarily a short intelligence briefing would follow, but since we were directly off the coast of southern California, evidently it was deemed safe to fly without intelligence. Rivs and I paid scant attention to the voice droning over the TV as we jotted down various pieces of information pertinent to the flight on our kneeboard index cards.

"How's the air force holding up?" I asked Rivers.

"Not bad; 505 is down for a phase inspection, everything else is full up. It looks like CAG's going to let us keep eight jets on the flight deck." The twelve squadron Intruders had survived the crane aboard nicely, and the air wing commander (CAG) wanted to keep eight Swordsmen A-6s accessible for flying on the flight deck. "All the armor plating has been installed; it's going to add 250 pounds to each jet," Rivers continued.

The underside of the A-6's fuselage had been beefed up with metal plating to give further protection to certain vital areas under the aircraft's skin. The penalty in doing this was the additional weight, which meant that we would have to land with 250 pounds less fuel. It was a trade-off, but bullets had priority for the time being.

"Hopefully it's a waste of time," I said. The TV went silent. Rivers pulled out his pocket emergency procedures checklist and opened it up to the numbered briefing section. We ran through each item quickly, with the confidence of knowing that we had flown in the shipboard environment with each other many times. Complacency of routine was a constant danger, and Rivers stressed the more critical items on the checklist: engine failure off the catapult, inadvertent taxi off the flight deck, in-flight fire, and a dozen other emergencies. Having a wife and four boys waiting at our home base of Whidbey Island, Washington, helped Rivers devote his full concentration to the contingencies portion of the brief. Ten minutes later we were at the bottom of the page, with 45 minutes to go before we needed to "walk" for our flight. Rivs dove back into his stack of folders, and I grabbed my coffee cup and headed for a refill.

I didn't have the motivation to tackle the pile of forms that was building a home in my mailbox. Instead I sat back down and watched the TV screen, which was now transmitting the black-and-white image of the platform camera. The flight deck was alive as various aircraft taxied toward the catapults and the first wave of carrier qualifications prepared to launch. I searched for the Intruder with 502 on its tail—the jet that Snax and the CO were in, the jet that we would jump into once they had finished. It was not in the landing platform camera's field of view. The "plat" camera maintained a 24-hour vigil of the flight deck. I soon grew restless. Hell, nothing was worse than just sitting and waiting. I headed back to my mailbox.

Thirty minutes later I had proven the assertion that paperwork was a distraction to flight planning. With my head bowed and a look of perplexity on my face I struggled with the wording of a performance evaluation that I was writing for one of my power plant mechanics. He had recently been promoted to second class petty officer, and I needed to evaluate his performance in his previous rank for documentation into his service record. I was fairly familiar with the petty officer in question, and it was not a dearth of positive subject matter that had me stymied. My problem was that I had allowed my thought process to revert from the superlatives of navy-speak evaluation writing to ordinary English. To characterize a worker as "excellent" on an evaluation was the equivalent of calling him mediocre. "Good" was the kiss of death to further advancement. The trick was finding new and inventive ways of saying "outstanding" in each of the bulletized remarks on the eval. Once in the proper mind-set the BS would flow effortlessly, but you had to completely divorce yourself from any recognizable form of English to transcend to this blissful state of eval-writing Nirvana.

"Well, are you coming?" I looked up and basked in Rivers' glare of exaggerated impatience.

"Is it that time? Well, we mustn't keep the commanding officer waiting. I got up and followed Rivers toward the ready-room door.

The painted green ready-room door slammed back into me as I stepped through the hatchway (navy-speak for door), Rivers' way of giving me a bit of grief, and himself a head start in the minor ritual of suiting up in our flight gear. I turned left out of the ready room, made another quick left past our squadron maintenance control, and saw Rivers' heels disappear into the paraloft shop 30 feet away. The parariggers (PRs) were enlisted men who maintained and serviced the aviators' flight and survival gear, including their parachutes.

Rivers was already half dressed when I opened the door, so I hustled over to the line of wall pegs and started pulling down my 30 pounds of flight gear. I picked up my helmet covered in reflective tape and set it aside on the floor so I could reach my G suit, hanging underneath it. The G suit, or anti-gravity suit (its more appropriate longhand name), was nothing more than a tightly fitting piece of inflatable nylon that covered the calves, thighs, and abdomen. I wrapped the green nylon around my waist, slid closed the zipper at my side, and began to pull the G suit leggings around my calves. I closed the leg zippers over the full length of my legs, stood up, and stretched until the tight fit no longer bunched up my fire-retardant Nomex flight suit overalls. The G suit's 2-foot-long hose hung at my left side like some strange appendage. Once in the left seat of the A-6 cockpit I would plug the quick-release fitting on the hose into the pilot's side console. With the onset of "G" loading in flight, the G suit would automatically inflate and literally squeeze the blood out of my legs and stomach, maintaining a supply of oxygen-rich blood to my brain so I would not black out. The combination of a G suit and a practiced breathing of grunts and diaphragm pushes could significantly increase the strength and duration of G's an aviator could endure before losing consciousness. Falling asleep while airborne was generally regarded as a bad thing, and could result in death or serious injury—just like tipping a Coke machine, only with a lot more noise.

The next step in the pilot dress-up game was the torso harness. Naval aircraft kept the aircrew parachutes attached to the ejection seats in the jet. The aviator needed some way to quickly attach, or free, the parachute each time he entered or exited the cockpit. The torso harness was a maze of straps with a nylon bucket seat for butt support, and two quick-release heavy metal fittings that attached to the parachute. The ideal fit was tight enough in the shoulders so it was difficult to stand up straight, which added to the impression of being wrapped in a green cocoon. A metal D ring hung ponderously off the right side of the torso harness, the preferred method of attachment to a hoist line lowered by a helicopter if one was unlucky enough to eject.

Two items were left hanging on my designated hook—a bulky, pocket-laden jacket, and two pieces of sewn-together green webbing, each with a buckle. The jacket was our SV-2 survival vest. Pulling the beaded handles waist high at one's side would inflate two bladders via $CO_2$ cartridges and provide adequate flotation for a downed aviator in full flight gear. A saltwater-activated sensor would discharge the $CO_2$ automatically if a pilot or B/N was injured in the ejection and was either unconscious or unable to pull his handles. In the pool during recurrent survival training we practiced treading water for 5 minutes in full flight gear without flotation. Swimming with steel-toed boots was bad enough, but the extra waterlogged weight of the SV-2, torso harness, and G suit made it extremely difficult even in the calm conditions of the pool. We put a lot of faith in those beaded handles and oversized air bladders.

In addition to keeping one's head above water, the SV-2 carried all the survival gear that an enterprising young aviator with the instincts of Daniel Boone needed to stay alive and get found by the good guys. Prominently accessed via the outside of one of the large front pockets was a parachute shroud cutter to free tangled parachute lines while floating downward. In a typical lowest-bidder operation, the shroud cutter had been designed, and accepted, completely backward. The request had been to design the hooklike shroud cutter with a switchblade mechanism for one-handed operation. What the navy got instead was a regular switchblade, illegal in most states, with a folding shroud cutter that required two hands and fingernails to extract. The complex technical solution was to duct-tape the switchblade closed and to keep the shroud cutter permanently extended. The U.S. Navy had hundreds, perhaps thousands, of these illegally backward shroud cutters circulating in the inventory. Thank goodness for duct tape.

In the same general vicinity as the shroud cutter was a waterproof survival radio and several signaling devices for a downed airman to attract the attention of an aircraft dispatched to search for crash survivors. The various instruments were diverse enough to provide an effective manner of signaling in virtually any set of conditions. For the daylight there was smoke, flares, and a mirror, and for darker situations there was an additional handheld flare, and a strobe light. Once in the ballpark, a rescuer would hopefully hear a small whistle if the underbrush was too thick to spy the grounded aviator. Rounding off the standard SV-2 gear was a plastic flask of water, a large World War II–vintage survival knife, a tiny compass, and a flashlight with white and red lenses for increased or decreased travel of light. Five pounds of optional equipment were permitted at the discretion of the aviator, and might consist of items such as extra water, space blankets, a smaller and sharper knife, and a fishing kit.

There were two reasons for the weight limitation of 5 pounds. A truly overweighted SV-2 ran the risk of ripping open its pockets in a high-speed ejection and spilling out its valuable contents. The limit also ensured that the heaviest of aircrew would not exceed the advertised limitations of the A-6's ejection seat. The seat had to be able to fling the pilot or B/N high enough under most normal flight conditions for the parachute to fully deploy prior to the aviator impacting the ground. All of the survival gear was tied into the SV-2 by a 500-pound test parachute shroud line in a last-ditch effort to retain it if the force of an ejection began to tear the vest apart.

The final items left on my hook were two webbed leg restraints. The nylon straps crossed each calf, were separated by a 6-inch gap, and were then buckled on the inside of the leg. Small clasps just above the boot heel snapped into a separate clip attached to the bottom of the ejection seat. In the event of an ejection, the leg restraints would be pulled tight and held against the bottom of the ejection seat until the parachute deployed. The possibility of an errant leg catching the windstream as the seat left the cockpit and being twisted into an unnatural position was reduced with the use of leg restraints. The only method of preventing so-called flail injuries on the upper body was by maintaining the practiced body position of elbows in, and hands tightly clasped to one of the two ejection seat handles either overhead or between the aviator's knees. If an airman was unfortunate enough to eject at any speed above about 250 knots, the chances were good that he would sustain some sort of flail injury regardless of body position and the use of leg restraints. One could only hope that the injury would be a minor sprain versus a broken bone or a severed limb. I glanced over at Rivers, who was staring intently at the landing platform TV.

"Is 502 on deck yet?"

"Can't tell," Rivers answered and turned toward the door.

I pulled the oxygen mask out of my helmet and snapped its protective cover to my SV-2 just below my chin. I attached the mask's hose to the front of my survival vest with Velcro, picked up my helmet in one hand, navigation bag in the other, and was once again in the familiar position of following Rivers' heels. We made two right turns out of the pararigger shop and started the walk down *Ranger*'s starboard side toward the stern of the ship. Every 20 feet or so there was a minor pause to our progress as we stepped over the 18-inch-high knee knockers designed to contain flooding water or provide the backstop for a watertight hatch. Visitors to an aircraft carrier were hard pressed to make it 30 minutes without skinning a shin on the omnipresent hazards.

Rivers picked up the pace of a man all dressed up and needing a place to go. The enlisted troops in the passageway stepped aside partially in deference to our rank, but more so as a practical matter so we could fit our tall, bulky forms through the narrow maze of hatches. Rivers strode over a final steel knee knocker, shot a look at the placard above one of the hatches to his left, and, satisfied with its label, stepped through it. I turned into the familiar ladderway, which led to *Ranger*'s lone superstructure, the island, three levels above us. Grasping the chain-link rail on each side, I took the steep steps two at a time so I could keep sight of Rivers ahead of me. My breathing became more labored under the weight of my flight gear, and I saw with a touch of relief that Rivers had slowed down. Naturally, I couldn't let the old guy outpace me, but I didn't want to break a sweat before we had even reached the flight deck.

I caught up to Rivers standing at the top of the third ladder with his fire-retardant skullcap on and his helmet poised to cover his head. I quickly followed suit, snapped my chinstrap, and put down my clear visor in preparation for flight deck operations. Once flight stations were called away on the 1MC loudspeaker, only those properly attired were permitted on the flight deck. You also needed a pretty damn good reason to be up there. Extra people on the flight deck meant unnecessary exposure to risk, and naval aviation was all about acceptable and unacceptable risk. I rolled my fire-retardant Nomex flight suit sleeves down and, satisfied that I was completely covered except for the lower part of my face and my hands, I signaled Rivers that I was ready to go.

Aviators enjoyed one exception to standard flight deck attire that others could not copy—gloves were optional. Aviators were not required to wear gloves, ostensibly because they might impede a pilot trying to extricate himself from his parachute in the event of an overwater ejection. More realistically, many aviators simply found it difficult to manipulate flight instruments and controls with gloves on. Regardless, the remainder of the flight deck uniform was rigidly enforced: steel-toed boots, legs and arms completely covered in flame-retardant material, helmet on with visor down or goggles on, and some form of flotation jacket. It was most practical to take preventive measures against the twin threats of fire and water; the other flight deck dangers were more difficult to guard against.

Rivers acknowledged my nod of go ahead and cracked open the 5-foot hatch to the starboard side of the island. Even in this most protected sideshow of the carrier deck, the noise level of jet engines, propellers, and catapults was initially overwhelming to the sound-protected ears beneath a helmet. The stiff breeze made as the carrier cruised into the wind alternated between the smell of salt spray and JP-5 jet fuel as the taxiing aircraft turned their tails and redirected their exhaust. I ducked my head through the hatchway and found a relatively wide-open expanse of safe area where the bomb farm was normally situated. The starboard side of the island was too small for aircraft movement, and its approximately 20-foot width was usually reserved for the forward staging of aviation ordnance. Ordinarily only a small path could be negotiated through this portion of the flight deck, but having just left port, it remained free of bombs and missiles for the time being. The chain to the bomb chute was up, barring accidental transit through one of the few portions of the carrier deck's perimeter where no horizontal web of steel cables was strewn to catch a sailor about to go overboard. The 3-foot catwalk of steel webbing lined both port and starboard sides of the ship, but had an intentional gap at the bomb farm so ordnance could be pushed overboard quickly in the event of a fire or flight deck calamity.

Rivers covered the 50 open feet quickly and cracked the hatch to flight deck control. I followed close in trail. The majority of the noise and commotion immediately ceased with the slamming shut of the heavy steel hatch behind me. Replacing the impression of utter confusion on the flight deck was one of a surreal dreamworld. Although it was day, natural light was restricted to a few select windows, all with sturdy metal frames and many inches of bulletproof glass. Aviators in full flight gear dominated half of the small compartment, with their helmets at their sides. In the other half those wearing yellow shirts ruled, and they stood in a constantly circulating semicircle around the giant tabletop representation of aircraft on the carrier deck.

Everyone on the flight deck had a specific color jersey for quick identification of his particular function. Taxi directors were in charge of aircraft and elevator movements, but more importantly, they maintained order and carried out the plans devised in flight deck control for getting jets where they needed to be. Taxi directors wore telltale yellow shirts and had a peculiar love-hate relationship with the air wing aviators. Yellow shirts were the ones who tried to taxi you too fast only inches from the flight deck edge when you were still shaking from a fast-paced daytime flight and recovery. They were also the ones who coaxed, urged, and just plain willed you to taxi with precision and safety after you had landed on that last night cycle when you were not sure if you had any reserves left in you. We could make the yellow shirts' job more difficult, but they could make ours pure hell. Maybe not rule number one of carrier aviation, but certainly in the top ten: Never piss off a yellow shirt. Yellow shirts were a group of highly disciplined (while working) professionals who took deserved pride in the enormous responsibilities they exercised. They sometimes viewed pilots as prima donnas, pilots occasionally viewed them as disrespectful, and both were usually right. But each group had a grudging respect for the other—there was a mutual understanding that both needed to be proficient in their respective jobs if the flight deck was to be kept as marginally safe as it was.

There were six other aviators crammed into our half of the space, all waiting for their jets to land so they could hot-seat into them. Every couple of minutes a shout would come across the room from the yellow shirts' side: "605's on deck, hot pump, hot seat."

The replacement flight crew would get their helmets back on, zip up their SV-2 (if they had gotten that relaxed), and foray out into the teeming activity of the flight deck in search of their jet. This was the worst part of carrier qualifications—waiting. Inactivity gave the mind an opportunity to wander to places that were not productive, dwelling on negative possibilities instead of positive probabilities.

"Crew for 502, next plane on deck, going to 'L' 1."

Rivers and I got up and put our helmets on. "L" 1 stood for Aircraft Elevator 1, and that would be where we would find 502 secured to the flight deck. I looped the strap of my nav bag through my left hand and pulled the oversized lever to the hatch open with both arms. Rivers followed me and quickly closed the hatch behind him in an attempt to trap some of the relative quiet inside the cramped space. I walked forward and stopped for a moment to get my bearings as I reached the edge of the island, and the far forward portion of the flight deck came into view. A new wave of propeller and jet noise washed over me; both bow cats were operating, and each had a single Intruder or EA-6B Prowler formed up behind it. I listened to the background hum from around the corner of the island; an E-2 must have its props spinning on one of the waist cats. All the carrier aircraft were painted gray in an attempt to camouflage themselves with the sea and sky. It should work for the desert as well, I thought.

There was an A-6 on half of "L" 1 with engines turning, its crew seated under the closed canopy while fuel was pumped into the chocked and chained jet. Next to the Intruder was an empty spot where we could expect one of the yellow shirts to park 502. I looked toward the unobstructed portion of the landing area forward of the island, and saw a recently trapped A-6 begin to fold its wings. The yellow shirt taxied it clear of the angle deck.

I yelled "502" to Rivers and pointed to the jet.

Rivs gave me a thumbs-up and we waited for our jet to be parked. Two minutes later, blue-shirted sailors swarmed around 502 and chained her securely to several of the steel-ringed padeyes that covered the flight deck. I walked briskly in a deep crouch under the midsection of 502's neighbor, steering well clear of her exhaust, a hazard even at idle thrust. Rivers continued around the front of 502, giving a wide berth to her jet intakes, and stood by the right side while I waited at the pilot's boarding ladder on the left for the skipper to finish unstrapping and climb down.

The purple-shirted fuelers, the grapes, had a fuel hose extended from the catwalk fueling station on the port side of the ship and were waiting to see if they should fuel before or after the hot seat. Their quizzical looks were answered by the opening of 502's canopy. Commander Starling stepped out onto the A-6's fold-out boarding ladder, reached back into the cockpit for his nav bag, and started backing his way down the 7 feet to the flight deck. Our CO was a complete professional who exuded competence. He rarely found it necessary to raise his voice when not on the flight deck. He reached the bottom and immediately turned to me with his hand cupped to his mouth.

"Jet's up and up. Takes a little left rudder." The skipper yelled into the wind, competing with a Prowler screaming at full power on cat one. I lifted the edge of my helmet slightly under my right ear so I could make out his assessment of 502: nothing broken on the jet, slightly bent airframe, requires a little left rudder trim to compensate.

"Got it," I responded in kind to his thumbs-up. "Thanks, Skipper." I turned toward the Intruder's access ladder and started to scramble up to the relative safety of the cockpit.

I grasped the inside rail of the Intruder's canopy bow and pulled myself up the last few feet until I was looking down into the cockpit. I placed my nav bag as far aft as it would go on the left console, taking care not to place it where it could accidentally fall onto the G suit test switch. A pilot only needed to have his G suit accidentally inflate to its muscle-squeezing capacity once during a precision evolution like tanking or landing to remember this small precaution. I scanned the ejection seat in a quick but thorough manner and ensured that both handles were in the disarmed position and all the safety pins had been removed. Having accomplished this singularly important safety check, I waited no further to pull my long legs into the cockpit. I straddled the stick and plopped down into the ejection seat. Rivers was mirroring my progress, and we turned to each other simultaneously. Rivers moved his hand horizontally over his head, verifying via hand signals that all my body parts were clear of the canopy rail. I looked over my shoulder to make certain no one had followed me up to assist me, saw that the canopy was clear, and gave Rivers a thumbs-up. Rivers reached over to the center of the instrument panel and held down the canopy toggle switch to the closed position. We each took one more look around the canopy rail as the glass and metal dome came forward in its tracks, clunked into position, and enveloped us in a feeling of secure quiet. I took a deep breath and started to strap in.

I snapped myself to the seat with six buckles: two for the leg restraints; two at my waist to keep from floating in less than one G flight; and two at my shoulders, connecting me to the ejection seat and its attached parachute. A grape was gesturing to me from the bottom of the boarding ladder, anxious to get on with the fueling. I tapped my refueling switch to the ground position and gave him a thumbs-up. During our brief Rivers and I had discussed the position of the ejection seat safety latches while we received fuel on the flight deck. Normally we would have armed our seats so we could eject as a last resort if a fuel-fed fire engulfed the Intruder. We were parked directly in front of *Ranger*'s island, however, and an ejection would shoot us straight up into the 20-knot wind over the carrier deck, which would immediately push us into the array of sharp antennae and steel guide wires 100 feet above us. We would have to either fight our way out of a flight deck fire on foot, or take our chances sitting tight and hope it would be put out before it penetrated our canopy or blew up the jet. Refueling fires were not common, but like many naval aviators, I knew someone who had died in one. That was enough to catch my attention.

Our fuel gauge started to rise, and I turned my attention to the score of switches, knobs, and dials that covered the forward instrument panel and the two consoles at my sides. The skipper had made certain that everything was set up for the outgoing crew. All I needed to do was adjust my seat and rudder pedals and verify that each switch was as it should be. Rivers was busy analyzing the status of the alignment of the inertial navigation system and updating our correct position. It did not take more than a few minutes for the high-pressure fueling line to pump 12,000 pounds of gas into our Intruder, bringing our total fuel to just under 16,000 pounds. Our computations during the brief showed that the maximum fuel we could trap with was 5,400 pounds. Extra gas was usually on-

loaded to afford loiter time if *Ranger* could not take us into
the landing pattern immediately. We had gotten word that we
could expect to wait awhile overhead the ship before it was
our turn to carrier-qualify. We took on enough gas to leave
ourselves the flexibility to stay airborne for 2 hours if need be
before we could land. It was easy to dump fuel to get down to
landing weight. It was impossible to create gas out of nothing.

I watched the grape drag the fuel hose off under his arm
back to the catwalk. He had not cleared the flight deck before
my attention was directed to the front of the plane, where a
yellow shirt was gesturing at us. I glanced at Rivers: "Ready
to go?"

# Chapter Five

# . . . thro' the mists of the deep

"All set . . . okay, let's go," Rivers replied as he put the finishing touches on his inertial navigation update.

I put my fists together above the canopy rail, where the yellow shirt could see them. With my palms upward and my thumbs pointed out, I rapidly moved my fists apart. The yellow shirt acknowledged my signal with a repeat of the thumbs-out, took each arm in turn, and ran his opposite hand down the length of it in a signal to the blue shirts under our jet to pull our chocks and unchain us. In seconds our Intruder was free, and the yellow shirt opened and closed his fists, palms out to us, in a signal to release brakes and taxi forward. I reached for my upper and lower ejection handles and pushed each respective safety latch down to the armed position. Seeing out of the corner of my eye that Rivers had done the same, I pushed in the metal parking brake handle with my left hand and gingerly moved the throttles forward. I mashed down on the nose wheel steering button on the control stick and gently moved my rudder pedals, rocking the A-6 ever so slightly from side to side in an effort to break the lock that the textured deck plates had on our tires.

We began to move forward, and the yellow shirt dropped his left arm, telling us to turn our jet to the right. We opened the distance between our neighboring Intruder, the yellow shirt increased the cant of his left arm, and I put in a harder turn to the right. Moments later we were in the relatively open space behind the jet blast deflector for cat one, and the yellow shirt moved both arms from overhead to his sides in an exaggerated motion. Rivers reached over to the center console with his left hand and moved the wing fold handle to the down position. I took my eyes off the yellow shirt for a fraction of a second and verified that my wing was indeed dropping. Once down and locked into position, I grasped the flap handle by the throttle quadrant and lowered the Intruder's flaps and slats. We had taxied forward another 10 feet or so when the yellow shirt stopped us, and dropped to his knees to gain a footing against the residual jet blast from a Prowler on cat one going to full power.

Our A-6 rocked back and forth, a result of the Prowler's exhaust traveling up the jet blast deflector and making contact with the vertical stabilizer at the tail of our jet. I pulled back on the top of my oxygen mask to blow away the acrid burn of the Prowler's exhaust that had migrated through our air-conditioning system and into my eyes. Rivers took advantage of the temporary lull in our taxi director's activity to read the takeoff checklist.

"Wings."

"Spread and locked." I pushed my hand against the wing fold handle to make certain it was flush.

"Trim."

"Zero, zero, and five nose up." The rudder, flaperon, and elevator trims were set for the cat shot.

"Flaps."

"Flaps, slats, stabilizers shifted, boards are in." I checked that the flaps and slats were fully extended, that the speed brakes were in, and that we had the extended rudder and elevator authority of a shifted stabilizer required for takeoff.

"Fuel."

"Normal, normal, two lights, fuel ready is off," I ticked off, verifying that our fuel quantity indications and switches were normal, and that the wing tanks were not yet under the pressurization that would transfer fuel once we were airborne.

"Controls."

"Visually checked, free, stab aug's off." I looked over my shoulder and into the mirror on Rivers' side of the cockpit as I cycled the rudders, flaperons, and elevator, then I glanced down to verify that the autopilot was not engaged.

"Seats."

"Armed top and bottom, in six ways, you're hot top." I double-checked that I was fully strapped into the ejection seat, that my seat was armed at both handles, and that Rivers' upper ejection handle was in the armed position.

"Harness as you like it, pop-ups and antiskid."

"Off and off." The final items were to ensure that the antiskid braking and automatic deployment system of the flaperons to full up for maximum drag were not armed. Both of these systems were for shore-based operations, where the tailhook was not normally used to stop the aircraft.

Rivers had just finished when the yellow shirt, still fighting the dissipating jet blast from the Prowler that had catapulted moments before, stood up, leaning into the wind, and started to taxi us forward. Vast billows of steam from the catapult track temporarily obscured my view of him except for his outstretched hands. He gave us a rapid signal to lower the tailhook, and after seeing that it had properly extended, he motioned for us to raise it. This was the only opportunity for us to verify that the tailhook was capable of being dropped before we were catapulted.

The jet blast deflector, a massive steel wall about 40 feet long and 8 feet high, swung back down on its six huge hydraulic hinges and became flush with the flight deck behind the catapult. The yellow shirt made a throwing motion with both of his arms and passed us off to the catapult taxi director, who was standing in the cat track. Our new yellow shirt moved his arms side to side over his head frantically in an effort to get us to pick up our taxi speed. I pushed the throttles forward,

and stole a glance into my mirror to check that our tail was
clear to prevent the increased thrust from hurting somebody.
The yellow shirt was responsible for ensuring that it was safe
for us to come up on the power, but that would not change the
fact that it was my jet that might blow an unaware sailor over
the side.

I refocused my undivided attention to the yellow shirt as
we approached the catapult track. If we did not taxi perfectly
straight onto the cat, the Intruder's wheels would not line up
correctly, and we would have to be physically pushed back by
a dozen sailors to try again. The yellow shirt's wildly exaggerated hand signals had dampened down until his hands now
barely moved, and the minor turns were communicated by
slight nods of his head in one direction or another. A form
came into my peripheral field of view to the left and forward.
The new figure ran to the side of the A-6, holding a large
board over his head. On it read the number "44,000." I
showed him my left hand palm up and moved it up and down
until the board had been changed to "45,000." Satisfied with
the new catapult weight, I gave him back a thumbs-up; 45,000
pounds would now be the weight setting for the catapult
during our Intruder's cat shot. Too high a setting and damage
might be caused to our nose gear at the catapult attachment.
Too low a setting and the force of the cat shot might not
be strong enough for us to reach flying speed. The aircrew
were the final judges of what the correct weight would be,
and determining that weight was a standard part of preflight
planning.

Our Intruder slowly reached the shuttle that would physically connect us to the catapult. I added power to get us over
this last small hump, and quickly pulled back the throttles
when I felt us go ever so slightly over the top of the small
piece of metal and clunk our nose gear down into place. The
yellow shirt clamped his hands into two fists. The taxi director took several steps to the side of the A-6, gave a look
over to the safety observers, snapped his heels to attention,

and shot his right arm out horizontally and his left forearm
vertically, with his elbow tucked at his side. I advanced the
throttles, and the Intruder began to shake and shimmy against
the holdback fitting recessed in the track of the shuttle. The
4-inch metal holdback fitting was specifically designed to
withstand the pressure of an A-6 at full throttle, but would
snap with the additional force of the catapult pulling against
it. The yellow shirt turned us over to the white-shirted catapult officer to my left and forward. The catapult officer was
one of the few officers who worked full-time on the flight
deck. He would have the ultimate responsibility for ensuring
that the jet had been connected correctly and that all safety
parameters had been satisfied. He gave a determined glare up
and down the cat track, raised his left hand, and rapidly began
to twirl his forefinger and index finger over his head in an abbreviated motion.

I pushed the stick forward and to the left, and then moved it
toward all four corners of the cockpit to check for full throw
of movement in the flight controls. Outside safety observers
scrutinized the plane, making certain that every control surface moved as it should and that there were no fluid leaks or
loose panels. The Intruder's engines howled in protest to the
stationary position to which they were bound. The noise in
the cockpit was deafening, and the engine instruments raced
upward to their limits. I scanned the instrument panel rapidly;
everything indicated normal full thrust. I keyed the intercommunication button on the throttle quadrant. "Good strut lock
light—ready, Rivers?" I said into my oxygen mask. The nose
landing gear strut was locked hydraulically in a brace for the
shock of the catapult.

"Let's go."

With my left hand locked around the catapult grip to keep
the throttles from moving aft during the cat stroke, I raised
my right hand to the top of my visor and rendered the catapult
officer a crisp salute. He briskly returned the salute and in-
spected up and down the deck, and then left to right one last

time. Having received a thumbs-up from all his observers, he bent down on one knee and touched the deck with his left hand in so rapid a motion that it appeared as if the deck plates had given him a shock. Across the cat track, standing face-to-face with the catapult officer in the catwalk, a young sailor with both arms raised in the air took one last look up and down the deck, almost daring someone to raise his crossed arms overhead in the suspension signal. Having no takers, he reached down below the scupper rail and pushed a single button.

Instantly the 45,000-pound Intruder was transformed from a state of quaking potential energy to streaking kinetic as it was literally hauled ahead of the thrust from its churning engines to a flyable airspeed. My head was firmly planted in the headrest, my left arm fully extended, my hand squeezing the cat grip, and my right arm cradled to catch the stick as it moved aft when the relative wind brought the elevator to life. The Intruder accelerated from zero to 150 knots, 180 mph, in 2 seconds. My ears rang with the sound of the shuttle rocketing down its track and then slamming to a standstill at the deck edge. Tunnel vision narrowed my sight—I strained to maintain focus on my ADI and backup standby gyro. The cat shot felt good—we were flying.

The wheels were barely off the deck when I shot my arm from the throttle to the landing gear handle. Gear up, set the jet in a climb attitude on the ADI. Both engines check good. I resisted the urge to do a clearing turn, a serious faux pas during carrier qualifications. Clearing turns were minor banks to the side to provide more spacing with any aircraft that might be getting airborne simultaneously off of an adjacent catapult. During CQ the cat shots were staggered so the first few rusty seconds airborne could be flown straight ahead. The A-6 continued its acceleration through 180 knots, and I translated airspeed to altitude. We climbed through 100 feet. Next, I raised the flaps and slats, and with the decreased drag we quickly arrived at our standard departure altitude of 500 feet. I pushed the stick forward, let off the pressure with the electric trim button on the control stick, and the jet accelerated to 300 knots. I reset the throttles and continued straight ahead at 300 knots and 500 feet as I flipped off the bayonet fitting on my oxygen mask and bared my face at our new-found freedom. What a kick in the pants.

The California marine layer of clouds at 1,500 feet was thin in spots, but with the sun still relatively fresh in the sky it had not yet had the chance to fully burn off. Rivers switched the number one radio's preset frequency from the ship's land/launch to departure. We continued out straight ahead on the cat shot's heading. We had reached 7 miles in front of the ship on the TACAN gauge when Rivers keyed the mike.

"Departure, Rustler 502, 7 miles."

"Radar contact, Rustler 502, your signal is marshal, cleared to climb, switch to button 17."

Rivers twirled the radio preset knob until the digital readout showed 17. "Marshal" was the call sign of the air traffic controller for the aircraft awaiting recovery, and also was the name of the procedure for the jet's circular holding pattern. I advanced the throttles to the stops, pulled back on the stick, and dipped the wings until the Intruder was climbing at 300 knots and was heading 30 degrees to the right of our initial heading. We punched through the cloud layer and were suddenly presented with an unobstructed view of the world above 2,000 feet.

"Marshal, Rustler 502, 280 radial at 11 DME, climbing through 5,000," transmitted Rivers.

"Rustler 502, radar contact, marshal overhead mother, angels 20."

"Rustler 502 marshal overhead at angels 20," Rivers repeated into the radio.

"Well, I guess we're not going anywhere soon." I keyed the intercommunication button and spoke into my oxygen mask. "At least they gave us some altitude right off the bat."

The low overhead holding altitude for A-6s was 4,000 feet.

By initially directing us to hold at "angels 20," 20,000 feet, marshal was telling us that we would be waiting for a while. The higher that a jet flew, the less fuel it burned, and accordingly the greater amount of time it could stay airborne.

"It looks like this stuff is getting ready to burn off. Bet it goes to Case 1 soon," Rivers replied.

The carrier had three standard aircraft departure and arrival profiles, depending on the weather. Case 1 was for days when the ship could be seen from virtually anywhere, and little to no radio communication was required. Case 2 was a bit of a hybrid and was designed for weather that was better than 1,000-foot ceilings and 5 miles of visibility, but had a cloud layer obstructing the view of the ship from overhead flight. An instrument procedure was flown to safely get below the clouds without running into another aircraft, and then the profile returned to a Case 1 visual approach. Case 3 was for bad weather and night operations. The Case 3 approach was flown entirely on instruments until approximately three-quarters of a mile from the back of the ship, when visual reference was made to the angled deck. *Ranger* was currently operating Case 2, but when the clouds cleared up she would switch to the faster-moving Case 1 pattern.

I looked at the TACAN distance readout, the DME, and satisfied that we were well outside the 10-mile radius reserved for aircraft circling overhead, I began a lazy, arcing turn back toward the ship. We passed through 10,000 feet and I pulled back on the stick to transition to a 250-knot climb, keeping the throttles against the stops at military-rated thrust, the maximum power the engines could produce. I peered over my left shoulder in the turn, and I could begin to make out the specks that were the various aircraft orbiting overhead *Ranger*. I kept my angle of bank at a relaxed 15 degrees so we would not close within 10 miles of the ship, and climbed into the brightly shining sun. The low marine layer of clouds started to evaporate, and bits and pieces of the ocean below us began to appear. Rivers had his visor up and was clearly enjoying the feel of the sunshine on his face.

"Still solid overhead the ship." I looked down at the solid white of clouds.

"They'll be able to pick up the pace if it goes to Case 1. Probably another half hour or so," Rivers answered back.

Our Intruder was stabilized in a 250-knot climb when we broke through 19,000 feet. I pointed our Intruder directly at the TACAN needle locked on *Ranger* while scanning the skies for any other jets at our altitude.

"Looks like it's just us up here; lucky us," I said, and engaged the autopilot. I brought the throttles back to the minimum thrust required to keep flying. This power setting would give us our maximum endurance angle of attack, that airspeed at which we would conserve the most fuel. It was such a slow airspeed that we were right at the edge of aerodynamic stall, which if it happened at 20,000 feet with no one directly below us would not be a big deal.

Flying around the carrier was a constant exercise in fuel conservation, often culminating in the dumping of thousands of pounds of gas into the air when the overhead jets were instructed that the deck was clear and that they should "buster," or hurry down, to land. It took only one good scare going low on fuel out over the open ocean to make a true gas-hoarding believer out of anyone.

Aerial refueling was an option for a pilot who could not catch a wire and had one too many trips around the bolter pattern. Aligning a jet's refueling probe with a 3-foot basket slung on a hose 20 feet behind another jet at night was not exactly soothing, however. If a nerve-racked aviator could engage the basket successfully and stay in it while fuel was transferred, it would buy him several thousand pounds of gas. This translated into a few more opportunities to excel in the carrier's landing pattern. The stress could be cumulative, but if the ship was conducting "blue water ops," out of the range of a divert airfield, then you had better get over it, because there were no other runways and no other options besides ejection.

Our radio was still tuned to marshal, and we occupied ourselves by listening in on the progress of the stack of aircraft circling overhead. Every couple of minutes an airplane would be told to switch frequencies to approach, and they would be vectored out behind the ship and below the cloud layer until they could see the boat. The air boss on board *Ranger* was evidently confident that the weather conditions would soon improve. It was his job to oversee the launch and recovery procedures of the air wing. The air boss was a veteran carrier aviator who sat in his minitower overlooking the flight deck, making the second-to-second decisions concerning the overall conduct of flight operations.

Ordinarily, Case 2 aircraft would be lined up at some distance from the stern of the ship. The "boss" was keeping them close to the carrier in the Case 1 overhead circle to be ready to fill *Ranger*'s landing pattern the second the clouds burned off. Until the skies cleared, aircraft would be vectored in as singles or pairs in the slower-moving Case 2 recovery. Evidently we were not going anywhere soon; there was no place to keep our Intruder parked on the flight deck, and there was no room yet in the landing pattern. We could expect to stay overhead at 20,000 feet until those two conditions changed; the pilots circling below us needed to become carrier-qualified, and their jets either taken below to the hangar bay on the flight deck elevator or catapulted with a new crew to join us in high holding.

The surge of the day's activity had placed us firmly in the grasp of the shipboard routine. For the first time in hours I relaxed my concentration temporarily and remembered that we were possibly only weeks away from war. The sun was almost too bright for my tinted visor as I watched it track across the sky westward. We waited.

Our Intruder's eight-day clock ticked the time away slowly

while *Ranger* steamed westward 40 miles south of San Clemente Island. By 1400 the scud layer of clouds had burned off completely, and we could track the progress of the carrier qualifications visually from our autopilot orbiting perch 4 miles above the ship. The recovery had gone to Case 1, and the aircraft holding below us had switched their radios to monitor the ship's land/launch frequency, waiting to be called down by the air boss. I was almost at the point of getting rid of a bit more coffee through the hornlike relief tube when marshal broke the monotony.

"Rustler 502, marshal, descend to low holding, switch button 6."

"Rustler 502 going to low holding, switching," Rivers read back lethargically into his oxygen mask.

We needed to snap out of the sleepy nonchalance we had slipped into. I clicked off the autopilot, pulled the throttles to idle, flipped the Intruder onto its back, and let its nose fall toward the ocean below. I waited until the ADI showed a 40-degree nose-down dive and let it stabilize there. Our A-6 shot straight ahead of the ship, and the airspeed indicator went through 450 knots. Once we were outside of a 10-mile radius of the ship I started an easy turn back toward *Ranger*, and then pulled on 4 G's as we approached our low holding altitude of 4,000 feet. Fully alert now, Rivers was eagerly scanning the horizon, looking for fellow Intruders we could join up on in formation. I beat him to it.

"Cross circle, can't tell if its one of ours or a Jakal." I directed Rivers' attention to the lone A-6 7 miles away opposite our orbit over the ship.

"Doesn't matter; let's join on him," Rivers returned. Flying formation in the Case 1 pattern would speed up the process of getting both aircraft to a position to land.

Once level at 4,000 feet I pulled hard to the left at 4 G's until our nose tracked up in line with the other Intruder's fuselage. I kept the throttles at idle, and our airspeed bled off;

400 knots, 350, I added power to catch it at 300 knots. The standard overhead airspeed was 250 knots, unless, of course, you were trying to save gas. I wanted to join up expeditiously, but I was having a difficult time judging the other jet's speed. I pushed the throttles up to keep us at 300 knots and kept our jet pointed to the inside of our target's circle. We rapidly joined. I yanked the throttles back to idle when the A-6 ahead of us looked about 2 miles away, and let our airspeed decay to 250 knots. We were still closing quickly.

I made a piercing glimpse into the obvious: "Shit, he must be slow." The Intruder got quite large in our windscreen. I extended our wingtip speed brakes, increased the angle of bank, and stepped on the right rudder, putting our A-6 into a slip. By cross-controlling our jet I was in effect flying it slightly sideways. The increased drag knocked our airspeed back at a clip. I looked completely outside now, judging the closure with the other jet by eye. Once we appeared to have it under control I let out the opposite rudder and angle of bank and retracted the speed brakes.

"Pretty smooth, huh?" I asked Rivers. He just looked at me and shook his head at the less-than-crisp manner in which I had effected the rendezvous.

We crossed underneath what turned out to be a VA-155 Jakal at the standard 10 feet, came up on the other side, and tucked ourselves into a close parade formation position. The B/N from our sister A-6 squadron stuck his thumb back to his face in a drinking motion in a hand-signal query of our fuel state. I glanced down at our gas gauge: 8,500 pounds. I passed our fuel remaining via hand signals, and received a thumbs-up and the "take cruise" command from our new flight lead. Aviator seniority was ordinarily bypassed during the impromptu rendezvous overhead the ship in the Case 1 pattern. The Jakal Intruder had cleared us out to the more relaxed cruise position about 20 feet to the lead aircraft's right side. We listened in to channel 6 on the radio.

Things were quiet, which was good. Ideally the Case 1 recovery was made with no radio communications whatsoever. In the close quarters of the Persian Gulf this would be particularly important so as not to highlight the ship's location to the Iraqis. During carrier qualifications it was expected that all aircraft would call the ball to the landing signal officers when they reached three-quarters of a mile behind the ship, but any other radio calls should be quite limited. What we heard now were the standard "ball calls," with an occasional "Power!" or "Right for lineup!" thrown in by the LSOs to remind everyone that they were still just the tiniest bit rusty from having been ashore for 2 weeks. It sounded like the landing pattern was saturated, so we settled down to Phase 2 of our afternoon wait. I moved the stick back and forth slightly in an attempt to ease the repetition of flying off the relatively stationary position of the lead Intruder. Every once in a while I would make an exaggerated turn of my head to the right to work out the kinks that were developing from looking into the constant left-hand turn.

We were far enough away from the Jakal A-6 that I could glance down occasionally to view the show on the flight deck. It looked like they were still using catapults 1 and 2, and that there was a constant stream of various types of aircraft going from the angled landing area back to them on the bow. I alternated my time among flying formation, watching the launch and recoveries, and monitoring our fuel as it dipped down to 6,500 pounds. Apparently we were going to make good use of every pound we had taken on more than 2 hours previously. The minor excitement of our rapid descent and join-up with the Jakal had completely worn off when a few minutes later we got the first indication that anyone on *Ranger* knew we existed.

"Jakal 405, Rustler 502, your signal Charlie," the air boss transmitted.

Immediately Jakal 405's tailhook came down and white trails came shooting out of both wingtips and the tail of the

Intruder's fuselage. Jakal 405 obviously had a lot more gas than we did, and too much to land. Our fuel gauge now read 6,100 pounds. We could wait until we were a bit closer to the ship before we had to determine if we needed to dump any gas to get down to landing weight. I pulled the handle to the tailhook, gave Jakal 405 a thumbs-up to indicate that his tailhook had extended properly, and he returned the courtesy. I increased our angle of bank as the Jakal began to make his play for the most direct route to get lined up 3 miles behind the ship at 800 feet above the water. The distance between our two jets opened slightly, and the Jakal put on a 3-G turn to align himself with the course *Ranger* was steaming. His wingtips were now emitting trace wisps of fuel, but gas was still pouring out of the tail of his jet. I glanced down and saw that we were 5 miles behind the ship, roughly on heading, and descending through 2,000 feet.

"That's 5,900 pounds of gas; what do you say we get rid of 300 to 400 pounds?" Rivers asked.

"Sounds good," I replied and flipped the toggle for the fuselage fuel dump switch.

Rivers stuck his finger prominently at the fuel indicator as an unavoidable reminder that we were pissing fuel out the back end of the Intruder at a rate of 1,500 pounds per minute. It would not take very long for us to get into an in extremis situation if we forgot we had the dumps on.

We closed the distance to *Ranger* to 3 miles. I bumped up the throttles and sucked it up into a tightly knit parade formation position, only 5 feet from the Jakal's wingtip bouncing in the airstream. There was no tactical advantage to flying this close outside of the clouds, but it was proper procedure, and you could count on any number of friends and acquaintances watching and grading our entry into the carrier landing pattern. We were about to enter "the break," the most dynamic part of the day carrier landing, the most fun, and the landing maneuver most often screwed up. It was not uncommon for a landing signal officer's grading comments to read "awesome break, bolter." Unfortunately, looking good got you only so far; you had to perform all the way to the spine-crunching slam of the wheels onto the carrier deck.

"Fuel's good; get the dumps," Rivers directed; I complied.

Our flight of two Intruders had accelerated to 375 knots in the descent, and I found myself jockeying the throttles around the same general setting to stay in position on the Jakal. I needed two daytime landings, of which only one was required to be a trap, and I wanted to ensure that I got the most out of both of them before we were sent out this evening for the night portion of the fun.

The break was a maneuver designed near the dawn of carrier aviation to perform two basic functions. In the old days an airplane approaching the ship was in a uniquely vulnerable position to enemy action. The landing aircraft would have to eventually lower his landing gear and flaps before trapping aboard the ship. An airplane configured in this manner possessed greater lift on the wings, enabling the aircraft to fly a slower approach speed, which made landing on the moving target of an aircraft carrier significantly easier. With increased lift, however, came increased drag, and a very slow acceleration to an airspeed at which the approaching airplane could defend itself against an enemy interloper. The break was designed to minimize the time that a landing aircraft was at a slow speed and vulnerable to enemy attack.

The secondary advantage that the break enjoyed, and the primary one in the age of jets and effective radar early warning, was that it absolutely minimized the time required to recover a large number of aircraft on board the ship. This meant less time the carrier needed to steam into the wind and cruise a predictable courseline. Similar types of aircraft could enter the break in a flight of as many as four airplanes in tight formation, or they could enter as a single jet. The breaking aircraft would fly toward the stern of the carrier on alignment with the course she was steering. Approaching a mile, the breaking aircraft would move ever so slightly to the right of the carrier, covering the ship below with the jet's left wing. By the time the aircraft was over the stern of the ship it needed to be at 800 feet above the water and at some speed greater than 300 knots. The faster the airspeed, the more dynamic the maneuver was, the more difficult it became, and the more fun it was to fly. Breaking anytime after reaching the farthest aft portion of the ship, the fantail, was fair game, assuming that the aircraft ahead of you was far enough into his approach that your jet would not encroach on his. Breaking as early as the fantail meant that the preceding aircraft had better be touching down when the pilot commenced his maneuver, or the interval between the two jets would be too close.

Once sufficient interval existed with the preceding aircraft, a pilot initiated his maneuver as soon as he felt he could safely land from it. After taking an extremely careful look around to ensure that he had not missed any aircraft in the pattern, the pilot would stand his wings up in a quick, crisp manner in a left angle of bank, virtually at 90 degrees to the water. Simultaneously he would slam his throttles back to idle, extend his speed brakes, and depending on how fast he was going, pull anywhere from 3 to 6 G's. The G force yanking the aircraft around in the opposite direction from the carrier's course would cause the Intruder to rapidly lose airspeed. The pilot would gradually let out his angle of bank as the jet slowed so the aircraft remained rock steady at an altitude of 800 feet. Once the breaking pilot had come through a full 180 degrees of turn, and was now facing the opposite direction from which he had entered the break, he would let the aircraft descend to 600 feet as he continued to decelerate.

The moment the jet reached a slow enough airspeed the landing gear and the flaps would be lowered, and the increased drag would cause the aircraft to decelerate at an even greater rate. Immediately passing the stern of the carrier, the pilot would begin another 180-degree left turn. He would make constant, small corrections to arrive behind the ship, perfectly lined up on the center of the angled flight deck, at 350 to 375 feet, on approach airspeed plus or minus 2 knots. If the break had been performed correctly the pilot would be able to pick up a slightly high to centered "meatball" when the aircraft rolled out on the landing area's centerline at three-quarters of a mile.

The meatball, or ball, gave the pilot a precise indication of the proper glide path that needed to be adhered to if the landing aircraft was to catch the preferred three wire on the carrier deck. Four cables were strewn across the ship's landing zone at approximately 40-foot intervals. A few feet too high on the glide slope and the targeted third cable would be missed, leaving the single four wire remaining to stop the 125-knot jet. If the Intruder flew over the carrier's stern a few feet too low it would drag its tailhook into a two-wire arrestment. A bit lower and the jet would catch the one wire, normally an indication that the A-6 had come perilously close to scraping up against the ship's fantail, an unforgiving rounded wall of steel plates 60 feet above the waterline and the carrier's propellers.

The remainder of the approach was executed with the pilot looking completely outside at the meatball for glide slope, the landing area's centerline, and his angle-of-attack indexers out of the corner of his eye for exact airspeed.

On the Intruder's glare shield at eye level were three tiny vertical lights spanning a total of 2 inches: a green chevron at the top, a red chevron at the bottom, and an amber circle, or "doughnut," in the center. These were the angle-of-attack indexers. Power was for changing the jet's rate of descent; nose position was for the aircraft's speed. Speed and rate of descent were the two intrinsically connected parameters at the heart of the carrier landing. An amber doughnut meant that the jet was "on speed," or at exactly the correct nose-up attitude to catch an arresting wire. A red chevron indicated that you were fast, with the aircraft's nose too low and its tail too high for the hook to engage the steel cable. A green chevron meant that the A-6 was too slow and was approaching a stall, that point where the wing is canted up at such a steep angle that the wind separates from it and stops producing lift. The difference between an amber doughnut and a dangerously slow green chevron was about 3 knots.

The carrier's landing area was at an angle so aircraft could launch off of the bow and simultaneously land on the stern. The angled deck gave a landing pilot somewhere to go if his tailhook did not engage the steel cable and arrest the aircraft's forward rush. Regardless of type of aircraft, the procedure for a missed arrestment, a bolter, was the same—full power, maintain the on-speed attitude of the aircraft's nose, speed brakes in, and take her flying again straight out the angled deck. Every landing at the ship was consummated by full thrust when the wheels touched the deck. If the arresting wire had been engaged by the tailhook, it would bring the aircraft to a screeching halt regardless of the jet's power setting. If the tailhook did not catch a wire, then the engines were already at the power required to do a touch-and-go landing and get back airborne. Bolters, if performed correctly, were not dangerous or unusual. A bolter might only cost a pilot a bit of frustration and a less-than-desired grade from the watchful eyes of the landing signal officers. On the other hand, repeated bolters were often the sign of a new or severely shook-up pilot who was having a little extra trouble with his scan of meatball, lineup, and angle of attack.

Jakal 405 was bouncing around quite a lot, and I struggled to maintain a tight parade position. Formation flying appears to be effortless and glassy smooth from the ground. What is actually happening is that each of the tiny jolts that the lead aircraft experiences in the wind stream are magnified with increasingly greater corrections required by each successive wingman in line. To provide the illusion that the various jets are somehow connected requires constant, timely corrections that move the control stick in a flurry of concentrated motion.

I needed to keep it dressed up nice and pretty for about 10 more seconds until we were past the flight deck and our shipmate spectators.

"There's a Prowler at the 90; I don't see anyone else." Rivers kept me updated on the status of any other aircraft that might be in the landing pattern. With only one EA-6B already 90 degrees through his turn to final at *Ranger*'s stern we would not have long to wait before we broke.

"Airspeed?" The 5-foot distance from the Jakal made me reluctant to take my eyes off him for even a second at this speed.

"It's 390 knots, 800 feet, we're lined up approaching the fantail." Rivers volunteered the rest of the information I needed to fill in the gaps of my mental picture of our progress. My eyes stayed glued to the Jakal out my left windscreen and slightly above us.

My fixation on the lead Intruder gave me a full side view of the Jakal bombardier/navigator. He had been moving his head around methodically, looking for any other aircraft in the landing pattern. Apparently he was satisfied that the Prowler was the lone jet out there. He turned his helmeted head toward me, put his fingers to the oxygen mask at his lips, and moved his hand outward in the "kiss off" signal. A fraction of a second later the Intruder was whipped into a left-hand roll, and I was staring at Jakal 405's belly. I took advantage of the sudden freedom that my eyes had secured and immediately punched the sweep second hand on my clock as I scanned my instruments. Heading, 260 degrees. I made a conscious effort to keep the wings level. There was a tendency while flying formation to keep turning slightly toward the lead. Now that the Jakal was gone I needed to pay strict attention to our course so we did not drift left and were in proper position when it was time for us to break. We were well ahead of the ship now, and all that was visible outside the canopy was water and sky. The second hand ticked past 15.

"Ready?" One last opportunity for Rivers to bail me out if

I had forgotten something. Rivers replied with a thumbs-up. I verified that the clock had reached 17 seconds, slammed the stick to the left console, pulled the throttles back to idle, and extended the speed brakes. I took one last look over my shoulder to make certain we were clear of other traffic and then moved my eyes into the cockpit. Altitude, instantaneous vertical speed, airspeed, angle of bank, heading, and back outside again; the entire scan took less than 2 seconds. The carrier came into view in the turn, and I kept the G meter pegged at 4. I made a quick reference to the TACAN distance (DME)—2 miles from the ship. The Jakal must have broken at the bow—pretty aggressive for carrier qualifications, good for him. Our heading approached 100 degrees, and I started to let out the angle of bank: 250 knots. I reached out with my left hand and slammed the landing gear handle down, then felt back to the throttle quadrant to the familiar shape of the flap handle. I pulled the handle aft. I made a quick wing dip to correct for a slight overshoot in our turn, and we steadied up on a 080 heading as we approached the bow of *Ranger* off to her port side. I descended to 600 feet and ran through the landing checklist from memory.

"Gear down, flaps down, stab shifted, boards are out. Pop-ups and antiskid are off, switches are off and safe, 15 cycles, hook down. Fuel's good." I saw Rivers pull the hook handle one more time out of the corner of my eye. Although similar to the takeoff checklist, several crucial items had been added to the landing checklist. Armament switches were checked off or in a "safed" position. It was no fair slamming an Intruder onto the flight deck with live bombs if all the safety switches were not correctly positioned. The auxiliary brakes were verified pumped up to capacity and the hook was double-checked down. If you planned on using the hook you better make damn certain it was down. Nothing was more frustrating than the deep sinking anxiety of flying a near-perfect pass and not feeling the jolt of hook engage, bringing the A-6 to a shoulder-strap-stretching halt. Now was our final opportunity to dump a little gas if we were still slightly above our maximum landing weight. Every item on the list I had rattled off checked out okay.

My attention was riveted to *Ranger*'s position and the Intruder's deceleration. We pulled directly abeam the ship, and I added power to catch our decaying airspeed. The red "fast" chevron on my glare shield turned to an amber doughnut. I fought to keep it there. I glanced down at our TACAN DME—three-quarters of a mile from the ship, perfect; 550 feet, a bit low, I would need a slightly slower rate of descent when we started our turn to final. We flew by *Ranger*, our Intruder at 125 knots, the carrier going the opposite direction at about 15 knots. I barely could see the backside of the ship when I began my turn. I added power to compensate for the loss of lift in our 25-degree angle-of-bank turn. Inside, outside, my head was not still for a second. The throttles were in constant motion, correcting for every deviation from what my eyes were telling me was the place I needed to put the Intruder to end up at three-quarters of a mile behind *Ranger* with a centered ball, on speed, on lineup. Each tiny gust of wind or minor change to *Ranger*'s course affected the equation. I began to sweat.

Four hundred fifty feet above the water and through 90 degrees of our turn. *Ranger* looked perilously close; I had to remind myself that the ship was moving away from us and that the wind was blowing us farther aft. Try not to cheat by looking outside, I told myself. The carrier's angle deck was canted 10 degrees to the port of the ship's course. Flying strictly visually encouraged the tendency to make the turn too rapidly, resulting in an angling approach to the stern of the ship. That extra 10 degrees of turn translated into more time to get the Intruder established exactly on the angled deck's centerline.

Rivers read off our vertical speed downward in feet per minute—"350, 400, 400." My scan gradually shifted to the picture outside our cockpit. The meatball came into view—

slightly high, good. The ball would tell us where we were on the glide slope, but our vertical speed would tell us the direction of the trend in which we were going. By the time the ball actually moved up or down, it was too late; our Intruder would be too low or too high and we would be forced to make a more aggressive correction. Constant, small corrections were the name of the game, working all the way down the glide slope until the thump of the wheels hitting the flight deck woke a pilot from his concentration-induced trance. We were nearing the end of our turn to the "groove," the last three-quarters of a mile straight in behind the boat.

"Rustler 502, hook up." Damn. Rivers punched the hook-retract button in response to the instruction from the landing signal officers. We needed two landings to become day-carrier-qualified, and evidently the air boss was only going to let one of them be a trap.

I advanced the throttles slowly in a staggered pattern, walking my left palm forward. The Intruder's wings rolled to the horizon, slightly high ball, lined up, and on speed.

Rivers confirmed our acquisition of the meatball to the LSOs and gave them our fuel state—"502 Intruder ball, 5 point 3."

"Roger ball, Intruder, winds are right down the angle."

My eyes were now completely outside: meatball, lineup, angle of attack. I held the stick with my fingertips, barely willing it to move, nudging the nose minutely with each power correction, adding power with each small wing dip. Fifteen to 18 seconds was the optimum time to spend in the groove. Any more than that was just an opportunity to screw it up. We approached the fantail and I began to add power out of reflex. I could feel the bottom drop out slightly as *Ranger*'s island blocked some of the wind; I added more power. No more comments on the radio from the LSOs, good—I had a shot at an "okay" pass. One last wing dip crossing the fantail, and I lost the image of the ocean out of my peripheral vision. My hands were in constant motion, the ball's movements becoming more sensitive the closer we got. Fly it all the way to touchdown, I coaxed myself, don't freeze up and drop into the one wire.

The Intruder's wheels slammed into the flight deck at a 600-foot-per-minute rate of descent. I immediately redirected my focus from the ball to straight ahead; I pushed the throttles forward to the stops, and retracted the speed brakes with my left thumb. Damn, even though we had been expecting it with our raised hook, the touch-and-go was disconcerting. It just wasn't natural to slam into the deck and not feel the accompanying tug on the shoulder harness as the jet was yanked to a halt. We lifted off the flight deck, and I held the stick more firmly in an attempt to maintain an amber doughnut in our angle-of-attack indexer. The Intruder felt squirrelly with the increase in power and looser flying of the takeoff maneuver. Once we had climbed to 100 feet I made a 10-degree correction back to the right to parallel the ship's course.

We were going through 400 feet when we heard "Rustler 502, cleared downwind" from the air boss. We reached 600 feet while still in the turn back toward *Ranger*'s stern.

I ran through the landing checklist quickly. Rivers pulled the hook handle, and we were barely finished when I began the turn back to *Ranger*'s angle deck. We should have been more comfortable on this second pass, but I was feeling behind the jet and off balance from the touch-and-go. I could see that I would need to make some aggressive plays to get set up for the groove. When we rolled out at three-quarters of a mile I saw that we were slightly low and had made the turn a bit too quickly. I momentarily leveled the wings, then put back in a left turn to get us lined up. I added power and fixed the low ball quickly, but I had a sinking feeling that the best I was going to get out of this pass was a grade of fair. The touchdown of the Intruder's landing gear was married to the tug of the tailhook this time, and was a welcome relief to the last 5 minutes' hectic pace. My face was pressed forward in the screeching halt, and I watched the water race toward us beyond the deck edge. Our A-6 came to a standstill. I brought the throttles back to idle and reached down to raise the flap lever.

A yellow shirt ran out to our right side, and Rivers punched the retract button after he motioned for us to raise our hook. Rivers' helmet turned to me, and though I couldn't see his face through the oxygen mask and visor, I knew it was a look of bored impatience, waiting for me to tell him that the flaps were up and it was safe to fold the wings.

I watched the indicator by my knee: "Flaps are up." I was rewarded with a turn of his head. The yellow shirt started to taxi us forward while our wings were still folding upward. I didn't expect that we would be going back to the cat; if there had been space or time for extra traps we would not have done the touch-and-go. I resigned myself to the fact that we had spent the past two and a half hours airborne for a 5-minute flight in the landing pattern and only one trap. Oh, well—flight time was flight time.

The yellow shirt passed us off to another taxi director forward of cat two on the port side bow of the ship. Two F-14 Tomcat fighters were left waiting for cat one to get them airborne, and cat two had ceased operating. The steam emanating from the catapult's inner workings had dissipated, and several sailors in green float coats were covering the cat track with a protective rubber strip. Our new yellow shirt brought us all the way to the bow to give the men working on catapult 2 time to finish before turning us back to taxi the hundred yards aft to park in front of an S-3 Viking sub-hunter.

Without the heat from the now setting sun, the clouds started to form again over the ship. Our taxi director gave us a sharp left turn to align us several feet away from the parked S-3, and abruptly brought us to a halt. Three other A-6s had landed after us and were following our lead to their resting spots on cat 2. Several sailors ran under the jet as I set the parking brake and waited for the signal to cut our engines.

Seconds later we had flipped the safety latches on our ejection seats, and Rivers had the canopy coming open with residual hydraulic pressure as the Intruder's two engines wound down. I took my time straightening up the cockpit and putting my kneeboard pad back into my nav bag. It might be a long night.

# Chapter Six

# Gave proof through the night . . .

I climbed down the boarding ladder, enveloped in the screech of an arresting wire being yanked out of battery: the final Tomcat trapped for day CQ. The F-14 was quickly chocked and chained, and there was a visible relaxation from flight quarters; simultaneously everyone abovedecks took off their helmets and goggles and rolled up their sleeves. The newfound silence was soothing; it felt like we were on a ship again now that we could hear the wind and the waves beneath the keel. There would be a brief hour-and-a-half respite while we waited for the sun to drop low enough below the horizon to qualify as nighttime. Rivers had unzipped his survival vest and was looking pretty laid back by the time we met at the nose of 502 and started walking toward the port catwalk.

"What time do we go out tonight?" I asked, hoping for an early "charlie" time to carrier-qualify. Our assigned "charlie" time would be the approximate minute we could expect to leave high holding for our approach to the carrier. During CQ it was an extremely approximate time.

"We're in the first hot seat. I think it's sometime around 1930. How's the division doing?" Rivers had not wanted to ruin our quiet time airborne with shop talk, but work was never far from his mind.

"Fine; everybody's unpacked. The AMEs are still looking

for a new space, but I think they might work something out with the air wing seat shop in the hangar bay." The AMEs maintained the ejection seats and air conditioning systems of the A-6. I was hoping that their supervisor would be able to schmooze his way into a corner of the relatively spacious air wing ejection seat work center, which was conveniently located directly off of the hangar bay.

"Have you been through berthing yet?" We walked down the steps to the catwalk, turned left, and headed aft.

"Just raced through once. I'm going to try and get down there before the night hop."

VA-145's two primary enlisted berthings held 135 and 75 men, respectively. During particularly crowded periods at sea it was not unknown for individuals to have to "hot rack," and share the same bed with someone who worked an opposite 12-hour shift. This was an especially odious prospect because shipboard work is intrinsically dirty, and sleeping in someone else's grease is not a very pleasant prospect. Sharing a rack also took away the last vestige of privacy or personal space that a person might enjoy on the ship.

We cracked open the hatch to the O-3 level below the flight deck. The carrier was divided into three "levels" above the waterline, except in the island, where the levels spiraled up a dozen higher. Below the waterline each of the ship's "floors" were called "decks."

The conversation stopped, and we proceeded single file down the passageway and over the knee knockers. Three ladders and a stroll farther aft and we were back in the pararigger shop, taking off our flight gear. It was helpful to know at least three or four ways to get from the flight deck to the ready room vicinity. It was essential to know various ways to get from the ready room or your stateroom to the flight deck in the event the ship was at general quarters and designated watertight hatches were secured. If it was a drill, you could expect to have to journey through the maze of hatches to fly a training sortie. If it was the real thing, you might need to go fly a strike, or you might be trying to find the quickest way off of a sinking ship. Gray steel all looks remarkably similar. The location placards at the top of each hatch certainly helped, but on a 1,000-foot ship the esoteric numbering and lettering system did not make shipboard navigation intuitively obvious.

I finished disrobing my familiar heap of flight gear and took the obligatory walk through the ready room. The schedule board was a bloody mess—that was more like it. Now I felt like we were really at sea—things were changing faster than we could react, but the group sentiment seemed to be a casual resolve to deal with it and not sweat the load. There was nowhere else to be, nothing more important to do. We had 6 months to sort it all out. I walked up to Tony at the duty desk.

Tony, Snax, and I shared a spacious "stateroom." Our room consisted of about 6 feet by 15 feet of living space for chairs and pacing. The walls were lined with lockers and fold-down tabletops to act as desks, and three beds, or "racks," each 3 feet wide, were stacked to the ceiling. Curtains on each rack kept the light out somewhat and provided the only semblance of privacy available on the ship. A single sink and mirror rounded out the accommodations, with a trip out the door and down two passageways required to get to the head and showers.

Tony was an easygoing Naval Academy graduate. This immediately placed him as a pariah in the hierarchy of our stateroom. He was married and had two boys back at our home base of Whidbey Island, Washington. Snax, a bachelor like myself, had gotten his naval commission through ROTC, and I had earned mine through Aviation Officer Candidate School. Tony was the only one of us who had not experienced going through college as a civilian. Despite this setback, and a shock of black hair that stood at the front of his good-looking face like Woody Woodpecker, Tony was fairly well adjusted socially for an Academy graduate and did not wear a uniform to bed at night. Snax was a tall computer geek with a

runner's physique who happened to be one of the most skilled
bombardier/navigators in the navy.

"Promoted?" I asked in my best sarcastic sneer.

"Yeah, you believe the candy-assed SDO wanted to eat?
Now I gotta miss out on my afternoon rerack." Tony was the
senior lieutenant in the squadron, which made him the senior
watch officer. He wrote the watch bill for the squadron duty
officers but didn't have to stand the duty himself. "Racking"
was sleeping; "reracking" was sleeping some more.

"Well, you look good back there. Out of place and incom-
petent, but good." I couldn't believe that I had been in the
ready room for 30 seconds and I had not yet filled my coffee
cup. I walked over to my chair to get my mug as I continued
the conversation. "All unpacked?"

"Yes, sir, all done. Been flying, ate, I'm pretty much on top
of the whole situation. Did you see the cruise patch design?"
Tony ran the squadron "administration." The "admin" was an
organization of all the officers that raised money through
patch sales and dues so a hotel suite with all the trimmings
(i.e., beer) could be tendered at each of the ports we would
visit. Tony was an aspiring artist; he didn't object strenuously
enough when offered the job, and he was "volunteered" to
design a patch specifically for this cruise to sell to *Ranger's*
five thousand consumers. He also got to keep the books and
drum up salesmen from VA-145's officer ranks; it could be a
real pain in the ass.

"Negative. Where is it?" I asked.

Tony opened up a folder on the SDO desk and handed me a
piece of paper. Sketched in pencil was a circular patch with
a rough drawing of the Persian Gulf and the neighboring
states of Iraq, Kuwait, Saudi Arabia, and Iran. An American
flag–draped arm led to a fist that was clenching a crushed
Iraqi flag. "Operation Desert Shield" and "CVW-2" (Carrier
Air Wing 2) were superimposed over Iran and Saudi Arabia,
respectively. Around the gold-rimmed circular trim was "Arabian Gulf 91 . . . USS *Ranger CV-61*." In an impulse of po-

litical correctness to somebody other than the Iranians we had been informed that the "Persian Gulf" was now the "Arabian Gulf." Shoot, we hadn't bombed the Iranians in years. The only thing worse than a knee-jerk reaction was an extraordinarily slow knee-jerk reaction. I had to admit, though, the patch looked good.

"Nice job; it should sell. Have you ordered them yet?"

"If the guys like it I'll mail off the order tomorrow. They say it should take about four weeks to make and get back in the mail out to us. I'm hoping to have them by the time we start home." I couldn't tell if Tony was kidding. It would be four months at the earliest before we began to head home, and for navy mail to take this long to get a box of patches out to *Ranger* would be unusually slow, but not unheard-of.

"Homeward is where all the ports should be. We've got time." Unfortunately, we probably did have a lot of time before we got into a good liberty port other than the Philippines.

The Philippines, or "PI," were great fun, but not very admin-friendly. Everything there was so cheap it was not really worth it to get a group hotel room. You couldn't leave the hotel after the curfew imposed to thwart terrorists anyway. And who wanted to be stuck in one place? That was what the carrier was for.

"No, really, you look good behind that desk." I gave Tony a parting shot: "You should try it for real sometime." I went over to the coffeepot to fill my cup.

Looking at the schedule board, I was only mildly surprised to see that Rivs and I were hot-seating into the skipper's jet again. Our commanding officer's flight was one of the few that had not been impacted by the SDO's red pen. And 1930 it was; we had 30 minutes before we were supposed to brief. I walked up to Rivers.

"Dirty shirt before we brief?" There was always time to eat. Officers on the carrier had two options for meals: the "clean-shirt wardroom," where a khaki uniform was required, or the "dirty-shirt wardroom," where flight suits and flight deck jerseys were welcome. The food was roughly the same, although the presentation, if you could call it that, in the clean shirt was a bit like Denny's, while in the dirty shirt it was closer to McDonald's. It was a no-brainer—dirty shirt.

"Let's go," replied Rivers. "We can take a walk through berthing on our way back to the ready room."

The dirty shirt was on the O-3 level under cat 1. The rumbling during flight operations helped induce a healthy appetite. Or make you lose it—I always forgot which it was. We walked through the cafeteria-style line, picking up a tray as we viewed the options through the sneeze guard. Elephant scabs, a.k.a. veal parmigiana; macaroni and cheese; or the daily standby of a "slider," otherwise known as a hamburger. I was feeling in an Italian mood, so I opted for the veal. It didn't much matter—the grease content was the same. Out past the food line I picked up my utensils out of a large stainless-steel rack and looked around for a familiar face. Snax and the skipper were just getting up to leave, and Rivers and I walked over to the soon-to-be-empty table with our trays.

"Hello, Skipper. How'd it go today?" Rivers asked in reference to the CO's personal landing performance.

"We're doing pretty well; got everybody day-qualified, but just barely. CAG says the air wing's got until tomorrow and then anybody who's not night-qual'd will have to wait until we steam by the next island with a divert field." The CO's mind was evidently on the air wing commander—CAG—and the big picture. Rivers let it pass, and we took our seats.

"Long time no see. How's dinner?" I hadn't seen Snax since last night in the stateroom. He had gotten up early to brief the first flight with the CO.

"Marvelous; the cake dryer is working perfectly. You guys just getting back?" Snax replied with a tinge of bored sarcasm. It might have had something to do with the jet fuel in the water system, but the nightly tray of wardroom cake was always as dry as a Bedouin's breath.

"Yep, they saved the quality flight time for us. Got a whole trap out of it. See you in a couple of hours." I stood up to go to the salad bar.

"You jumping into our jet again?" I nodded my head. "We'll try not to keep you waiting." Snax turned to follow the CO out the wardroom door.

I reached the salad bar and forced myself to fill a plate with whatever looked fresh. From here on out the fruit and vegetables would age until we replenished with fresh produce, and it was anybody's guess when that would happen. I remembered our last cruise steaming circles in the North Arabian Sea off the coast of Oman. For months the closest thing we got to fresh produce was some shredded cabbage and bland, tasteless "Iran-a-lope" from the desert. I never did find out what that stuff really was.

No time for socializing; Rivers and I gulped down our meals, and gave our trays to the mess deck sailor with the navy-issue birth control glasses who was hovering over the tables waiting to bus our empty plates. We headed to the ready room for a much-condensed brief and then moved on to the para-rigger shop. Our flight gear had barely had time to cool down from our sweat on the last flight. I put the damp gear on quickly, finding it easier to do so now that it had been stretched out from its restricted, dried-out state. One night trap was all that was required to get back into currency, and we wanted to be ready just in case the skipper and Snax took off directly into the landing pattern. We struck out for the confined space of flight deck control.

We broke out into the cool night air and, for a few moments, stood at the starboard side of the island by the bomb farm to let our eyes adjust. The passageway lights in the island had gone to red for better night vision, but climbing up the three ladderways to the flight deck didn't give us much of an opportunity to take advantage of it. The sun had dropped completely behind the horizon and we could hear the bow cats back in action. It had chilled considerably, and I regretted for a moment that I had not put on my long-sleeved, turtlenecked flight deck jersey under my flight suit. Oh, well, we would not be outside for very long.

Rivers opened the hatch to flight deck control. The battle lamps gave off an eerie red glow and accentuated the already dreamlike quality of the atmosphere. In addition to assisting flight deck workers with their night vision, the setting of night illumination on *Ranger* would limit the travel of white light over the water. The habits that would be required while steaming in a hostile environment needed to be constantly practiced and refined. I turned to secure the hatch and then stood in the doorway, afraid to move with my limited sight, until I could make out a yellow-shirted form moving toward my position, blocking the hatch. I took a few steps into the compartment and removed my helmet. Rivers had found a small bench to sit on, and I joined him. We were the only aircrew in flight deck control, so either we were early or somebody else was late. Better to be on the early side—leaving a crew sitting in the cockpit of a jet with their engines running was bad form, particularly if the pilot was the CO. The roar of the jets outside was too loud for conversation, so I went through the flight mentally in preparation.

The Case 3 pattern was micromanaged in comparison to the Case 1, particularly during carrier qualifications. We could expect more radar vectors than a normal night cycle, and the holding we would inevitably undergo would probably not be directly over the ship. Typically all aircraft scheduled to recover on a given flight cycle would marshal well behind the ship on the base recovery course, which was the reciprocal of the direction that the ship was cruising. For example, if the ship was heading 360 degrees, directly north, then the base recovery course would be on the 180-degree radial, directly south of the carrier. Aircraft would stack up in 1,000-foot increments starting normally at about 15 miles, with each higher jet spaced out at a progressively farther distance from the ship. The staggered stack of aircraft was designed so that when the lower jets began their descent and approach to the carrier, they would be a mile closer to the ship than the aircraft 1,000 feet above them. This would give a bit more separation between the jets as aircraft began to descend in the darkness, and there would be less concern about running into the aircraft that preceded your own. The Case 3 pattern was designed to allow for a 60-second interval between each approaching aircraft. There was a strict procedure to follow to ensure that the 60-second separation was maintained from the time a jet left the marshal stack behind the ship until trapping on board the carrier.

All marshaling aircraft would be assigned a "push" time, when they would be expected to be at their assigned orbit point, heading inbound to the ship, at 250 knots and initiating a descent. Completing a single circle around the marshal point in a comfortable turn took up several miles and several minutes, and a certain amount of planning was required to get each individual aircraft exactly where it needed to be at its assigned time. Speeding up or slowing down was one option, but this usually required more fuel and was an indication that the marshaling aircrew had screwed up their initial plan. By varying the distance that the jet flew outbound, away from the ship, and altering the aircraft's angle of bank to make a tighter or a wider turn, a crew could arrive at their marshal point on time at exactly 250 knots. Plus or minus 10 seconds was the acceptable error at the push point. After that a radio call was required, and the deviant crew could expect to receive a small radar vector to correct their mistake. Even at night, radio transmissions were held to a minimum to make it more difficult for any bad guys who might be trying to track *Ranger*'s course. There were different checkpoints with airspeed changes inbound to the ship, and as long as all the aircraft in the pattern flew the same profile, the separation between them would be maintained.

The catapulting procedures at night were basically the same as during the day. The main operational difference was that a pilot placed an even greater degree of dependence on the attitude direction indicator and backup gyro. This was due to the lack of a defined horizon to use as a reference to determine when the Intruder's wings were level. In the 1990s, flying was still very much a visual game. Technology and instrumentation helped tremendously, but as with most precision maneuvers, it came down to a pilot trusting his sense of sight. The darkness of night made everything we did just a bit more difficult, except for landing, which was a lot more difficult.

The steel bulkheads of flight deck control shuddered as a taxiing jet turned his exhaust into the island. The aircraft handling officer yelled, "Easy on the power out there!" into the radio connecting him to the flight deck yellow shirts. Stealing glances down at the engine power settings was another of the items that became more difficult for a pilot to do at night.

I sat on the hard, cold bench and was amazed, not for the first time, at how quickly we all had adapted to the carrier environment. The noise, the long days, and the challenge of flight operations were not at all reflected in the casual manner in which the aircrew and sailors who worked the flight deck treated the danger and the stress. Habit patterns and routine had kicked in, not a happenstance occurrence, but the result of literally years of training and desensitization to the commotion all around. Perhaps the greatest challenge facing us on this first day of cruise was to maintain the small, crisp edge of alertness for the next six months and not fall into complacency. It was immaterial how many cruises you had made or how many traps were indicated by the patches on your flight jacket; if you let down your guard for any length of time there was a good chance that you or someone close to you would die. It was just not possible to get so good at this game that you didn't have to consistently think and work hard.

Six other pilots and flight officers entered the space over the next 10 minutes, but it wasn't until 1945 that we received our first indication that our jet would be trapping. The plat camera blared out the ball call from an A-6 at three-quarters of a mile: "507, Intruder ball, 5.5." Definitely Snax's voice. Rivers and I began to zip up and snap together our relaxed flight gear.

A yellow shirt from across the room yelled, "507's a hot-seat hot pump, Hummer hole." We headed out the hatch.

The Hummer hole was a spot aft of the island where one of the twin-prop E-2C "Hummers" was regularly parked. Behind the island was one of the few places that could accommodate an aircraft the size of a Hummer. The area was a hodgepodge of various pieces of equipment. The huge flight deck crane was stowed there, as were extra tow tractors and electric power carts. A lone A-6 could barely squeeze in beside the E-2 and the menagerie of yellow shirts' gear, or simply yellow gear, as it was called. The aircraft in this portion of the flight deck sat facing the port side, barely clear of the foul line on the edge of the landing area. To get to the bow catapults it was necessary to taxi across the angle deck during the minute interval between landing aircraft. It was a bit unusual to park a jet hidden away in the Hummer hole during carrier qualifications. The aircraft would have to be hooked up by its nose landing gear to a tow tractor and pushed back into the tight spot, all the while fouling the landing area and keeping any other jets from trapping. We must be at a lull in the landing traffic, I thought; 507 must be the last of the first wave of aircraft to land.

We weaved our way around various wheeled vehicles of different shapes and sizes and took comfort in the fact that the Hummer's engines were not running. Dodging the two enormous propellers was a particularly unnerving task, with the invisible blades buzzing by at decapitating speeds. I had my flashlight aimed at the deck plates in front of me as I walked, looking for trip hazards in the form of chains and the long aircraft tractor tow bars. The red lens made it more difficult to see, but I did not want to risk blinding someone with a flash of white and destroy his night vision. Besides, white illumination on the flight deck usually resulted in a nasty reminder from one of the yellow shirts that it was against ship regulations. We turned the corner around the last tow tractor and I shone my light up at the nose of the A-6 in front of us: 507.

The tow tractor was still attached to the Intruder's nose gear, but it was not moving anywhere. I made a closer inspection of the parking job of the A-6 and saw that the tractor had pushed it in at an angle, and that it would need to be moved again before it was chocked and chained. The reason for the halt to the action by the tow tractor became apparent as an S-3, with its relatively quiet engines, crossed the round down at the stern, caught one of the steel cables, and dragged it out until the aircraft was no longer in view. As soon as the S-3 sub-hunter had raised its hook and the arresting gear wire began to retract, the tow tractor pulled out into the landing area to respot 507. The yellow shirt at the wheel of the tractor had just cleared the landing area, pushing the Intruder into correct alignment, when an F-14 fighter appeared at three-quarters of a mile behind the ship. By the time the Tomcat had trapped, 507's tow bar had been removed and the tractor sped off on another flight deck errand.

We got to 507's boarding ladder too late for the fuelers. The elephant trunk of a fuel hose had already been connected, and the skipper and Snax were captives under the glass canopy. Rivers and I stayed on our respective sides of the jet as we waited for the impatient outgoing crew to finish filling up our A-6 for us. Eventually the CO climbed down his boarding ladder, gave me a quick thumbs-up, and set off in a hurried crouch for *Ranger*'s island. I climbed up, strapped in, and made a quick check of the cockpit instrumentation and our fuel load. The skipper had taken the gas all the way up to 18,700 pounds. That meant that not only were the fuselage and wing tanks full, but the cylindrical drop tank that was attached to the center of the 507's fuselage had its limit of 2,700 pounds in it as well. The Intruder had five attachment points, or stations, for bombs, missiles, or extra fuel tanks. The center station was usually reserved for gas. I took a wild guess that our night CQ was not going to be any shorter than our day qualification flight.

Rivers closed the canopy, we armed our seats, and I made a circle with my red flashlight in lieu of a thumbs-up for the yellow shirt. The taxi director's twin yellow lights came alive in the darkness, and he gave the signal to break us down from our chocks and chains. Moments later, we were taxiing across the flight deck at an uncomfortable speed in a race to clear the landing area before the next aircraft attempting to land had to be waved off for a fouled deck. We managed to save the approaching aircrew the disappointment of having to take another stab at landing as we rolled clear of the angle deck and came up in front of the island. I anticipated the yellow shirt's direction to slow down and almost brought 507 to a complete halt before we started a much more cautious and slow taxi forward. The catapult crews had worked out any bugs they might have had during the day, and a steady stream of jets was shooting into the air.

Rivers extended our wings, the jet blast deflector in front of us began to lower, and the little bit of light that we had enjoyed disappeared in a wall of steam from the catapult. I went through several repetitions of the engine failure off the cat procedure in my mind, following each step with a movement of my hand to the appropriate controls so I could readily access them, and react more quickly if the need arose. Left hand to the landing gear handle, simulate gear up, put my hand palm up to the panel immediately above the landing gear, feel for the emergency stores jettison button with my thumb, move my hand down to the left console and feel for the fuel dump switches. Do it again and again until I didn't need to glance at where any of the levers, buttons, or switches were. If we lost an engine off the catapult shot my eyes would need to be glued to the ADI, airspeed, and radar altimeter. If we were to fly we would have to immediately lose any extra weight and eliminate the drag of the extended landing gear.

My scan would be on the ADI to ensure that our wings were flush with the horizon, our airspeed to make certain we didn't stall, and our Radalt so I could call for the ejection before we hit the water if the jet was descending. I practiced this simple but critical ritual before every night cat shot.

Wings down, flaps and slats down, the yellow shirt passed us off to the taxi director working cat 2. I wiped out the stick and rudders in all four corners of the cockpit without taking my eyes off the two lighted wands in front of me, and Rivers rogered the backlit weight board as being correct. The ship was slowly rolling from side to side and fore and aft. The only way I could tell that the Intruder was moving was that the yellow lights in front of me continued their steady rhythm coming together, and then pulling apart over the taxi director's head. My additions of power were fruitless as the bow raised up in a swell. Seconds later we came down the backside of the wave and rapidly accelerated. I pulled back the throttles and eased on the brakes. We clunked into the shuttle, and the yellow shirt stepped to the side and signaled us to take tension. I moved the throttles full forward and felt with relief that the A-6 stayed in its position. I moved the controls through their full range of motion once again and gripped the catapult handle slightly tighter than I had during the day. All I could see outside the cockpit were the lighted wands of the catapult officer while he waited for us to relay our readiness for launch. No peripheral vision, nothing but a black hole in front of us; absolute vertigo enveloped me, and we were not even airborne yet. I asked Rivs if he was ready to go.

"Let's do it," replied Rivers. I loosened my thumb from my clenched fist, found the external lights master switch at the end of the cat grip handle, and flicked it up. The corners of my eyes came alive as the Intruder's navigation lights beamed on our wingtips. The cat officer returned our salute of night lights and touched the deck. I stuck my head firmly back into the headrest, took a deep breath, and started to scan the instrument panel while the jet shuddered and shook in its strain to be unleashed. Two seconds, 3. Why so long? I thought about glancing to the side at the cat officer but decided against it. Taking the cat shot with my head at an angle would only increase my vertigo. Hold tight a little longer . . . then "Whoosh!" Two seconds later we were off the deck. Landing gear handle up, engines look good, it feels right. Rivers reads out our airspeed, we have more than enough, we are flying. There is no greater test of faith in carrier aviation than the night cat shot. For the most part, the crew is simply along for the ride.

We climbed rapidly in the cool night air. Rivers checked out with departure and in with marshal. *Ranger*'s air traffic controllers gave us immediate instructions.

"Rustler 507, marshal on the 060-degree radial at 25, angels 10. Case 3, CV-1 approach, altimeter 2994. Expected final bearing is 240; stand by for your expected push time." Rivers wrote it all down on his kneeboard and read back the instructions to the controller. I steered our jet slowly around *Ranger* and climbed to our marshal altitude of 10,000 feet. By the time we got pointed to our assigned radial we could tell it was going to be a long wait. No one was receiving push times yet, which meant that we could all expect to hold in the marshal stack indefinitely until the ship sorted out whatever plan they had for us. Without a defined time to leave the holding pattern there was nothing more for us to do but put on the autopilot and circle.

I remembered a squadronmate's story from a late-night holding pattern last cruise. They had been the designated tanker for the flight cycle, which meant that they would orbit overhead the ship for 2½ hours just in case another aircraft found itself low on fuel. Without any distractions, and after a long day, the pilot flicked the autopilot on and started to nod his head trying to fight off the sleepies. Evidently he lost the battle, and he woke up sometime later, a bit disoriented and not aware of how long he had been out. After he realized that he was in a jet, and flying, he noticed the slumped-over figure of his B/N next to him, sawing wood. Unaware that he was

capable of moving his neck so fast, the pilot slammed his
gaze over to the fuel gauge and breathed a sigh of relief—
they had been out only about 20 minutes and had lots of gas
left. The possibilities made for more than a few jokes for a
long time after that. I pictured the two of them cruising oblivi-
ously straight into Red Chinese airspace, not responding to
radio calls and tracers fired across their nose. It's those wacky
guys again, the sleepy twins, just chilling out and enjoying a
bit of rest. What a couple of nuts.

As funny as it was—mostly because it didn't happen to
us—I was fairly certain that the inoculation of the day's
coffee would keep me from experiencing the situation firsthand. We entered the marshal stack and began our endless
circling.

"Hear anything about Bama?" I asked Rivers.

"He's still fighting the medical issue; I don't think he'll be
able to get back into an ejection seat, but maybe they'll let
him fly something else. Don't really know," Rivs replied.

Bama was a squadron pilot who had the misfortune of
ejecting on takeoff at Whidbey Island just about a year ago.
He and his bombardier/navigator, Pink, were doing a maintenance check flight of an A-6 that had recently been delivered
to the Command. Somewhere along the line in the reworking
of the refurbished jet's flight controls an incorrect pin had
been installed into the horizontal stabilizer linkage. Bama
and Pink started their takeoff roll at Whidbey, and everything
felt just fine. When the lightly fueled A-6 reached about 80
knots, something frighteningly wrong began to happen.

The horizontal stabilizer, which controlled the vertical
movement of the A-6, had gotten stuck in the full-nose-up position. The control stick felt absolutely normal, but the combination of the stabilizer commanding full nose up and gusty
winds forced the Intruder airborne well before a safe flying
speed at about 90 knots. The jet went nose up for 100 feet, entered a full stall as the surprised crew tried to figure out what
was wrong, then rolled left and back rapidly to the right.

While Bama continued to try to push the nose back down and get control of the aircraft, Pink realized that the situation was going to get significantly worse as the jet continued its rightward roll. He yelled "Eject!" and reached between his knees and pulled his ejection handle. The sound and motion of Pink's ejection seat breaking through the canopy glass, as it was designed to do in the A-6, was enough to snap Bama out of his concentration in trying to save the plane, and he ejected as well. Pink's seat shot him straight up in the air, the parachute filled, and Pink got one swing in the chute before he impacted the ground.

The 1 to 2 seconds that Bama delayed cost him quite a bit more. By the time he pulled his ejection handle the Intruder was about 50 feet off the ground and at a 90-degree angle to the right. The rocket motor in the ejection seat shot Bama straight across the hardened January terrain. Bama was still in the seat when he hit the ground, trailing his limp parachute behind him. His leg was caught and mangled between the side of the metal-framed ejection seat and the dirt before he was finally thrown clear of the seat. To make matters worse, once Bama did get free, his parachute was inflated by a gust of wind and proceeded to drag him 100 yards until he hit a tree. Bama was clearly lucky to be alive, but he would never fly a tactical jet again.

The story highlighted the importance of a few seconds of reaction time when things began to go wrong, but it also pointed out a glaring problem that Intruder aircrews had been striving to get rectified for years. There did not exist, as there did in virtually every other ejection-seat aircraft in the U.S. inventory, an ejection system where one crew member could eject both pilot and B/N. The lack of a "command ejection system" in itself had not caused any accidents, but there were many cases where it would have saved a life had it been installed. After my first skipper left his command of VA-145, he was killed flying a test flight at Patuxent River, while his B/N managed to eject safely. He just happened to be the only fatality I knew personally, but there were others. In the world of positive images for Congress and $100 toilet seats, our ejection seats had been put on the back burner.

"Does he know yet if his leg is going to completely heal?" I asked Rivers. I brought the throttles back a bit more to save fuel.

"Can't tell; may not know for a long time. The docs aren't giving out a whole lot of information. I guess they just don't know." Rivers gazed out at the stars. "I just hope they don't screw around with his disability if it comes to it."

We made idle conversation to kill time, but our moods had been soured. Carrier qualifications had a lot of filler time for pilots, but it was even worse for B/Ns. Landing at the ship was one of the few endeavors in the Intruder where the bombardier/navigator could provide the most assistance possible, but the pilot could still screw up the pass. On the other hand, the B/N didn't have his name posted on the Greenie board in the ready room, where any missteps would be public record for months. The only controls the B/N would use during carrier qualifications were the radios. Where a B/N became invaluable was in their experience and their second set of eyes. Without a newer jet's heads-up display the pilot had his hands full, particularly at night, trying to assess and correctly respond to the mass of information available. The B/N could help direct the pilot's attention to where it needed to be at any particular moment. A timely vertical speed call-out, or "check your lineup," could easily prevent a problem from becoming serious enough to catch the LSO's attention. We pilots were the trained monkeys with the specific hand-eye coordination skills. The B/Ns liked to think of themselves as our trainers, coaxing our egos and steering us in the right direction. I suppose there was some truth to this.

"Snickers bar?" Rivers pulled two candy bars out of his SV-2 survival vest pocket.

"Sure." I gladly took the "pilot" candy. Whatever it took for a B/N to get his pilot safely on the deck of the ship. After a long night a dose of chocolate from the B/N's stash of pilot candy often did the trick. Just like feeding a monkey.

We flew circles for an hour and a half, always to the left, watching the lights of the aircraft above and below us at 1,000-foot intervals. It was a nice change of pace to escape the bustle of activity of the aircraft carrier and fly aimlessly, but to do so twice on the first day of deployment was a tad much. Finally the radio came alive with the sort of information we were concerned about: push times. The marshal controller started off by broadcasting a time hack to ensure that all of his wards in the holding pattern were working off of the same clock. Ten seconds was not much allowable error to give away any time to an erroneously set watch. Starting from the bottom of the circle, times were assigned to each aircraft to push out of the stack. The majority of times were separated by 60-second intervals, but between every third or fourth aircraft a 2-minute sequence was inserted to accommodate any aircraft that would need to be fit back into the pattern due to a wave-off or bolter.

"Rustler 507, your expected approach time is 1-5."

"Roger," Rivers answered. "One-5."

We had until 15 minutes past the hour to be pointed directly at the ship on a 240-degree heading, exactly 25 miles away, at 10,000 feet and 250 knots. It was currently 2003, so that left us 12 minutes to get ourselves set up. I bumped up the throttles and turned back directly to our assigned point in space. Easier to get to the starting point, and then figure out how to eat up the remaining time and return to that same piece of sky. Rivers and I decided on a basic plan that would have us fly a set turn rate that would get us back to the push point at our assigned time. Of course, this did not account for the winds or the fact that the carrier was moving away from the marshal stack at about 15 knots. We would compensate by turning a little early and accelerating to 250 knots on our final turn toward the ship. It always looked good when there were about 10 minutes to go.

It became apparent 2 minutes from our push time that we were leaning toward the late side. I tightened up our turn until we were afforded a clear view of the lone jet remaining in the stack below us. With a minor power addition we worked it out, and we left the marshal orbit 5 seconds late.

Rivers keyed the mike: "Rustler 507 commencing, 8.7, 2994." We had dumped our remaining wing fuel, which left us with 8,700 pounds. The altimeter setting of 29.94 was verified to make certain our aircraft had the proper barometric correction dialed in and our altitude information would be accurate. I brought the throttles to idle, extended the speed brakes, and maintained 250 knots in the descent. We dropped into the blackness at 5,000 feet per minute.

We passed 20 miles from the ship's TACAN and descended through 5,000 feet above the ocean. I put the speed brakes back in, and we shallowed out our plunging dive toward the water. Two minutes later I leveled off the Intruder at 1,200 feet, and we drove the jet in at 250 knots the last couple of miles until we reached our slowdown point 10 miles behind *Ranger*. The landing gear and flaps and slats went down, and we decelerated to 150 knots before I halted our airspeed decay with an addition of power. Here was where the real work started. I used my trim button judiciously, trying to get our A-6 to the point where she would fly perfectly straight ahead with my hands off the controls. At 6 miles from the boat I snuck a peek out the front window and saw the small row of centerline lights on the carrier deck in the distance. I put my eyes back into the cockpit and flew my instruments before I scared myself trying to figure out how to stay aligned with the tiny column of lights moving from side to side with the wind and the waves.

We had slowed down to our final approach speed, and I had the reassurance of a constant angle-of-attack amber doughnut in my peripheral vision. The crosshairs of needles I was referencing on my ADI became more sensitive with each passing second, and I was making constant tiny corrections to keep them both lined up in the center of my display. One was for glide slope, the other for lineup. If either was out of parameters at three-quarters of a mile it would be an automatic wave-off. Three miles and 1,200 feet, the horizontal needle began to move downward as we reached the glide path. I adjusted the power back and we started down to center the raw data of the needles; we did not have the assistance of flight directors to dampen out the required corrections.

Rivers called out our vertical speed in feet per minute of descent—"600, 700, 800"—as I tried to catch the glide slope. We had gone a little high. We caught it—"700, 600, 700"— and the needles were centered again.

"You're on centerline, 700 down, I'm starting to see a ball." Rivers became my outside world so I could slave my eyes to the needles and the ADI. "Two miles, the TACAN distance cross-checks." Rivers verified that the needles were giving accurate information by referencing them to what our correct altitude should be at a distance of 2 miles.

The farther out from the ship we were, the harder it was to judge alignment with the carrier deck. The angled landing area was just too short, and each slight heave or roll of the boat in the water made it extremely difficult to gain a perspective without benefit of a horizon. There were few to no lights on the horizon at sea, and it was extremely difficult to ascertain exactly when the Intruder's wings were level and inducing no drift left or right. At a mile I risked a few furtive peeks outside, then went quickly back to my instruments to verify what I thought I was seeing.

The final controller on *Ranger* made one last radio call: "Rustler 507, three-quarters mile, call the ball."

The transmission from Rivers was directed to the landing signal officers on the windswept platform at the stern of the ship: "507, Intruder ball, 5.5."

"Roger ball, Intruder. Winds are 18 knots, slightly port." The LSO indicated that we could expect the wind to push us slightly to the right.

Rivers was rattling off vertical speeds at a steady rate as I made the transition to an outside scan: "700, 750, 700." He restricted the content of his calls to numbers so I would not confuse a radio command from one of the LSOs with something he had said.

I took one last look at my needles and made the leap to flying completely visually. Meatball, lineup, angle of attack. A quick glance at my ADI to check that our wings were level, then all outside. The ball started to sag ever so slightly, I thought. Rivers snapped me out of my indecision: "750, 800, 800." I added a handful of power and got the ball back to the middle. Where's the centerline? I added more power and made a small wing dip to the left. There—green out of the corner of my eye, more power to keep from going slow—shit, too much! The lens went a full ball high: "600, 500, 500." I pulled the power off even as I heard "Easy with it" transmitted over the radio. Dammit. Then, "650, 700, 750." Stop it there, reset the power. A rapid wing flash to the right, but I kept the throttles where they were this time so the Intruder would sink just a little in the slight turn and settle back on the glide path. I was concentrating so intently on the ball in close that I didn't notice we had crossed the ship's round down. I added a touch more power, the landing gear smashed into *Ranger*'s deck, and I was jerked forward into my shoulder straps. My left thumb shook imperceptibly as I flicked off the external lights and I looked for the yellow wands of the taxi director. Home.

With the night trap out of the way I was considered carrier-qualified. Coming off the flight deck, I felt the familiar mixture of fatigue and exhilaration from the completion of a full day of flying. Rivs and I took our time getting out of our flight gear, cleaning off our oxygen masks, and hanging our sweat-soaked skullcaps last on the metal hooks so they would dry by the morning. I looked at my watch and saw that it was 2105. Fifty-five minutes until the wardroom opened up again for the late-night feeding.

"Midrats?" I asked Rivers, making the decision to forgo a workout at *Ranger*'s gym.

"Sure. We've got time to kill. Let's swing through the ready room and try to catch the LSOs." I was glad that Rivers had suggested waiting for the LSOs to give me my grades. I didn't want to appear too eager, even to Rivers.

Rivers walked out into the steel gray passageway. It often struck me how timeless *Ranger*'s lower decks were; with some imagination it was easy to picture the interior of a World War II–vintage vessel. *Ranger* was an old ship by the current standards of the U.S. Navy. As a Forrestal-class carrier she was quite a bit smaller than the newer nukes, but that did not necessarily mean she was any less comfortable to live on. *Ranger*'s flight deck may have been smaller than her more modern counterparts', so there was less room for error in landing, but belowdecks the spaces were proportioned somewhat similarly between the new and the old. With each foot in length or increase in tonnage of the nukes came more aircraft and more personnel to fly, repair, service, and supply them. The greater number of men on the nuclear-powered vessels compared to the conventionally driven *Ranger* took up the majority of the increase in living space belowdecks. Living quarters were roughly comparable in respect to size; there were just more of them on a nuke.

From speaking with friends who had deployed on nuclear carriers I had learned that there was one aspect of comfort that the nukes were clearly superior in, and that was in the ship's temperature control. There was rarely a problem thoroughly air-conditioning a nuke, but the Forrestal-class ships had trouble keeping many of their spaces cool while steaming in the tropics and Middle Eastern climes. Ingenuity and a touch of extra effort in two areas, however, gave *Ranger* a leg up over any other carrier in the U.S. Navy. These were her gym and the normal fare at midnight rations, or "midrats."

*Ranger*'s gym was built on a huge steel loft at the far aft end of the hangar bay. The free weights, lifting machines, and aerobic bikes were in the open air as long as the hangar bay doors leading to the flight deck elevators were open. Absent was the claustrophobic feeling that other carrier sailors experienced crawling around shipmates in a cramped, low-ceilinged space deep in the bowels of the ship. The equipment was relatively new, and it was clear that several consecutive ships' captains had recognized the importance of physical fitness and burning off steam while living in the confines of the floating city. This was also reflected in the liberal policy of allowing personnel to run on the flight deck at any time during daylight as long as flight operations were not being conducted. These simple steps made great strides in maintaining high morale on *Ranger*.

Most carriers made a point of having a special "pizza night" for officers once a week. Because pizza ingredients were not particularly perishable, they were usually available. Normal dinner might be hard to stomach, but if you could hold out until midrats at 2200 on pizza night there would be relief. The wardroom on *Ranger* took the subtle, but surprisingly influential to morale, concept to its next logical level, and came up with the unprecedented and unmatched idea of having pizza at midrats every night in the dirty-shirt wardroom. What innovation, what daring, what a plain old good idea! No carrier, to my knowledge, ever did the same, and I don't know why. At any rate, the gym and a perpetual pizza night made *Ranger* aviators happier as they cycled through the process of pumping in the calories and then pumping iron to burn them off.

I sauntered after Rivers toward the ready room. The unusual flurry of activity as we opened the door emblazoned with our Swordsmen logo could only mean one of two things: either a short-notice all-officers meeting had been called (that was unlikely, because we still had officers flying), or there had been a mail call. The sound of tearing envelopes gave it away. We beelined to our mailboxes. Cargo flights were made daily this close to the States, and evidently many families and friends had made the effort to say one last good-bye before *Ranger* headed west. The letters must have been dropped in the mail the second we left home, or perhaps before. My mood dropped as I saw that a stack of airmen evaluations were still covering the top of my mailbox.

"How'd you do, Rivs?"

"Barb and the boys. I'm gonna save it for later. How about you?"

"Skunked. Hold on a sec, will you?" The LSOs entered the ready room fresh from the flight deck platform still wearing their flight jackets replete with "Rectum Non Bustus" patches. The landing signal officers' motto and message to the air wing pilots were identical—"Don't Bust Your Ass," particularly on the steel round down at the stern of the ship. They were immediately swarmed by the ready room pilots, all waiting for their jet's side number to be called out so the LSOs could debrief their landings for the day.

One of the younger-looking LSOs asked a squadron pilot, "505? That you, George?"

"Yep, I charlied around noon and 1930" came the answer, and the LSO jotted down the correct last name beside the shorthand notes grading the pass.

The LSOs worked in teams, and usually there were four to six on the platform at any time. Any one of them might be "controlling" the pass, calling for more power or corrections to line up. Although he would grade the landing, he might not be experienced enough to do so without some guidance, and always present on the platform was an LSO who was qualified by the air wing to "wave" any pilot, in any type of aircraft. Most landing signal officers came from the individual squadrons and performed their function on the platform as a collateral duty. The exception to this was the wing LSO, who was a senior lieutenant or lieutenant commander and who was present as the full-time adult supervision on the platform during flight operations. He maintained the option to override the radio directions of the controlling LSO and to change any grade he found unwarranted. He was not attached to any squadron, but reported directly to the commander of the air wing himself.

Rivers walked up beside me while George was getting debriefed. "What do you think?" he asked.

"I think the day touch-and-go was solid, the trap sucked, and I don't know about the night. We got the 'easy with it' call, but the deck might have been moving. That sound about right?"

"It was a pretty dark night; don't know about the deck. I think we faired the day trap." Rivers confirmed my doubts.

My turn: "502? Around a 1230 charlie?"

"That's me, Hunt." I stood there waiting, as if some substantive part of my fate were in the hands of the white-shirted LSO.

"Right, two passes. First one a little high, a little lined up right start, a little come down to land. Okay touch-and-go. Second one, low angling start, flat in the middle, a little settle into a fair two wire. That sound right?" The LSO listened politely, but I realized that if I disagreed with him, which I didn't, it wouldn't matter anyway.

"I'll buy that. I was in 507 at about 2030." I waited for our night trap.

"Got it. A little high start, a little overpowered on deck down in the middle, a little settle to land. Okay three wire." The movement of the flight deck in an ocean swell had exaggerated my picture of how high we had gone in the middle portion of the pass, at about a third of a mile from behind the ship.

"Thanks; take it easy." I felt satisfied with my overall performance for the day. Rivers gave me a little good-job pat on the arm and we turned away from the LSOs as they continued to debrief the remaining pilots. By qualifying each performance at the back of the ship in such stark terms the LSOs left no room for the sugarcoating of a bad landing. In the world of naval aviation everybody had a big ego, but the truth was far more important than hurt feelings when it came to landing on the ship. The LSOs had a tough job trying to get a pilot to learn from his mistakes without alienating him personally. The pilots needed to exercise a great degree of professionalism if they were to honestly look at their flying skills and make a serious effort to improve the deficient areas the LSOs pointed out. I was hungry.

"I'm going to swing by my stateroom, Rivs. See you up at the wardroom at ten?"

"Yeah, good idea. I'll see you up there." Rivers wandered off to talk to another one of his division officers about something as I headed for the door.

I had not been to my room since I had left there at about 0900. I wanted to drop off my stack of paperwork, but more importantly I wanted to wash my face and sit down behind a closed door for just a minute. More than five hours strapped into the ejection seat for two traps and a touch-and-go. I felt a drain to my energy level that I knew I would gradually become accustomed to, and quickly learn to power through. But on this first day of cruise I needed 2 minutes by myself to regroup and let my mind catch up with events.

We were only hours away from San Diego, but we would not set foot on American soil for another six months. When we were airborne it was easy to ignore such sentiments, but I found it was better to deal with them gradually and early on in a cruise, as opposed to burying them and letting them ambush you when you were not prepared.

I thought of my fiancée, Laurie, in Baltimore, and my parents, both teachers living in Damascus, Syria. Syria was awfully close to the action. Six years of my childhood had been spent in Athens, Greece, where my father had taught high school, and my mother was a librarian. I tried to convince myself that they could read the political undercurrents of a foreign country. I wondered how the events of the next six months would unfold and affect their lives. For the first time I fully realized that my actions truly impacted others, not simply on a personal scale, but in the case of my parents as part of a broader physical reality. Whatever we might end up doing when we collectively confronted Iraq's military in a few short weeks, it would most likely have farther-reaching ramifications than I was used to thinking of in the crisp, real-time universe of carrier aviation.

My brief moment of reflection over, I headed up to the dirty-shirt for some pizza.

# Chapter Seven

# . . . when free men shall stand

Another day would elapse before Air Wing 2 completed the carrier qualification of her pilots and *Ranger* was allowed to plot a course westward on 10 December 1990. The officers and men of the *Ranger* Battle Group began to shed the last remaining vestiges of the trudging pace of the eight-month air wing training cycle, workups, with the final hurdle of CQ complete. During workups we had practiced general quarters drills with old, ratty gas masks of Sergeant York vintage. Safely away from the possibilities of pilferage ashore, we were each issued brand-new masks that actually fit. The masks had a high-tech appearance that inspired a dual message: Hey, this is serious stuff, but that's okay because we've got these shit-hot gas masks to protect us.

Man-overboard exercises became second nature, and the goal of an on-sight accounting of every one of *Ranger*'s five thousand personnel was completed in less than 20 minutes. A new twist to the time-honored training on board *Ranger* emerged with the introduction of gas masks and chemical/biological/radiation exposure suits. The demonstrated resolve of Iraq to use chemical weapons in its war against Iran, coupled with Iraq's twin missile impacts on USS *Stark* in the Persian Gulf in 1987, had most definitely not gone unnoticed. The compact package of gas mask and protective gear, to be carried at all times by all personnel, was a physical reminder that this cruise would be different.

I found myself trying to keep busy constantly to avoid reflecting in my mood the political swings of the U.S. Congress and press: one day leaning toward war, the next day appeasement. The few minutes in the rack before being overcome by sleep were the exception to the regimentation of my thoughts during this third night at sea. My mind bounced back and forth, wondering if this would all turn out to be much ado about nothing. My emotional mix was not separating into any truly discernible themes yet, but merely abstract feelings. I did not want to go to war, but if it was going to happen, then I certainly wanted to be in the middle of it. Fear, excitement, a sense of history, mission, and purpose. An adolescent anxiety that I might miss out on something big vied with "Let's just have a boring cruise and forget about it." These were a few of the many individual thoughts that never seemed to pull together into a single, unified focus. Not that it mattered. For all intents and purposes I was along for the ride, at least for now.

On 11 December, we left the comfort of proximity to landing fields ashore and began flying blue water operations. Any animosity toward *Ranger*, the symbol of our captivity, evaporated from our collective thoughts temporarily as we catapulted with the knowledge that there was only one landing strip in town and tailhooks were not optional. The training missions we did fly on our first days at sea were not terribly applicable to what we might expect to accomplish over Iraq and Kuwait, but they were generic enough so as not to impede *Ranger*'s steady progress into the setting sun. We searched out civilian merchant vessels and tracked their course. Rivers and I helped plan a practice war-at-sea attack, a scenario that seemed hopelessly outdated and unlikely, with our simulated target of the maritime power of the Soviet Union now in disintegrated fragments.

We had all expected that the flying during the transit to the Persian Gulf would be spotty and limited in the effect it would have in keeping our skills sharp. We struggled to get our training where we could. On our night war-at-sea exercise, Rivers and I disciplined ourselves to fly the mission at 200 feet above the water and 480 knots. Not a big deal with no mountains to run into, but unnerving nevertheless flying that low and that fast strictly on instruments.

Low-level flying, particularly at night or in the clouds, was inherently dangerous. In the three years I had been stationed at Whidbey Island, two A-6s had crashed into the Cascade Mountains, killing a total of four young men. This was the accepted accident rate that had come to be thought of as "normal," and was viewed by the navy community as a necessary price to pay for combat-readiness.

Occasionally, media or congressional attention would spike up the interest level, additional investigations into training and safety would be conducted, and minor recommendations would be made. Eventually, however, there was no escaping the basic premise of the night low-level attack mission, which required putting aircrews at risk. The ultimate irony was that we had to train hard in peacetime, and accept certain losses, so we could fulfill our mission in war more safely and effectively. No one I knew seriously argued against the necessity of the dangerous training—we accepted it as part of the package. Besides, it could never happen to me. You had to believe that, to fly your machine aggressively through the dark-as-pitch valleys night after night.

The last A-6 to crash had been piloted by my roommate and friend John while we were going through initial A-6 training. As with most aircraft accidents, we will never know exactly what happened or why, other than that they flew too low for too long. A minor distraction, or perhaps a major one like a fire light, may have divided their attention for those critical seconds prior to impact. Or they may have pushed themselves just a bit too hard. The only thing certain was that they were dead, and there was now a charred, twisted-metal crater on the side of an unnamed hill. It paid to revisit such

memories seriously and frequently; they might be all that
could sober up the adrenaline-soaked spirit and keep the
pilot's hand from pushing the stick forward that last little bit,
all hopped up on the juice of speed and danger. The sacrifice
was not in vain. It sharpened the awareness and skills of
other A-6 pilots, and just may have saved their lives. I know it
did mine.

Our squadron tactics department devised various flight
profiles to simulate instrument-only, high-G, low-level turns.
Exhaustive preflight planning through topographical analysis
was the only way for an Intruder pilot to regain any certainty
that he was pulling his jet in a direction clear of hills and
mountains. It was impossible to predict the exact locations of
the enemy positions shooting at you, and therefore the least-
threatening route in the immediate vicinity of the target. A
pilot doing high-G, low-level turns at night relied on more
than a little faith and a lot of gut feeling. There is an old low-
level adage that would be a platitude if it were not written in
the blood of countless aviators: The ground has a "PK," or
"probability of kill," of 100 percent. All the fancy flying in
the world might dazzle a surface-to-air-missile radar operator
to no end, but if you fly yourself into the ground, he still wins.
And, of course, you are dead.

We practiced mock bombing and HARM missile attacks
against oblivious merchant ships. We did what we could, but
it was difficult to keep the edge with no bombs to drop or terrain to hug. We ended up conducting more "make-believe"
training at sea than we ever did at home with the benefit of a
simulator.

As long as there were flight ops, however, there would be
excitement. On the third day out from San Diego two F-14s,
in separate incidents only hours apart, trapped just a few feet
to the right of the angled deck's centerline. No one was hurt,
and each Tomcat caught a wire, but the row of A-6s parked
amidships on the port side of the ship's island didn't fare
nearly as well. Each F-14 wingtip managed to career into the

prominent noses of the parked Intruders, and in the space of an afternoon the entire West Coast fleet was out of A-6 replacement radomes. The three that were on board for the unlikely possibility of incurring a breakage to the fiberglass nose cone were enough to repair the stricken Intruders, but if any more were seriously damaged during the remainder of the cruise, A-6s would start dropping out of commission for months. Given *Ranger*'s track record of three in one day, these didn't seem like terribly good odds with almost six months at sea remaining. As fate would have it, not a single additional radome was destroyed during the ensuing deployment.

Without the distractions of shore to "bother" us, much could be packed into an 18-hour day. When I wasn't flying, my time was consumed with paperwork: evaluations, awards boards to determine how to allocate squadron-awarded medals, writing up those selected awards, sailor of the year, sailor of the quarter, reviewing training records—the list went on. It was all part of the morale suppression plan, navy retention at its finest. Perhaps it was an integral component of a grand design to help us appreciate the escape of flying all the more. . . . No; it was too early in the cruise for self-delusion.

The executive officer, our XO, kept a tight rein on the squadron spaces, and zone inspections were conducted to check for cleanliness and general order. Rumors began to circulate that the gates at Subic Bay in the Philippines would not be opened as a response to terrorist threats. But that was all right, because there would be 16,000 Marines camped out on the base for our battle group's 10,000 sailors to get chummy with. It started to sound safer in town with the terrorists.

This was the general tenor of the light fly days while transiting to and from our carrier's assigned station. I took daily time out to go to the gym or run on the flight deck to burn off the building tension. The air wing had a safety stand-down, perhaps a reaction to the mishap with the Tomcats two days before. Flying was not permitted, and the full day was devoted to training and safety awareness. The ritual was designed as a "let's step back and take a look at what we're doing" type of reorientation to prevent a future accident. The navy is pretty good with statistics, so I have to believe that there were fewer accidents because of safety stand-downs. But it always seemed to me that one of the primary reasons for mishaps on the carrier was that everybody was perpetually and hopelessly behind in their work, and rushed to get things done. The thought had crossed my mind that if we turned a safety stand-down into a nonflying day, where people could catch up on their more mundane tasks without enduring endless meetings, then we might all be a lot safer.

*Ranger* steamed on, and at a point 1,200 miles equidistant from Hawaii to the southwest and the mainland to the east, the seas began to build. The word was that several of the flight surgeons were seasick, which we all found exceedingly amusing, although I'm not quite sure why. Perhaps it was because we were ordered to get our flu shots that morning. Or it may have been the diabolical eagerness with which the navy doctors attempted to coax all the married men into getting vasectomies. There were few occasions for the fresh-out-of-medical-school flight surgeons to practice cutting, given *Ranger*'s complement of young, healthy males, and they jumped at every opportunity to get their scalpels bloody.

We were only six days into the cruise, and the air wing was treated to another no-fly day. Fortunately, this time we indulged in a much more entertaining form of air wing gathering, called Fo'c'sle Follies. These staged events showcased the funniest (and often crudest) people from each of the squadrons in barely rehearsed skits in the ship's anchor locker, the fo'c'sle. The fo'c'sle was the closest space, with the exception of the hangar bay, that the ship had to an auditorium, and it was relatively easy to maintain a semblance of privacy so the enlisted troops would not hear the disrespect being bandied about. All of *Ranger*'s bigwigs were invited, and usually attended, but it was the admiral, the ship's captain, and the air wing commander who were the obvious targets. Officially the purpose of the events was to dish out various air wing awards representing achievements in landing performance and milestones in the individual numbers of *Ranger* traps accumulated. The cruise was divided into three to four separate line periods where the landing grades would begin to be tallied fresh from the start, and all the air wing pilots had an equal opportunity to receive a "Top Ten Tailhook" award. The judging was strictly objective, and was directly dependent on the average of all of the landing grades bestowed on each individual pilot by the landing signal officers during the line period.

This first of several Fo'c'sle Follies for our 1990–91 deployment reflected the achievements of the squadron pilots during precruise air wing training. We all sat around the hot and humid cavernous fo'c'sle in fold-out chairs, massed in the groupings of our particular squadrons. The atmosphere was intended to be casual, and with the exception of the air wing LSOs, who acted as masters of ceremonies, the crowd was decked out in flight suits. The air wing's LSOs wore their traditional white flight deck jerseys, khaki pants, and steel-toed boots, all the better to kick up shit with. The only people sitting between *Ranger*'s 30-ton twin anchors who did not seem completely at ease were the squadron commanding and executive officers. Despite their attempt to fit in and go with the flow, there was always the tiniest bit of concern that their boys onstage, unleashed with a limited license to buck authority, would overstep their bounds. The possibility of one of the senior brass in the front row retaliating in a more serious manner lurked in the subconscious. In these days of pre-Tailhook notoriety, and an all-male complement on combatant naval vessels, it took a lot to break out of the confines of an acceptable parody during the time frame of the officially sanctioned Follies. Nevertheless, the senior squadron leadership was well aware that they were ultimately responsible for their boys' performance and taste, or lack thereof. Pushing the limits was covertly encouraged, as it was in all facets of tactical military flying, but breaking the limits was strictly taboo. Naturally, the difficulty was in figuring out exactly where those limits were.

With just the few frantic days since we left San Diego to prepare, and only the marginal opportunity of training workups to expose major faux pas and screwups, the Follies were somewhat predictable, rather tame, but quite funny all the same. One squadron did the obligatory "butt man" routine. A row of guys painted their bare naked asses with caricatures of various shipboard dignitaries and held a "conversation" depicting the incompetence and idiocy of all those senior enough to supposedly be in control of the big picture. This crudest of the night's events was not particularly clever, and the insight it provided was certainly not appealing. But it was a no-brainer skit that was a sure sell in accomplishing what was perhaps the underlying goal of the Follies: to set a defined arena where the everyday barriers of professionalism and decorum could be shattered temporarily. Hopefully this would enable the air wing aviators to return to their business of following orders that routinely endangered their lives with a little bit less steam in their pressure cookers. "Butt man" was about as far as it could go, and the precedent had been set that it would not land a CO or an XO in the brig as long as the "conversation" was within the nearly impossible-to-define limits of not being excessively disrespectful.

We were 2 hours into Fo'c'sle Follies by the time the last of the skits was "performed" and the milestone patches had been handed out to aviators achieving a hundred or more *Ranger* traps. The last two events were predictably the most important: selecting the ten individuals with the highest landing grades from the wing's hundred-plus pilots, and the award for the best average landing grades by a squadron. This was the carrot for each carrier aviator to push his hardest during each attempt behind the boat. The stick was the ship's steel round down and the threat of never having your body recovered from the depths of the ocean. Our squadron did not end up winning the "hook" for the workup line period, but we made a respectable showing, and we filed out of the fo'c'sle more relaxed and eager to get a fresh start on our next line period of landing grades. None of the squadron skippers was invited to the air wing commander's spaces for a heart-to-heart talk, and apparently the admiral had gotten a few laughs out of the evening. Overall, a resounding success. It was 2205, and I fell in line with the rest of the air wing on their way to midrats.

The flight schedule came out, as usual, at 0100 the next morning, and I saw with frustration that my name was absent. Three no-fly days in a row might help with relieving the weight of paper from my mailbox, but it did nothing for my morale. The longer we were away from port, the longer the days dragged on, and the days without flying were the worst. It made it all the easier to lose perspective and forget why we were deployed on the "Gulag 61" at all. Invariably the lowest of moments came after several days without flying, when there were no reminders of the larger issues surrounding us. I marveled at how the enlisted troops could handle it without losing all motivation and sense of purpose. Every day at sea was a day without women, families, babies, flowers, silence, privacy, buildings, cats, dogs, and an endless list of the microcomponents that composed our mental images of home and its accompanying feelings of security and warmth. The mounting oppression of the ship's rote routine would melt away in an instant once airborne, but without that escape our morale was compressed daily to ever greater levels of lethargy and inaction.

It was a given that the daily regimen of shipboard life would put all aboard on edge—there were too many competing stresses for any normal person not to be affected in some manner. For the enlisted ranks the complete lack of privacy and rigorous work conditions were the leading factors. Sharing a room with dozens of others was simply difficult to bear under normal circumstances. Throw into the mix 12-hour work shifts every day while at sea (in other words, no week-ends), family separation, constant noise, and temperatures in the tropics that the shipboard air-conditioning could not keep up with, and a level of emotional intensity was produced that simmered just under a boil. For the men who worked on the flight deck, jet engines were at every glance ready to suck you in and spit you out in a jellied form of yourself. Propellers turned so quickly that they were invisible except for a stripe of yellow paint to help prevent a bone-tired trooper from putting his head down into the howling night wind and walking through their deadly arc.

"Diversity" was an understatement when examining back-ground and skin-deep identity. All fifty states, Guam, Puerto Rico, and the Philippines were represented, and every race and religion imaginable was among the ship's embarked complement of close to five thousand men. Most of the en-listed sailors were high school graduates, some had gone to college, and a few had advanced degrees. Their commonly experienced contradictory emotions of frustrated boredom and absolute uncertainty coexisted as the daily routine varied little, but the actual environment outside the dark recesses of the ship changed with each new stretch of water beneath the keel. The daily excitement might entail guessing what was for chow, while deeper in the psyche were visions of tropical ports in the positive, or antiship missiles breaching the water-line in a dark mood. The vast majority of the enlisted ranks were young—17 to 19 years old—and all were male. Sexual frustration was a way of life when sequestered from the oppo-site sex for months at a time. What the nonofficer mass of hu-manity did have in common was fundamental and a bedrock in the apparent confusion of the floating city.

Ultimately, and most definitely by no accident, the greatest unifying factor was that each individual was part of some-thing bigger than himself: He was a sailor in the U.S. Navy. Unit cohesion and morale were not just the happenstance niceties that might improve production or profits in the civilian world. They were singularly important factors that, only if achieved, would enable completion of the aircraft carrier's two primary objectives: to accomplish its assigned mission, wherever in the world that might be and whatever it might entail, and to bring everyone home alive. Without the esprit de corps tipping the scale ever so slightly away from the fear of the unknown and the doldrums of the mind, these two objectives could not be accomplished. Most who have been in the military understand the utter necessity for common resolve and identification intuitively. To seriously stray from it meant that shipmates would die, and more importantly, the carrier's mission capability would be put in jeopardy. It was a constant battle to keep the balance shifted to common purpose and away from common despair, but most recognized that it was in their best interest to do so, to fulfill the most basic of needs. Those who did not were ostracized, in extreme cases through official means, but minimally in the social structure of the boat. Peer pressure was a most powerful tool, but failing that, commanding officers still had the authority in 1990 to prescribe three days of bread-and-water confinement in the ship's brig. Occasionally it took a sixteenth-century remedy to remind a soul that they were indeed embarked on a naval combatant on the high seas.

The times, and general condition of combat-readiness in the navy, decidedly moved the overall mental state to positive morale. The draw-down following the end of the Cold War had not yet begun in earnest, and effective training was the norm. There was a sense of common purpose through Saddam Hussein—this would not be just another cruise, steaming circles in nondescript water for six months, and then returning home with the nagging doubt of whether it had all been worth it. Rapidly evaporating was the junior officers' shipboard mantra "Sleep until you're hungry, eat until you're tired." This time there was an additional strand to the thread that bound us all together, and it made everyone work just a little bit harder and complain just a little bit less.

It became increasingly difficult to get up early on consecutive no-fly days, but with the initiation of the flight schedule on the deck 10 feet above us, sleeping was no longer an option. I wrapped my towel around my waist, opened the stateroom door, and squinted my eyes into the white lights as I made my way to the showers. I glanced to my right at the remaining doors in VA-145's dead-end cache of officers' spaces that we called the alley. The alley was a unique arrangement of rooms for a carrier to have. The closed door at the beginning of our row of eight squadron spaces created a physical dividing line between the rest of *Ranger* and the minicommunity where half of the Swordsmen officers lived. With the exception of the daily visits of the "coop cleaners" who picked up our laundry and vacuumed and dusted the officer spaces, there was no official reason for anyone else to open the alley door and enter our domain. Our relative seclusion and neighboring staterooms strengthened the bond among the officers in the command.

I shuffled through the alley door and continued down the passage to the left, my flip-flops barely clearing the knee knockers and making a smacking sound with each step. Sailors and khaki-clad ship's company officers filed past me in the opposite direction as I entered the main passageway on *Ranger*'s port side. The never-ending cycle of the ship's work schedule, and the overlapping proximity of work spaces and staterooms, made for some odd pictures in the carrier's labyrinth of hallways at all hours. Here I was barely covered in a towel, soap in one hand and shampoo in the other, trudging along with my slitted eyes fighting the glare while all around me officers and men were in the middle of their workday routine. It was not uncommon to be slouching your way to the showers, trying to be inconspicuous in your half-naked state, and be rendered a hearty "good morning" by the CAG or even the admiral on some official errand. The actual time might be in the afternoon or the middle of the night, but "good morning" was always appropriate for the out-of-place aviator struggling to get to the "invigorating" streams of a carrier shower. I was never completely comfortable making the trek to the shared shower facilities, but that was okay because navy showers were supposed to be anything but comfortable.

I left the bustle of the main passageway and turned in to the damp, mildewed shower room, looking for an unoccupied stall. From the sounds of it only about half of the room's dozen showers were occupied, and the occasional sharp exclamation of shock told me that the water temperature was at its normal perfection. *Ranger* was blessed with hot and cold running water, occasionally at the same time, but over the course of the months I suppose it all evened out to a nicely metered temperature. A dripping Snax exited one of the stalls. I contemplated which of the stalls held the most promise for a bearable shower.

"What's the word today, hot or cold?" I asked with feigned enthusiasm.

"Well, we've actually got a bit of a mixture. It started out cold, but turned to raw steam halfway through. I think it's back to cold now," Snax replied as he dried himself off. "What do you got going today?"

"Nothing. I'm not on the schedule, not even for a spare. How about you?"

"Spare SSC with the skipper. I think he might be getting out of it; he's got some CO's meeting with the CAG. You should see if you can scam the hop." A surface search and contact flight, SSC was a fairly relaxed evolution. We would search for ships in an assigned sector within about 100 miles' distance from the carrier, and then take pictures of them for the intelligence guys to evaluate and plot.

"Yeah, I guess I'll wander around the ready room a bit more aimlessly than usual this morning and make my availability known. Thanks."

Our operations department kept track of the hours and traps each of the squadron aviators possessed for the deployment.

Each pilot and B/N was supposed to fly an equitable number of flight hours and traps. But you never knew; on a short-notice cancellation by the skipper there might be a scramble just to get the flight airborne, and when the schedule began to unravel, it paid to be in the right place at the right time.

"Who are you talking to about diving in the Philippines?" Snax and I had both packed our scuba gear into the overhead locker space in our staterooms and were hoping for an opportunity to use it on this cruise.

"Just Quiver so far, but I think he's got some folks from 131 who might want to go. I hope it doesn't turn into a gaggle," Snax answered. Quiver was a Whidbey friend in the Prowler squadron.

With six days in the Philippines there was no point in wasting time trying to organize a major diving trip. We would each need to stand some sort of in-port duty on at least two of those days, and getting our schedules in synch for one afternoon was probably the best we could hope for. With all of the turmoil around us now it seemed too ambitious to attempt to dive at all. But we both knew that things would settle down in the next two weeks before we reached port, and we were looking forward to a diversion to keep us out of the local bars for at least one afternoon.

"Okay. See you back at the room." Snax wrapped his towel around his waist and headed out into the passageway.

I stepped into the shower and found that we were back to operating at full scalding temperature. Using the technique we had all refined to perfection, I held down the push button on the handheld showerhead and sprayed it straight up into the air. By the time the mist drifted back down to my shoulders, it had reached a bearable temperature, and I did my best to soak down. Lacking a steady stream of water with which to rinse off, I opted to forgo the soap today and let the gathering humidity run off of me in an attempt to loosen some of the previous day's grime. It would have to do. Who could complain? At least we had water. I was certain the poor slobs sitting in tents in the Saudi desert since August would have been ecstatic for a scalding shower. Well, I thought, they get the fresh air and sunshine—lots of sunshine. We get the water. I completed my morning routine at the stateroom sink, got dressed, and headed down to the ready room to see what surprises lay in store for me in my mailbox. I had just walked in when the assistant maintenance officer (AMO) caught my attention.

"Pete, have you seen the Amcross in your box yet?" asked the AMO.

"No, Steve. What's up?" I asked.

The American Red Cross provided the navy with the service of notifying ships at sea of messages of a serious personal nature. Most of Amcross correspondence was in a negative light, but far too rarely they actually contained good news, such as a wife's uneventful labor. Amcross messages carried the weight of independent verification of the specific event with them. Inevitably there were the few sailors who would go to great lengths to get off of the ship, and that included concocting a story of hardship at home. Most such attempts were nipped in the bud when it was determined that the sailor in question had a mother who died not just last week but on the previous three cruises as well. Unfortunately, some were valid, and once corroborated by the Red Cross, the pertinent information was relayed to *Ranger*. Navy policy dictated that only in the case of the death of an immediate family member—a wife or child, mother, father, brother, or sister—would the sailor be permitted to leave the ship. The policy needed to be this way due to the simple fact that there was not a single person on *Ranger* who did not fill a 12-hour work shift with his efforts. The navy could not furnish the personnel for all of the squadron billets as it was, even in these times of record recruitment, and everyone who returned home left his shipmates with an extra 12 hours of work to divide among themselves. Obtaining a replacement was almost unheard of; if there had been extra sailors available ashore, they would have deployed with us to begin with. The number of sailors who would be allowed to leave had to be limited by a strictly adhered-to policy, no matter how heartless it might seem at the time.

"It's one of your chiefs. Father was just diagnosed with cancer; it looks terminal."

Shit. I allowed a moment of sympathy to transit my thoughts, and then it was back to business. "Let me grab the message out of my box and see if I have any questions."

I walked over to the wall-mounted boxes and took out a privacy folder at the top of my stack of new paperwork. I read the single paragraph, which could not possibly answer all of the questions that the soon-to-be-informed son would have.

"Can you let him go?" Steve asked. As the chief's division officer I would have some input as to whether he would be allowed to leave the ship.

"I think so. Things are starting to run pretty smoothly; we can get one of the first class petty officers to fill in for him. Maybe he can hook back up with us in the Philippines."

Chief petty officers were the noncommissioned officers who supervised the squadron's sailors and ensured that operations ran smoothly and nothing fell through the cracks. The aviator officers in the maintenance department held overall responsibility and accountability, but the chiefs handled the daily running of business when it came to repairing and servicing the squadron's fleet of twelve A-6s. If we were any later into deployment I was not sure I would be able to make the same recommendation.

"All right. Why don't you go and tell him what's going on. Let him know that we can't give him an answer just yet on leaving the boat. I'll try to find out if Rivers has spoken with the CO yet." Steve turned to go.

I definitely needed some coffee before I set out on this next endeavor. I sat down and pumped the caffeine into my system as I reread the Amcross message and looked for any nuances or details I might have missed. Several minutes later I was out of coffee and out of excuses. I made a photocopy of the message, guaranteeing that the chief had as much information as I did. I figured that the hangar bay was as good a place as any to begin looking.

There was a cool breeze coming through the open hangar bay doors when I stepped up the last ladder and out into the open space. I set out in a purposeful stride for the cluster of Swordsmen A-6s that were chained down in the forward half of the hangar bay. It didn't take long to find the chief. He was looking over the shoulder of a power plants mechanic beside the massive damage control door that could be electrically closed to separate the hangar bay into two separate chambers. I stood about 15 feet away until he was finished with the sailor and I could catch his eye.

"Chief, you got a minute? I need to talk to you." It was obvious that he could see something in my face; I had his undivided attention.

"What's up, sir?"

"Just a minute; let's talk over here." I steered him over to the starboard bulkhead away from the workers gathered around the hangared Intruder. "I've got some bad news." I tried not to torment him with delays or by sugarcoating the hard facts. "We got an Amcross this morning. Your father has been diagnosed with cancer; it doesn't look good."

I put the copy of the Amcross message in the chief's open hand to give him something to hang on to and stood there silently while he read it impassively. Navy chiefs have a reputation for gruffness and a hard-nosed, businesslike approach to life. I should have known better, but I was still a little bit surprised when I saw what I thought were tears well up in the chief's eyes. I was glad that we were out of sight of his men; it seemed that with the stress of carrier living a few of the sailors usually had an ax to grind. I didn't want to give any of the chief's subordinates ammunition to take advantage of later.

"What would you like to do, Chief?" I asked. It was always

difficult to tell how someone would want to handle their individual situation. Some people actually preferred to stay on board the ship and keep busy.

"I want off the ship, sir. When can I leave?" I could see with the hardening of his eyes that in his mind leaving the ship was a done deal; the only question was when.

"The maintenance officer hasn't talked with the skipper yet. I can't make any promises right now. I really don't know what he's going to decide." I didn't want to lead the chief into believing that the CO was leaning one way or another in his decision, but he did need to be reminded that the possibility existed that he would not be permitted to leave. "Let me try to find them so I can get an answer for you."

"I'm leaving the ship. Go ahead and find out when, but I'm leaving, sir."

There was no point in giving the chief a destructive outlet for his frustration. I just nodded my head. "I'm sorry, Chief. I'll get back to you as soon as I find something out."

The chief turned toward the bulkhead and stepped through a hatch, probably to go back to the chiefs' berthing to sit down, but perhaps just to pace the passageways in anonymity. I set off in the opposite direction, back to the ready room. I ran into Rivers outside the pararigger shop on my way.

"Rivs, did you see the Amcross this morning?" Rivers looked tired.

"Yes. I spoke with the skipper about it. I want to talk to Bill to see if we can let him go." Bill was the ground pounder in charge of maintenance control, the production side of the maintenance operation. He was in the best position to make an assessment of what impact the chief's absence would have on the smooth running of the department. "Have you spoken with your chief yet?"

"Yeah, I just finished talking to him. He's pretty upset, definitely wants off the boat," I answered.

"Okay; there isn't a COD until tomorrow anyway. Let him know that if he's going to leave, it will be tomorrow at the earliest." Rivers turned and began walking toward maintenance control.

The COD was the carrier's onboard delivery aircraft. The CODs were C-2 Greyhounds, the same basic airframe as the twin-prop E-2 Hummer but without the radar dome, and internally configured for passengers and cargo. The CODs were not attached to any specific ship, but were land-based and provided support for any carrier transiting through their area of responsibility. *Ranger* was steaming about 1,000 miles north of Hawaii, and that put us within COD range for at least a day. If the chief did not get off tomorrow he might not have another opportunity until we came within COD range of Guam in about a week.

"I'll go track him down right now and let him know." There was no point in holding back information. I headed to chief petty officer berthing.

The chiefs on a carrier lived in separate quarters from the rest of the men, and had their own mess hall for their meals. Most chiefs, by virtue of their rank, had been in the navy for at least 15 years and had made many 6-month deployments. VA-145's maintenance control senior chief, which was one rank above plain old "chief," had made something like fifteen cruises in his 20 years in the navy. If you added workups into the equation, that equaled about 10 solid years at sea over the course of his career thus far. Aviators tended to have more employment options available to them ashore, and the average 20-year pilot or B/N would complete five to six deployments at most.

The chief petty officers knew as a community that it was the nature of their job to spend a lot of time on the water, and they had worked the system to make their longer periods away from shore more comfortable. They all paid dues into their wardroom mess to guarantee that they had the best food on the ship, and that included in the comparison the admiral's private mess. It wasn't steak and lobster every night, but it was on a select few. I suppose it was a difference in focus between the officers and the chiefs. The officers spent most of their time planning how to get off of the boat and have a nice dinner. The chiefs had resigned themselves to the fact that they would not often get to leave, and were willing to pay, and pay a lot, for the luxury of higher-quality food. It was an event of enormous importance for an enlisted sailor to make the rank of chief, and attendant with the increased responsibilities of wearing a khaki uniform came many privileges that made extended deployments less onerous.

I found the target of my search and relayed the message about the COD. The time spent wandering the passageways looking for various people was a constant impetus to getting things done. The ship was just too big to locate someone quickly; if they were not in the ready room, berthing area, or work center, then it was strictly a hit-or-miss proposition. By the time I returned to the ready room, Rivers had an answer for me: the chief would get to go home.

Being the bearer of bad news was no fun; rubbing salt in the wound by telling the chief that he would not be seeing his father on perhaps his last living days would have been much worse. In a stroke of time-saving luck I found the chief talking with the first class petty officer I was going to assign as his fill-in. I left the two while the chief passed down the information he thought pertinent to help the first class keep things running in his absence. It was 1030 and I had not made a dent in the stack of evals and awards sitting in my box. I got to work.

# Chapter Eight

# The terror of flight . . .

15–18 December 1990,
North and West of Midway Island

Air Wing 2 had a fairly extensive supply of the high-speed
antiradiation missiles at our disposal. The ultrasensitive seeker
head of a HARM was designed to fly down the enemy radar's
beam and explode at its source, destroying the critical radar
dish. The ability to utilize HARM was of critical importance
to us in the Intruder community, because the A-6 would find
itself in the heart of the enemy's surface-to-air-missile defenses.
Now we could take an active part in defeating and defending
against SAMs while carrying out our bombing missions.

The HARM practice missiles were relatively new to the
command, and I did not want to squander an opportunity to
fly with one, hopefully in the next day or so. Operations was
doing its best to cycle each of the squadron's crews through a
flight with the blue-banded inert missile, with the intent of
giving everyone possible a chance to flip the appropriate
switches and work the sensitive missile-seeker head. It didn't
take much time to get back up to speed on HARM procedures, and feeling on a bit of a tactical roll, I decided to head
to the ship's intelligence center to see how the assessments of
the Iraqi air defenses were coming.

The Carrier Intelligence Center, CVIC, was on *Ranger*'s
O-3 level, port side, directly below the flight deck amidships.
Each squadron had its own aviation intelligence officer, or

AI, to brief aircrew when ashore and to provide any support necessary for targeting and threat assessment and analysis. On board the carrier the individual squadron AIs reported to *Ranger*'s intelligence officer, and they all made their home away from home in the CVIC spaces. The Carrier Intelligence Center was not large: three spaces and a hallway. The air wing intelligence officer had his own office, there was a vault for special classified materials above the top-secret level, and the remaining open space doubled as an aircrew planning area and a ministudio for the televised intelligence briefings during flight operations.

I walked out of the ready room and trudged slowly to the escalator just forward. *Ranger* had two escalators, one forward and one aft, and each traversed the three stories up to the O-3 level. They only seemed to work about half of the time, but they provided a straight shot up as an alternative to the winding maze from ladderway to ladderway. Predictably the escalator was not running, and I glanced over to the wall switch to see if it was tagged as out of service. The red "do not touch" tag was indeed there, stressing that men were possibly working on the machinery out of sight and the operation of the automatic stairs might cause an injury. I gave a low grunt and started up the stationary steps two at a time. I turned the corner at the top just in time to see Snax walking down the passageway, heading aft.

"Snax, hold up!" I yelled. He stepped to the right to let other traffic pass and turned in my direction. He gave a nod and waited until I approached.

"Hey, what's up?" he asked.

"I was heading to CVIC to see what's going on. What do you got going?"

"Nothing really. I was working on the skipper's ConOps strike; just took a break for some chow. Are you on any of the strike teams yet?" Snax queried.

"No, not yet. I think Rivers and I are doing something with

the one the Jakal CO's leading. So far I think Stilts is the only one read in."

Stilts was the pilot who flew with VA-155's CO. This early in the cruise the air wing would typically be working out various scenarios for strikes into the Soviet Union as a part of our ConOps, or contingency operations plans. With the Soviet Union crumbling and the situation in the Persian Gulf developing, the plans had been shifted to the more likely scenario of action over Iraq. Only the actual strike leads and their associated crew members seemed to be read into the plans by ship's intelligence at this point. The specific plan of attack, and even the nature of the potential enemy, became highly classified for obvious political reasons. We could expect that the basic outlines and strategic objectives would be limited to a select few personnel until it was absolutely essential to read the remainder of the strike players into the plan.

Historically, when we had been dealing with the Soviet Union as the primary threat, the air wing never reached this phase. We could expect to fly practice "mirror image" strikes against a hypothetical enemy target without ever being informed of where or what the actual target would be if the scenario developed for real. The purpose was to test the academic planning solution as it related to aircraft fuel requirements and general logistics without giving away any substantive details about what the actual attack would entail. During the Cold War we had grown used to devising plans that would not be used, and it was not such a bad thing to be left out of the planning process, which was usually long and laborious to the exclusion of all other duties, including flying. But now that the focus had shifted to the Middle East, and the likelihood of combat was imminent, nobody wanted to be left out of the action. I envied Snax's position as the skipper's B/N.

"How's it going with the planning?" I asked. With just a handful of missions divided among the Intruder squadrons' CO and XO strike leads, there were few junior officers privy to this most sensitive of information.

A senior, experienced member of a squadron would be assigned the overall responsibility to lead an air wing strike, both for planning purposes and as the lead for any airborne, on-the-spot decisions that needed to be made. For major, high-visibility missions the commanding or executive officer of one of the attack squadrons could expect to fill that role, although usually there were four to six other experienced pilots or bombardier/navigators in the command who were officially designated air wing strike leads.

"It's okay, mostly just a pain in the ass. It sucks being locked up in the vault all day. You have to get the AI to let you out to take a piss." I instantly felt a little better. Snax started down the passageway again, and I followed close enough to continue the conversation.

"Can you talk about any of the targets?"

"No, but I only know about the one we're doing. So far it's mostly fuel planning. We've got to put requests in for air force tankers early if we need them." Nothing but number crunching; I began to feel less out of the loop.

"Cool; better you than me, I suppose. You been flying today?"

"Hell, no, not for three days. The skipper keeps taking us off the schedule so we can plan. I'm telling you, it sucks." I was downright chipper by this point.

"Maybe I'll catch you at midrats. See you later." We both flashed our Department of Defense IDs to the sailor behind the glass window, and he buzzed the door open to the Intelligence Center. Snax turned right toward the vault, and I headed straight ahead to the planning center.

Several of the squadron AIs were working on various maps, charting SAM sites and troop positions in Iraq and the Kuwaiti Theater of Operations (KTO). All of the action must have been in the vault, because there were only one or two other aviators in the room, and they didn't look like they had any more definite purpose than I did. The room was dominated by the sound of CNN on the ship's TV; I guess that the intel guys didn't want to miss out on anything important. Made sense, I thought. Now, who's going to be in a better position to determine certain types of enemy preparedness in Iraq—an ensign hunched over a navy message board, or a reporter live on the ground? It was wise to utilize all of the resources at your disposal.

Some reporter was going through a commentary regarding statements from the Iraqis, and Saddam Hussein in particular. He was in the middle of his report, and apparently the Iraqis were boasting how their troops were battle-hardened and that our men would run at the first casualties. I joined in with the disapproving looks and "bullshits" that were muttered under the breaths of the various folks working in CVIC, but I felt an uneasy chill down my spine. As obvious as the attempt at intimidation rhetoric was, there was a certain element of truth to it. Not one of us in the various squadrons on *Ranger* had ever been in combat. As well-trained and confident in our abilities as we were, we also were aware that there is only one way to determine how you will react in combat, and that is to be in combat. The Iraqis had been at war with the Iranians for years, and not an antiseptic, made-for-TV war, either. This was the stuff of gas attacks, teenage conscripts (and eager volunteers), and atrocity as a way of life. The reality of the Iraqi experience of war was completely foreign to most, if not all, of us. There was no question that we were technically far superior in training and equipment. What Saddam was doing was challenging our nerve and our guts. It would have been bullshit to give any indication that there was any truth to what he was spouting off, but beneath the denunciations and flip answers I believe that a small question was raised in each of us: Will I be able to hack it? The practical way to answer was with a hardened "Hell, yes!" Of course, the sliver of doubt remained.

I walked up behind Bluto, one of VA-145's intelligence officers, and peered over his shoulder while he marked up a chart of the Persian Gulf with a felt-tip pen. "You figure out where I'm going yet?" I asked him with a serious expression on my face.

"I don't know where you're going, but I certainly know where you ought to go." *Touché.*

"Whatchya doing?" He was drawing various small rings, some out over the water in the Persian Gulf, some over Saudi Arabia.

"Tanker tracks for the air force. Tankers are supposedly available on request at these coordinates. I don't even know if any of our plans call for air force tanking," Bluto answered.

The air force fielded giant KC-10 and KC-135 tanker aircraft capable of off-loading hundreds of thousands of pounds of fuel to either air force or navy jets, but not both at the same time. The air force conducted their aerial refueling by having the tanker aircraft insert a probe into a receptacle on the top of the receiver jet's fuselage. The navy did things the other way around, and had a refueling probe attached to each individual jet's nose. We needed a basket of some sort to poke our probe into, and then hold in place by flying tight formation off the basket while fuel was passed through the tanker's extended hose. The air force could modify their tankers temporarily to provide us with a basket, but that meant it was strictly suitable for navy jets until they could retract the fuel hose and remove the basket.

On the carrier several Intruders and S-3s had been modified with aerial refueling stores to provide emergency fuel airborne during blue water operations, and as a limited boost to the fuel stores of a strike package going to a target. Our organic tanking assets were small compared to the amount of fuel the air force's huge converted airliners had to offer. The limited fuel that the air wing tankers could provide was ordinarily reserved for a few select fighters that might expect to engage the enemy while the strikers were inbound to the target. Despite the capabilities of the relatively long-range A-6 and F-14, exceptionally long bombing missions might still make it necessary to receive extra gas from an air force tanker. If this was required, much of the flexibility we enjoyed as a mobile airfield was lost. We did our best to plan our missions utilizing only the assets we possessed on *Ranger*.

"It's good to know that they're there. I guess we'll have to see how far up the gulf our carriers go. You don't know where that might be, do you?"

Bluto turned his weight-trained torso to me and said in a paternalistic voice, "No, my friend, we shall have to wait and see. And now it is time for me to go back to work."

Bluto's exaggerated enunciation was a trademark characteristic of his "I am Intel, you are guest here" act. It was all in good fun. I told him to go to hell and turned to look at the rest of the brightly colored maps that surrounded the cluttered space.

Without knowing where our potential targets were, the mileage rings depicting the locations and ranges of the Iraqi SA-2, SA-3, SA-6, and SA-8 surface-to-air-missile sites bordered on meaningless. Of course, the placement of each SAM site was not a random event, and you could be fairly certain that there were high-value military targets in the vicinity of each of the color-coded rings. I looked again and tried my best to guess what the targets in each sector might be. Some were simple to determine: charted military airfields and naval ports gave pretty solid indications of why a SAM was directly adjacent to them. Others were much more difficult. Some of the SAMs were in the middle of the desert, along barren coastline, or at the edge of a city. These could be protecting almost anything, and without being read into the current strike plans it was futile to try to imagine what each target was. I eventually gave up and decided that I had avoided my ground job long enough. I slowly made my way back to the ready room to see if my pile of evals had somehow miraculously disappeared.

No-fly days sapped the strength of will from the body and produced a lethargy that was tough to shake. Even a tanker would have been a welcome diversion today, I reflected. Not to say that all tanker hops were boring, just that most were, and if they were not boring it was probably not a good sign. I thought back to *Ranger*'s last cruise, a 6-month deployment that had departed San Diego almost 2 years prior. It had been my first cruise, and with little to compare it to, every flight was exciting. It wasn't until about halfway through that the tanker flights began to become tedious and routine, at least on paper. The ship was in its first of several months on station off the coast of Oman in response to the hostile relations we had been experiencing with Iran. This was truly drilling holes in the water. The only sights to see from the flight deck for week after week were the sea snakes swimming in the Indian Ocean below us, and the occasional storm that would blow quickly through the circle of *Ranger*'s wake.

My B/N, the Dude, and I were standing the alert 5 tanker for the last recovery of the evening. This meant that we needed to be in our tanker-configured A-6, with engines running, chocked and chained to the flight deck, ready to launch in 5 minutes while we waited for the last aircraft of the night to land. It was a boring and typically uneventful evolution, a "just in case" gesture to ensure that no aircraft would find themselves in an *in extremis* situation if they required more fuel airborne than the last cycle's dedicated tanker could provide. The Dude and I had originally manned our Intruder at 2000 to fly a mission looking for surface ships in the area, but a monstrous squall had enveloped the area as our launch time of 2030 approached. The driving rain in the dark night drove visibility down to zero feet at times, the winds constantly shifted, and the ocean swells had built up to where *Ranger* was rolling and heaving with tremendous energy.

Fortunately, the ship's captain decided to cancel our cycle, as it would be impossible to safely recover us. While the rest of the aircrew manned up in their jets shut down their engines and left for the dry comfort of their respective ready rooms, our yellow shirt refused to give us the signal to cut engines. Finally the Dude called the boss on the radio and asked him what the reason for our special treatment was. It turned out that due to our Intruder's configuration as a tanker, the air operations officer in the Carrier Air Traffic Control Center (CATCC) had assigned us the job of alert 5 tanker for the remaining five aircraft airborne.

CATCC was similar to a scaled-down version of mission control at NASA, where representatives from each air wing squadron would sit in a row of benches watching the platform camera view of the flight deck and listening to the radio communications as their squadron's jets approached the ship for landing. An experienced pilot or flight officer would be responsible for recommendations to the air ops officer, CAG, or possibly the captain of the ship for any jets that were experiencing difficulties from his squadron. The CATCC observers were chosen for their experience level and ability to react quickly. They might be making a recommendation that could have grave consequences, such as advising an aircrew to eject.

The boys in the Carrier Air Traffic Control Center were evidently, and justifiably, concerned that the five airborne aircraft would need extra fuel as they attempted to land in the maelstrom. We were in the right place at the right time, I suppose, and we found ourselves sitting in our Intruder, engines running, with a fuel hose attached to us to keep our jet perpetually topped off with JP-5. After an hour and a half of the ship steaming in different directions in a futile attempt to find a clear area for landing, the decision was made to try to recover aircraft before their fuel states dwindled further. Jet after jet shot the approach, arrived behind the ship, and was waved off at less than a quarter of a mile when the LSOs could not see the aircraft lights in the driving rain. None of the five aircraft that attempted to land ever saw the ship until they were flying above it at 50 feet in their wave-off, hoping that their course would keep them clear of the carrier's island. All that the Dude and I could see from our vantage point directly across from the LSO platform was an occasional tire as it dipped into view, which would disappear as the power addition of the wave-off caught up with the jet's descent and began to push the aircraft upward.

The circumstances were not boding well for our chances of making midrats tonight. The yellow shirt that had been getting soaked in front of us for the past two hours picked up as directions were transmitted into his radio headset. He looked up at our cockpit and gave his deck handlers the signal to break us down and go flying. I looked at the Dude in disbelief—not a single aircraft could make it aboard, so they are going to send us up, too? He just shook his head as our fuel hose was disconnected and we were taxied to the catapult. Our tires sought purchase with the wet, greasy nonskid on the flight deck with each roll of the ship. Shit, I thought, they can't make me go; we passed over the shuttle in the cat track; they can't make me go; the cat officer raised his lighted wand and put us into tension; they can't make me go: Whoosh! They made us go. Shit.

What I thought had been an appropriately low light setting for our instrumentation suddenly blinded me as what little ambient light that existed on the carrier deck disappeared. I forced myself to stare at my instruments and try to catch up with the jet. Climb, keep the wings level, keep climbing. We had barely gotten the flaps up when the departure frequency came alive.

"Rustler 513, your vector 075 to join on a low-state Tomcat at angels 7." I pulled the Intruder around to a 075-degree heading and kept us climbing until we got to 7,000 feet.

"Rustler 513, the Tomcat is in a clear area overhead Mother, joined on an S-3 tanker." We stared into the darkness, trying to make out the aircraft lights. "Steer 350, vector for the rendezvous."

I made out two sets of lights about 2 miles away and continued my rendezvous, much too fast for the conditions. I still didn't know exactly what was going on, but it was obvious the situation was deteriorating rapidly. The S-3 Viking came up on the radio.

"Rustler, we have no more give, we're out of here on a bingo profile to the beach."

The S-3 tanker was the last aircraft overhead the ship besides the Tomcat, and had only stayed in an attempt to squeeze a couple of hundred pounds of fuel that he probably couldn't afford to give away into the Tomcat. Everyone else had determined that they barely had the gas to fly a maximum-range "bingo" profile to the coast of Oman and hope that *Ranger* could arrange for a divert airfield by the time they got there.

"Rustler, get your hose out, please, we're at 1 point 8 on the fuel," transmitted the F-14.

Shit. He had maybe 15 minutes before he flamed out. The Dude extended the hose from the fuel tank attached to our Intruder's belly, and the Tomcat moved immediately into position. The Dude stared intently at his refueling panel, looking for an indication that the Tomcat had mated with the basket.

"He's in, negative flow," the Dude said, then to the Tomcat over the radio, "Negative flow Tomcat; back out so I can recycle and try again."

The Tomcat moved back out of the basket and slightly to the right. The Dude pulled the basket back in, and then put it out again. "Cleared in," transmitted the Dude.

The second attempt proved no more successful than the first, and we relayed our situation to the ship. "Rustler 513 is a sour tanker, negative give." You could almost hear the wheels turning in the red-lit Carrier Air Traffic Control Center. Seconds later and a decision had been made.

"Tomcat signal is barricade. Marshal on the final bearing at 3 miles and 1,200 feet."

The Tomcat slowly peeled off, and I felt their desperation. They couldn't make it to the beach, they probably had enough gas to attempt one landing, but that was it. If they ejected into this storm the chances of recovering the crew before sunrise was nil, which meant that all that would be recovered would probably be bodies. The ship had decided that the best odds were on rigging the emergency barricade across the flight deck, maximizing the chances that the F-14 would stop once its wheels touched down on the deck. But how were they going to get that far? We had just witnessed five attempts at landing, and not a single jet had made it through the storm successfully enough to get their wheels on the deck.

The minutes ticked by. Rigging the barricade was a well-practiced drill, but it took time to stretch the tremendously strong web of nylon straps across the flight deck and attach them to the 15-foot-high stanchions that would be raised into position, forming a wall across the flight deck. If the low-fuel F-14 came too close to the top of the 15-foot webbing, the Tomcat's wheels would catch the upper limit of the barricade and slam the jet upside down into the steel deckplates, with no opportunity to eject. Too low and they would hit the round down and explode in a fiery ball. Every second that the Tomcat crew waited, the closer they came to ejecting into the storm. I imagined that they might be a tad tense.

"Boss, how much longer? State is 1 point 1," radioed the F-14.

One thousand one hundred pounds left. They had to be burning about 5,000 to 6,000 pounds an hour flying that low. What do Tomcats flame out with? I knew that A-6s had flamed out with as much as 700 pounds indicated on the fuel gauge.

"Just a few more minutes; almost done."

"We can't wait," replied the Tomcat. "We're inbound now; if you can't take us when we get there, then we're going to have to eject alongside."

"Copy that. Come on in; LSO's on frequency."

I looked down from our vantage point 20,000 feet above the ship and couldn't believe what I saw—the lights of *Ranger* appeared through the clouds. The ship was in the clear.

"Tomcat, paddles, call the ball when you get it."

"Tomcat, ball, 600 pounds." The voice behind the ship was steady and calm.

Later that night we would watch the reruns of the landing platform video camera, showing the barricade being raised upright into position simultaneously as the Tomcat made his call at three-quarters of a mile from the ship, less than 30 seconds before touching down.

"You're on glide path, on centerline, showing a little bit fast." The landing signal officer worked his words with a soft touch meant to help the Tomcat pilot finesse the power off slowly and smoothly.

"Looking good, keep it coming, deck's down just a bit," soothed the LSO.

Seconds later and it was over. The Tomcat had safely trapped, and disaster had been narrowly averted.

For the first time in 15 minutes we thought of our A-6 and the options still open to us. There were several factors to consider, given the circumstances that had unfolded in the preceding minutes. We had plenty of fuel remaining to loiter, but there was currently a break in the storm directly over the carrier. The flight deck would be fouled for a considerable amount of time while the barricade and the F-14 were separated and removed, and the angle deck was scrutinized for any stray pieces of metal that would wreak havoc on a jet engine going to full power in the wires.

Just as I wondered how the four aircraft on their way to Oman were faring, the radio came alive.

"Rustler 513, Mother, request you attempt radio contact with divert aircraft and determine status. Griffin 702 should be the closest." *Ranger* had lost radio contact with the outbound jets, and with our Intruder the sole airborne asset available, we would attempt to act as a communications link.

"Copy that. Griffin 702, Rustler 513." We waited several seconds and tried again, this time with more luck.

"Rustler calling Griffin 702, go ahead."

"Griffin 702, Rustler 513, Mother requests status of divert aircraft."

"Roger, Rustler, four diverts all in contact with Masira tower, we should be low state at 1 point 8, they're starting to clear us to land. Will notify ship by best means when we are all safe on deck."

"Copy that, Griffin 702. Good luck." The Dude relayed the positive news back to the ship. "Approach, Rustler 513, say intentions for our recovery, please," the Dude continued.

"Rustler 513, approach, we should have a ready deck in approximately 20 minutes. Hold high overhead, Mother; we will call you down."

Evidently they were counting on the clear air staying over *Ranger* a while longer. From what I could see in the darkness it did not seem to be a bad plan. Lightning flashed in the distance, and it appeared that the bulk of the storm was beyond us.

We orbited over *Ranger* at 20,000 feet, and I retraced our steps to try to determine if we had missed anything. Our attempt at tanking was by no means standard operating procedure, and the Tomcat had quite understandably left our vicinity prior to visually verifying that our refueling basket had indeed retracted into its resting spot in our center fuel tank. I turned to the Dude and asked him how our refueling panel looked on his starboard console.

"I'm showing the drogue stowed. No visual confirmation, but everything looks right from here."

The "buddy store" refueling system we were using was fraught with mechanical problems and malfunctions, as had been proven by our recent inability to pass gas to the low-state Tomcat. I wondered if there was anything else wrong with the store.

The flight deck cleanup effort went on, and eventually from our perch high overhead we could see a line of lighted wands moving down the angled deck. The final step in the process of an FOD walkdown was under way. Controlling "foreign-object damage," or FOD, was a continual challenge in the cramped confines of the flight deck, where jets were routinely slung into the air and jerked to a halt. Fasteners and small pieces of metal inevitably came loose during flight operations and found their resting places on the carrier deck, presenting a constant hazard to equipment, readiness, and lives. If a jet engine sucked up a screw while taxiing to the catapult it would likely destroy the furiously spinning turbine blades and require that the entire engine be changed. The aircraft would not be available until it was repaired, which might be days, assuming that a spare engine was on board the ship.

The cost of replaced engines might well be reflected in a commanding officer's, the air wing commander's, or even the ship's captain's fitness report. A record of FODed engines was not terribly conducive to career advancement by the folks at the Pentagon's puzzle palace, where the ultimate promotional decisions were made.

Of far greater importance were the events that could be triggered by foreign object damage during a critical phase of flight, such as a catapult or a trap. Under certain conditions, an A-6 loaded with fuel or weapons could not fly on a single engine off the cat. Now we were talking about real money lost, more than $30 million, no chance at getting what might turn out to be a vital asset back into service, and the possible loss of two crew members' lives. Trapping was almost as susceptible to disaster from FOD as catapulting. A stray bolt going into a jet intake when it touched down and the pilot advanced the throttles to full power could make for quite a surprise if the tailhook did not catch a wire.

The efforts made to avoid an FODed engine were truly monumental. Several times a day the entire flight deck would cease all activities, and hordes of officers and sailors would stream out from belowdecks to participate in an FOD walk-down. Several lines of people, one after the other, would proceed down the width of the carrier deck picking up any piece of foreign material they encountered. If a loose rivet was found under an aircraft, that jet's commanding officer could expect to hear about it from his seniors. Any loose change, paper clips, or metal of any kind except for tools were strictly forbidden on the flight deck, and all of the tools required for work on an aircraft were inventoried several times a day to ensure that none had migrated to a potentially hazardous spot. A single lost tool would mean a definite cessation of flight operations for the squadron involved until the tool was accounted for; a loose screwdriver in a paneled-shut engine compartment could cause the same damage as a loose screw on the flight deck.

The emphasis on FOD verged on the bizarre, but it usually had its desired effect. It was not unusual for a carrier to conduct aircraft-jarring flight operations throughout a 6-month deployment and experience no engine-eating foreign-object damage. In the end it was all worth it.

The FOD walkdown line on the flight deck below us was in its third inspection of the landing area when approach began to give us vectors to *Ranger*'s final bearing. I spoke into the radio.

"Approach, Rustler 513, be advised that we have not received a visual confirmation that our drogue is stowed. Would you like us to plan a flyby of the LSO platform?" There was a moment of silence, and then the voice of our CO in Air Operations came over the radio.

"Five-thirteen, understand that you have a stowed indication internally."

"That's affirmative, sir. The Tomcat did not have a chance to look us over after retract."

"Okay; pull the buddy store circuit breaker and recover." By removing all power to the buddy store, the retract mechanism was supposed to automatically pull in the drogue if it was not already stowed.

"Copy that, Skipper." The Dude had found and pulled the circuit breaker, and his refueling panel still showed a retract indication, as it should.

The weather held out for us during the short approach, but

as we crossed the round down my fatigue caught up with me and I was slow in correcting as the jet settled. We trapped into the two wire, no big deal. Immediately after stopping I knew that something was wrong; we were not instructed to raise our hook or wings, and several sailors ran under our still-turning engines.

"Rustler 513, your drogue was out. We're going to shut you down there, clean it up, and tow you out of the wires," transmitted the air boss.

It turned out that the refueling basket had never retracted, and we had dragged it and 50 feet of hose smack into the round down at the back of the carrier. The impact reduced the forward whiplash tendency that the basket would otherwise have had. If I had not been slow with my power correction on landing and had not settled into the two wire, the basket would not have hit the round down, and the hose would have shot forward, possibly breaking off and cutting someone in half on the flight deck. For the second time that evening, the first being when the weather cleared for the Tomcat, I thought about how Murphy's Law had been countered by extremely fortuitous events. What a roller coaster of a night, with good luck following bad.

"You ready for a trip back to reality?" I snapped my attention back to the ready room around me. I suppose that my daydreaming had been fairly obvious, and Rivers decided to break me out of my stupor before I began to drool.

The pace picked up the next day. Rivers and I flew a hop with an inert HARM missile for practice attacks, and we made good use of the training aid, targeting various unsuspecting ships and radars from the battle group. We almost got the opportunity to actually drop a practice bomb, but the ship that was towing the bombing target spar decided to call it quits early before we arrived on the scene. We spent the remainder of the flight practicing high-G instrument turns in the best simulations of flying on the terrain clearance display that we could muster over the water. One needed a bit of imagination to maintain low-level skills when flying over the vast, flat expanse of the open ocean. On the other hand, Iraq was not a terribly hilly country, so perhaps we were conducting realistic training after all.

I was feeling more comfortable as the repetition of left- and right-hand turns progressed, and we steadily lowered our target altitude to 500 feet above the waves. The daylight presented a somewhat artificial scenario and a feeling of increased situational awareness. Rivers and I did our best not to look outside, and I increased the stick pressure until the G meter clicked to 4, and then held the turn in until we had come around 90 degrees of a circle. My scan moved easily back and forth among the instantaneous vertical speed tape on the ADI, the altimeter, our angle of bank, our heading, and the Radalt when it occasionally came back within limits in our tight turns. The radar altimeter would not function past 60 degrees angle of bank. One turn to the left, roll out without ballooning upward; another hard, level turn in the opposite direction. I kept repeating the sequence on the instruments until I felt I had developed a feel in the stick for the correct angle of bank and pull that would keep us level at a speed of about 480 knots. We decided that 500 feet was low enough for our practice maneuvers for now, and opted to save a further step down toward the water for another day.

In the sterile environment of flying over the ocean I was not having any trouble maintaining altitude plus or minus about 30 feet. I wondered what effect removing my peripheral vision completely in the darkness of night and the need to avoid enemy fire would have on my level of precision. I figured that I would most likely be afforded the opportunity to find out, and until then I would plan on using 300 feet as the lowest altitude at which I would attempt to fly my high-G turns at night. I was not sure if that would be low enough, given the advanced capabilities of the Soviet-made SA-6 missile in the flat desert, but any lower at night and the risk of running into the ground started to outweigh the risk of getting shot down.

After our flight, I headed down to the ready room to see what I might have missed in the past couple of hours. I picked up a copy of the *Navy Times* that had been lying on the SDO desk and started to read an article about the scheduled future replacement for the A-6, appropriately named the A-12. I suppose it was designed to have twice the capabilities of our 1960s-vintage bomber. The bat-winged, stealthy A-12 had been the center of a recent controversy regarding cost over-runs, and the threat of canceling the project had been bandied about. Several opinions were quoted in the piece, but the one that caught my eye was by retired admiral Dunleavy, an ex–deputy chief of naval operations for air, one of the gentlemen who used to kind of run things for us naval aviators. His point was an obvious attempt to reinforce the argument against canceling the A-12 program. He was quoted saying words to the effect that we needed the A-12 as a replacement for the A-6 because the A-6 was old and "losses in a conflict with a country like Iraq would be disappointing." I suppose that was one way of looking at it. But it sure didn't make me feel any better to know that senior leadership was lacking a certain degree of confidence in our aging Intruder's abilities—certainly not a month before we were supposed to enter the Persian Gulf, at any rate. I put down the newspaper and tried to dismiss the admiral's assessment as a political plug for the A-12; the alternative did not make the prospect of flying the next several months over Iraq particularly pleasant.

I did not rush immediately to my mailbox on this tenth day of the cruise; I was getting tired of the disappointing dearth of letters. I was surprised and excited to see that there were envelopes with Stateside postmarks on them, three of them! I pulled out the stack of papers with the three brightly colored envelopes on the top, and was taken a bit off balance when I realized that they were addressed to "VA-145 Pilot." Now with more curiosity than anticipation I opened the first, recognized the writing as that of a child, and felt a wave of simultaneous disappointment and guilt. Shoot, I had been expecting something from Laurie or my family, not a Christmas card written by an elementary school kid I had never met. When we got mail only once or twice a week, the bags of these well-intentioned cards had to be displacing a lot of the personal mail we were all waiting for. The guilt came back stronger; it was nice to have folks at home thinking about us; I just wish they could somehow screen these letters. The big media plug to send the Desert Shield troops mail had backfired for us magnificently, at least for now.

I decided to skip dinner and go to the gym; I could grab something at midrats in a few hours. I put on shorts and a T-shirt and grabbed a small white towel that was getting a touch of gray from unwashed use. The gym was packed, but after a 20-minute wait I snagged a Lifecycle. I rode hard while George Thorogood blasted from my Walkman earphones and helped motivate my workout. My imagination was transported away from the fifty sweaty bodies surrounding me in the dimly lit, gray hangar bay.

An F-14 was starting an engine with its exhaust pointed out the hangar bay door in an attempt to replicate some sort of maintenance problem, and the noise became deafening, even at idle power. I crammed the earphones farther into my ears and turned the Walkman volume up as far as it would go, but Lonesome George couldn't compete. Some of the less dedicated in the gym decided it was not worth the pain to get a workout, but the no-fly days had left me with a lot of pent-up energy. I pedaled harder.

It was extremely easy to lose perspective while living on the ship. The regimentation and lack of variety funneled the imagination and attitude in directions that were completely out of proportion to the circumstances. I found myself getting really pissed off at the F-14; it was destroying my one shot at a semblance of a daily ritual and the mental regrouping I found I could get by working out. I pumped my legs faster in my agitation and again checked that the music volume was at its highest level.

Five minutes later the hangar bay went silent, and my anger dissipated almost as rapidly as the noise. I rode on until I had completed an hour on the bike and was soaked from head to toe in sweat. I dismounted, went down the ladder that led from the gym's loft to the hangar bay, and walked over to the huge open door to look at the night waves for a moment. A few deep breaths and I felt completely invigorated, the noisy Tomcat not even a memory. I was back in my stateroom and heading for the shower with a bounce in my step in less than 5 minutes.

Keeping a sense of perspective was particularly difficult when we had long stretches without flying. Why were we out here, with the restricted freedoms of the ship? It was frustrating steaming by amazing sights we might never see because we were stuck in the cellar of this steel prison barge. No privacy, living on top of each other, dirty, and constantly feeling oily from the jet-fuel-tainted water and ever-present aircraft exhaust: nothing certain or stable, the ship moving side to side, fore and aft, and heaving up and down. Everyone was different in how they recaged their gyros, how they maintained their mental balance day after day, week after week, month after month. The sense of mission was what tied everyone together. For the aviators the brief escapes from the carrier while airborne provided tangible evidence that filled the senses with the reality that there was a full world out there, with sun, sky, and occasionally even a little bit of ground.

I finished up the night as I did most evenings, filling out my journal and trying to think of something new I could write in a letter. The routine was stale enough that I had difficulty thinking of events on a daily basis that Laurie or my family would be able to understand, yet would find new or exciting. I could vent my real feelings in my journal, though, without fear that one of my brief lapses in perspective would be taken

too literally in a letter, coloring my situation with a broad
band of darkness or melancholy.

I thought about Laurie in Baltimore, going to work at a
pharmaceutical company outside of D.C. How much news
did she watch? What images were she and my siblings getting
of the growing momentum toward war, a momentum that
seemed to build in perfect unison with *Ranger* closing the
gap to the Persian Gulf? The fact that I could follow along
somewhat via CNN was strange in itself—to my knowledge
no U.S. Navy carrier had been able to broadcast real-time
news to her crew before.

During our last training detachment the captain of the ship
had struck a deal with someone to get a satellite dish and reception of CNN while we were at sea, yet another indication
that this cruise was different. Normally the only available
channels were what was piped through by the ship's cable
station—movies, reruns, but nothing in real time. Now we
could mark the progress of peace talks Stateside while we
cruised ever closer to the center of the controversy.

Our last night in port San Diego had been a fitting introduction to the sways of public opinion that CNN brought with
it. Saddam Hussein had just released several groups of
Western hostages he had been threatening to use as human
shields. The ebb and flow of political emotion in Congress
was evidently cycling back toward peace at this token con-
cession. Didn't the word "appeasement" ring a bell with any
of you jokers? I thought. I gathered a bit of comfort from
President Bush's demeanor and message. He had been out
fishing in Maine, much to the chagrin of the press corps, who
evidently thought that he should be wringing his hands in
rhetorical fury in the capital. He had it right, I thought. Keep
the message clear to Saddam: Get out of Kuwait. No need to
show any undue emotion or excitement. There may come a
time for that later, but as the leader of the most powerful nation on earth, President Bush had acted correctly by not ap-
pearing to be overly concerned. The megalomaniacal Saddam

lived for the attention. It never ceased to amaze me how many Americans were quick to show their approval for the threat of force, but did not realize that occasionally words had to be backed up with deeds.

I doubted that my parents could get uncensored news in Syria. What were they hearing? Could my brother and sisters in the States possibly fill them in on the latest in any kind of a timely fashion? There was no way they could.

I hoped that my parents' guardian angel at the State Department was watching out for them. He had to be one of the busiest people in the world right about now. My mother's brother was Thomas Pickering, the U.S. ambassador to the United Nations. He definitely had his hands full trying to coordinate the amazing hodgepodge of a coalition that had unified against Iraq.

Uncle Tom had spent his life in the Foreign Service. He held the prestigious rank of career ambassador, was not a political appointee, and apparently had thrived in both Republican and Democratic administrations. It was difficult to keep track of his many assignments, but I knew that his first posting as an ambassador had been to Jordan, and then Nigeria. He had led the embassy to El Salvador during the crisis years of the early 1980s, and more recently he had been the ambassador to Israel.

He was one of those incredible people whose talents were matched only by his tireless efforts. He spoke an amazing host of languages: Arabic, Swahili, Spanish, Hebrew, and French. It kind of made me wonder with all that ability what had happened to me. I suppose it skipped a generation. Regardless of his demanding schedule, I knew that Uncle Tom would keep an eye out for his little sister in Damascus.

It was coming up on 2300. I closed my journal, sealed the letter to Laurie, walked it down the passageway in my flip-flops, shorts, and T-shirt, and put the letter in the outgoing mailbox. When the mail would actually leave the ship was anybody's guess. I headed back to the rack to get some shuteye.

I woke up to use the head in the early hours of the morning and stopped on my way back to my room to see if the day's flight schedule was posted on the back of the alley door. My brain started firing at a faster rate when I saw that Rivers and I were flying on the Jakal CO's mirror image strike—at last we would gain some insight as to what the Iraqi targets might be. I hit the rack for another 2 hours until it was time to get up, take enough of a shower to snap me out of my stupor, and make it on time to the VA-155 ready room for the 0600 briefing.

The longer we sat intently listening, the more evident it became that there would be no great revelations today. The simulated target would be the towed spar of one of the battle group ships, and our limited role in the strike was to simulate the firing of four HARM missiles at a phantom SA-6 site. Total round-trip distance for the strike package would be 900 miles, and other than a few minor turns for the Intruder bombers, it appeared that there would be no obvious attack profiles outlined that might give away a bit more substance. The only reason I could think of for flying the mirror image at all was to verify the fuel figures for the strike's planned altitude and airspeed. Time in the air was time away from the boat, so we made the best of it.

Our position of relative ostracism as HARM shooters, orbiting dozens of miles behind the bombers, did not sit well with Rivers. After the flight he made his intentions clear with me that he was going to lobby our CO to assign us to fly one of the strike A-6s when and if the actual mission was going to be carried out. It took less than a second for the nervous wave of excitement to wash over me.

"Good idea, Rivs."

# Chapter Nine

# Between their loved homes . . .

*Ranger* made determined progress westward, her boilers
churning 24 hours a day, 7 days a week. We passed the international date line and jumped from 18 December to 20 December in a day. The carrier's massive decks heaved and
rolled in the seas kicked up by approaching Typhoon Ross,
and the captain raced in an attempt to cut to the south of the
burgeoning storm. We hoped to make safe passage through
San Bernardino Strait, then head north to Subic Bay for resupply and onloading of weapons. The captain announced to
all ship's personnel that we could expect to spend 6 days
ashore, and would leave the Philippines on 3 January to be
ready to launch aircraft in the Persian Gulf no later than 0800
on 15 January.

The seas picked up to even greater heights, and the angled
flight deck twisted and turned in all sorts of unnatural
directions—the carrier heaved up and down 20 feet. A few
days before Christmas one of the air wing Tomcats boltered
or was waved off six times in a row due to the heavy seas.
*Ranger*'s captain eventually decided to cancel the flight schedule that evening—no point in taking a chance on losing a jet;
we would need every one in the months to follow.

The next day we were back in the flying business again.
The air wing practiced a night war-at-sea exercise in lieu of

167

any other realistic coordinated training available. The seas had not abated much, and after a 3½-hour flight, Rivers and I were both relieved when our Intruder came to a heart-pounding stop on our first attempt at landing on the dark, pitching deck. From the time I could first make out the fuzzy amber form of the meatball it did not stay still for a second. Only our constant rate of descent, and the landing signal officer's reassurance that we were on glide path, enabled us to land. The meatball's stabilization system could not possibly keep up with the rolling and heaving of *Ranger*. The ball cycled constantly from the top to the bottom of the lens, and the centerline lights made no sense with the random twisting of the ship. On the next cycle the LSOs decided to discard use of the automatic system and instead control the recovery with the manual wheel of the Movlas system. Movlas allowed the LSOs to physically put the ball on the mirror where they wanted it; if they thought a pilot was too high, they would show him a high ball; too low, a low ball. In this manner they could dampen out the effects of the rough seas and guide a pilot in using nothing more than their experienced eyes to gauge the glide path. It wasn't pretty, but everybody got aboard that night. Eventually.

Christmas Eve came and went, and in spite of the half-hearted efforts of some and the wholehearted efforts of others, it was essentially just another day on the boat. A few roving bands of carolers managed to set a quasi-festive atmosphere for the impending holiday, but it was no easy task to make the inner steel workings of a ship designed for battle cheery and light.

I knew I could not express my feelings tonight in the company of my shipmates. I was incapable of turning on and off my military bearing at will, and around my comrades it usually took at least a six-pack. That was definitely not going to happen tonight. Instead I went to my empty stateroom to compose a letter.

*24 Dec 90*

*Dear Laurie,*

*It's Christmas Eve, so what are you doing? I'm sitting in my room in my underwear sweating and writing a letter. I'm so sentimental about the holidays.*

*We're about 600 miles north of Guam, heading for the Philippines. Nothing has changed, I expect that we'll get to the Gulf in the middle of January, just in time for the fun. Flying has been erratic—I fly about every 3rd or 4th day. Otherwise it's been pretty busy—paperwork, studying, working out every day. I've lost 6 lbs. so far and the moustache is coming in pretty well. You won't recognize me (yes you will).*

*So far things aren't too bad—I know what to expect and things are moving pretty quickly. I'm getting more confident about the role that we'll play in the situation over there. I suppose that's natural as it gets closer and it becomes clearer exactly what we're dealing with. I think that we are all going to do fine.*

*I hear that it snowed in Whidbey. It would have been nice (and different) to have been in a snowy beach house with you, a fire, wine, curled up. That's OK, we'll have plenty of those. Enough of that stuff.*

*I've been thinking about you, but we haven't gotten any mail yet so I don't know what's up. I should get all your mail next week in the Philippines. I need tapes.*

*Well baby, Merry Christmas,*

   *Love,*
   *Pete*

Christmas was one of the few times at my home on Long Island where you could count on the family all being there. I think my father's killer eggnog played no small part in that. For most of my 28 years we had managed to be together, first as wide-eyed children, and then as festive adults, for a sleepless Christmas Eve and the traditional opening of presents in the morning. The total absence of family tradition made Christmas on *Ranger* empty and hollow.

How the tables had turned for my parents, with me worrying about them, in addition to the other way around. They were used to maintaining a low-level anxiety of concern for me. I was not for them.

I remembered when I was 9 years old the frantic exhortations from my father to climb back up the cliff face at the temple to Poseidon, the sea god, in Sounion, Greece. While living overseas my father would constantly berate me for snorkeling out too far—he was afraid he would be unable to swim the distance if he needed to rescue me.

In college I did not give them a break. On the evening before my parents were planning to fly to El Salvador to visit Uncle Tom the ambassador, they had to cancel their trip because I fell off a four-story fraternity roof. I joked that I had saved their lives by flinging myself off a roof and keeping them from going to El Salvador, a country in the midst of civil conflict and mired in violence. I knew their disappointment in canceling the trip, though, but could never admit to them my embarrassment and shame in ruining their plans.

Then there was the scuba diving. Not content with "normal" recreational pursuits, I felt compelled to visit *Andrea Doria*, more than 200 feet below the surface. They probably did not relax when I joined the navy. And now it looked like war. I hoped they were getting a silent chuckle at the butterflies they were giving me, worrying about their safety in Syria.

We Swordsmen prepared for a haphazard gift exchange by shopping at the only option in town, one of *Ranger*'s two ship's stores, where the extremely limited selection of possibilities promoted candy and pocketknife key chains as the hot ticket items. The real gifts went to a select few who were permitted to fly into Cubi Point airfield early to help arrange for the battle group's arrival in the Philippines. Unfortunately, all of the air wing pilots needed to get a night trap for landing currency immediately preceding our entry into port, and it gave us a brief rallying cry to bemoan the unfairness and injustice of being a pilot. It was an extraordinarily short-lived rally, more a squeak than a cry in the end.

Christmas Day had all the formalities available to *Ranger*'s complement of officers: a sit-down dinner in Wardroom 2, the land of no flight suits and normally the domain of the ship's "shoes." Aviators wore brown shoes on the few occasions when they could be coaxed or bullied into their khaki uniform, and everyone else who didn't fly wore black shoes. The term "shoe" had come to mean anyone who wore black shoes, or in other words, anyone who didn't fly. At least that was what the aviators called the surface navy folks, even if they did not refer to themselves in this manner. I am certain that they had a few choice descriptions for us flyboys as well.

*Ranger*'s two A-6 squadrons got together in Wardroom "Shoe" for a dinner that was served, not slopped out in line, and some camaraderie of the common spirit that we enjoyed through a shared mission and mutual roots in Whidbey Island. Afterward it was back to the ready room for the official exchange of gifts and some good-natured harassment of one another. With the last present opened and the final gag gift of insult hurled, the skipper started a video that the squadron wives had put together of the families at home. The single gents quickly got up and left as the room went dark and the eyes got misty while the video showed hordes of children running helter-skelter and creating general havoc.

The squadron took the night off and the paperwork treadmill ground to a temporary halt. I headed back to my stateroom and toyed with the option of reviewing several award write-ups I had neglected for the day, but ended up saying the hell with it; it was Christmas and I was going to do something a little bit outrageous and simply relax. The TV was grinding out the news as I entered the stateroom. Snax was paying half attention to the circular run of the same stories as he entertained himself with what I could only hope was non-navy material on his computer. Tony was busy watching his kids act like children with the rest of the family men down below. I grunted "Hi," walked to my desk, focused on the TV image, and plopped down in my chair.

Senate Majority Leader Mitchell was being interviewed regarding the crisis in Iraq, and he had raised an interesting possible turn of events: If we bombed Iraq, and Saddam followed through with his threat to attack Israel, the Syrians might change sides. If the bizarre alliance we were cultivating with the Syrians was that fragile, it opened up all sorts of possibilities into the conflict.[1] The Syrians had been one of the primary Middle Eastern allies of the old Soviet Union, and as such had been outfitted handsomely, as had Iraq, with some of the most advanced Soviet weaponry. Of particular concern to those of us on *Ranger* who wore brown shoes was the cadre of SA-6 surface-to-air missiles the Syrians possessed. It wasn't all that long ago that U.S. naval aircraft had been shot down over the skies of Lebanon either by, or with the tacit assistance of, the Syrian occupying forces. Now we were presented with the prospect of having their most effective antiaircraft defense set up on our side of the Allied lines.

From strictly a technical perspective, several issues of concern were raised: If our on-board warning systems detected that an SA-6 site was searching for us, how could we be certain it was an Iraqi or a Syrian system? The confusion that could be presented by having SA-6s on both sides of the battle lines must have been addressed by the "way smart" guys who wear the stars, right? Questions like these were above my pay grade, but not beyond my field of immediate and personal interest. The idea of Syrians in Saudi Arabia with missiles pointed at Iraq was as twisted a case of "my enemy's enemy must be my friend" as I could think of.

1. Although Syria and Iraq were both aligned to differing degrees with the Soviet Union during the Cold War, rivalry between their two lands dated back to before the Ottoman Empire. More recently, Syria's branch of the Ba'ath Party vied with Iraq's for supremacy in the more radical branch of the Pan-Arab movement. Syria had backed Iran in the Iran-Iraq war.

And what if the Syrians did choose to switch horses in midstream? Tactically it meant that Israel probably was in the war, and that all Arab support suddenly became quite soft. President Bush's unified coalition could be in tatters instantly, and we might find ourselves with half a million Americans sitting around the Middle East not sure which party they should attend. Hopefully Saddam would not launch a preemptive strike into Israel, and possibly provoke a tactically warranted, but strategically devastating, counterattack by Israel into Iraq. If we could only get the first punch in, perhaps enough of Iraq's offensive air capabilities could be eliminated to shield Israel and help to isolate her from the conflict politically and, more important, militarily. The thought of biochemical weapons impacting Israeli cities and the ensuing nuclear retaliation would seem to muddy the waters of our mission somewhat, and might reintroduce the word "Armageddon" to the region where it was born. Scary shit.

I had not heard from my parents since we had left San Diego. The situation was most certainly not cooling down, and I could only hope that the gravity of the possible responses in the current standoff were becoming as conspicuous to my parents as they were to me. Living in Damascus might have had particular charms, but I sincerely doubted that nuclear annihilation was one them. Merry Christmas, Mom and Dad. Suddenly I felt the urge to be busy again. I abruptly stood up and left the room without saying a word to Snax.

I needed some mindless but constructive activity to keep from dwelling on the negative possibilities for the remainder of the holiday, and I decided that surveying the state of my SV-2 survival gear might do the trick. I struck out with purpose for the pararigger shop, worked the combination lock on the door, and found myself in the comfortable solitude of my familiar flight gear. Here was tangible hope, things that would save my life, not futile second-guessing and vain attempts at insight to a situation that was impossible to predict. I took stock of my 5 pounds' allowance of extra equipment, added a second plastic canteen of water, and removed my winter-knit wool hat and gloves that had been in the front pockets since the beginning of autumn in the Pacific Northwest. I made a mental note to buy several bandannas in the Philippines; they would make great bandages and could double as any of a number of handy items in a pinch, and they weighed virtually nothing. Satisfied that there was nothing left to arrange in my SV-2, I turned to the lone desk and sat down.

I took two metal dog tags out of my khaki trousers pocket and read them once again: Peter M. Hunt, LT, USNR, 079-55-4328, Protestant. The Protestant had come after a bit of deliberation. I could probably best describe myself as a lapsed agnostic at the time, not having grown up with any exposure to organized religion and not having given it serious consideration in my adult life. While I purposefully had ignored the question of religion, I had not ruled out any possibilities. Our intelligence briefings had indicated that the Iraqis would probably be more hostile to an infidel who did not hold any religious beliefs whatsoever than to someone who merely had faith in the "wrong" religion. If I had been any less ignorant of religion at the time I might have viewed it as just a touch heretical, and a whole lot hypocritical, to stamp a popular religion on my dog tag in the hopes of self-preservation if worse came to worst. But I wasn't, and I took a small degree of comfort in my ace in the hole as I fashioned a parachute line through the freshly minted dog tag and wrapped it around my neck.

I took no comfort in the second dog tag. This one I blackened out with shoe polish to be inserted into my flight boot-lace when I got back to my stateroom. The shoe polish was so that the glint of metal would not give me away to any Iraqis who might be searching for a downed pilot. The tag itself was so that my boots, the sturdiest portion of my flight clothing, could be identified if there was nothing else left of me to recover from a crash site. I came to the realization that sifting through my survival gear was probably not a very uplifting way to spend Christmas either.

With Christmas behind us, the only distraction left to our still-unknown mission was our port visit to the Philippines. The training and preparation for operations in the Persian Gulf increased in intensity, a locale to which no U.S. carrier had been deployed since 1948. The day after Christmas was a mass of meetings and events as we approached the final opportunities to organize the thrust of our tactics and energies. With less than three weeks until President Bush's designated date for Saddam to withdraw his troops from Kuwait, the air wing needed to fine-tune the contingency plans we had roughed out, as well as mentally prepare the wing aviators for battle.

Air Wing 2's commander was one of the few actively flying aviators on the ship who had experienced combat firsthand, and he offered to speak to each of the ready rooms about what might be expected of an individual in his first test of war. Captain "Rabbit" Campbell was a blond-haired, laid-back fighter pilot who had been in the navy for more than 20 years. He was based in San Diego, and his relaxed demeanor fit in perfectly with the southern California image. He was the type of professional who was comfortably aware of his strengths and weaknesses, and therefore listened exceptionally well to suggestions and recommendations outside of his specific area of expertise, the fighter mission. All of us in the *Ranger* attack community respected and liked CAG immensely, and were eager to hear what he would say regarding what we might encounter on our first combat mission.

CAG entered the conversation with the easygoing repertoire he was known for, and he instantly had the undivided attention of all present, from the senior ranks at the front of the ready room to the new-guy JOs in the back. He was extremely frank, and not at all pretentious about what we might expect over Iraq. It was not the same for any two people, he said; each person is going to react slightly differently to the fact that you were consciously going to a place where people were going to do their damndest to kill you. His experience as a fighter pilot differed from our mission to a fair degree, and he discussed more of the mental aspects we could expect to encounter versus the tactical. His esteem in the eyes of the ready room became even greater as he deferred to our collective expertise in the air-to-ground arena.

That was it—no motherhood, no platitudes, no micromanaging advice, no false gods to rely on; he had given us something more valuable. We each left the ready room visualizing, some for the first time, how we wanted to see ourselves react to the stresses of combat. We might be caught flatfooted by an enemy defense or tactic, but CAG had planted the seed in our minds not to be caught unawares by the enormous psychological impact that the rapidly unfolding future events might have in store for us. The unsettling fact that CAG raised more questions than he answered was overshadowed by the renewed emphasis each of us now put on our mental preparedness and aggressive mind-set.

The pace of the flight schedule picked up as we closed to within 500 miles of Subic Bay. We had requested an air force tanker for practice refueling, and I got to try my hand at holding steady in the 50-plus-pound steel-rimmed basket of a KC-135. The night was dark, his lights were bright, and there were probably a few more excuses I could come up with, but regardless, my stabs at the basket, while successful, were certainly not pretty. I was satisfied with the fact that my Intruder's gyrations around the basket had not caused any damage to the A-6's radome, a now singularly difficult item to replace. It had been a while since I had tried tanking off of the more difficult KC-135, so I figured I would be a little bit rusty. Things would go much better next time around.

It had been 3 weeks and seven time zones since we left San Diego, and what meager flying we had done was exclusively over the open ocean. That changed when *Ranger* steamed through San Bernardino Strait and the air wing found itself within range of the bombing complex at Crow Valley. Crow Valley bombing range was maintained primarily to support aircraft stationed at Clark Air Force Base, but the navy was welcome to utilize its facilities of a scored bull's-eye and several scattered tactical targets whenever we were in the neighborhood. Unfortunately for Rivers and me, our antique inertial navigation system (INS) "dumped" and lost its alignment during the acceleration of the catapult shot. Without the INS we were limited to manual bombing deliveries using the bulky gunsight mounted on the glare shield in front of the pilot's forward window.

We didn't practice manual deliveries that often—they were inherently inaccurate, and it seemed quite unlikely that we would find ourselves in a daylight situation where it might prove workable over Iraq. Without the stabilization to use his radar or forward-looking infrared effectively, Rivers helped me do my best to fly that perfect airspeed, dive angle, and release altitude that would make a meaningful symbol out of the gunsight crosshairs. Without the aid of the inertial navigation system the computer could not be used for bomb release, and it did not take much deviation from perfection to cause a bomb to be flung hundreds of feet off target. I had a lot of respect for previous generations of pilots who manually bombed for a living, but then again, they had practiced it. My hits were respectable but nothing to brag about. More importantly, we had not hit any Filipino civilians with our 25-pound practice bombs. I considered the flight a great success.

The local population was the unknown variable that was added to any practice-bombing sortie in the Philippines. Much of Philippine society on the island of Luzon were poor enough that they found it worth the risk to scavenge for the scrap metal left behind by our small practice bombs, or any live ordnance we might drop. Despite the presence of a spotting tower, fences,

and danger signs, there were no guarantees that several Filipinos might not be in the bushes adjacent to the target, waiting to run out and get their prize. The metal they collected
would be fashioned into belt buckles and similar trinkets for
sale to the foreign military population at Clark and Subic
Bay. It was a competitive business for the locals, and waiting
for the bombing runs to finish could mean that another desperate craftsman might hurry away with the scrap metal. We
took each of the clearing runs through the target area prior to
dropping bombs seriously—these folks had a hard enough
life without the loss or disabling of their breadwinner, and I
certainly didn't need the hodgepodge of emotions of such an
accidental death on my conscience.

As dangerous as it was, Crow Valley was safer than the
other live ordnance drop zone in the Philippines, Scarborough
Shoals. On our previous cruise I remembered watching from
the air as a fleet of small "bonka" fishing boats waited just
outside the range for us to drop our load of 500-pound bombs
on the mini-island atoll. Five hundred pounds of high explosives can make a hell of a lot of belt buckles, but it also could
ruin a lot of lives. The Filipinos normally held their ground to
the outside of the danger zone until the runs were completed
at Scarborough Shoals. But occasionally there would be a
misread by small boaters thinking that the jets had left, and
they would race one another at a frantic pace to the semisub-
merged rocks. Before a pilot squeezed his commit trigger he
had to remove his gaze from his instruments and look one last
time outside for any tiny forms who might be people scurry-
ing along the rocks. I did not know of any accidents in our air
wing, but there were definitely some very last-second bombing-
run aborts to avert a disaster. I always felt more comfortable
dropping the somewhat safer inert practice ordnance in the
Philippines; it just was not worth the loss of a life.

Flying in the daylight over dry land and dropping bombs
was a lot to handle after the scarcity of quality training sorties
the past several weeks. Rivers and I did some sight-seeing on

our return to *Ranger*, and after two quick wing flashes that inverted our Intruder, we each got a God's-eye view of the naval installation and the neighboring town of Olongapo. The naval facility was divided into two general divisions: the port of Subic Bay, where most of the battle group tied up, and the naval air station at Cubi Point. There were no defined geographic features that separated the two, but much like on the carrier, the atmosphere changed noticeably when traveling between brown- and black-shoe territory.

The Subic and the Cubi sides of the base each had their own officers' clubs, and while there were no restrictions on visiting one or the other, few aviators frequented the black-shoe club and vice versa. It was not a matter of animosity or dislike, but simply a lack of common experience to share. We aviators had the reputation for being more obnoxious and wild, and we lived up to those ideals as best we could. The Cubi "O" club was a veritable museum, with plaques and relics from the Vietnam era and beyond. When a carrier was in town it was the scene of nightly camaraderie and carousing as drunken aviators told stories, and snarfed down the near-toxic mixture that made up the colorful "Cubi Specials."

Much has been written about the town of Olongapo, and most of it is probably true. Even as late as 1991 it was a Far Eastern version of the Wild West, with shotgun-toting bouncers providing the stability for the hookers and the nightclubs to engage in their business trades. The two main drags—Gordon and Magsaysay Streets—were block after block of bars, nightclubs, rickety hotels, and enterprising storekeepers who could replicate anything on earth. It was the land of the not quite right. The club singers could mimic the latest pop songs in perfect English (but could not speak a word), and craftsmen would fashion anything from model aircraft to ornate belt buckles to personalized banners and plaques. Just show the shopkeeper a picture or a drawing of what you would like reproduced, and leave the rest to him. But watch out, because you could rest assured that as perfect as the handiwork might appear at first glance, it was guaranteed that if you looked long enough you would find something that was not quite right. It might be a basic misspelling that would transform a sentence into a bizarre rendition of its original meaning, or a New York Yankees shirt with a football on it, but the little errors were not misunderstandings, they were a lack of understanding. The Filipinos were fantastic at copying what was in front of them without having the slightest clue as to what the true meaning of their handiwork was supposed to be. It was not their fault; the projects they worked on might as well have come from an alien universe, and they possessed no concept of what the crazy Americans wanted all the junk for anyway.

Our arrival in the Philippines on our last cruise had been heralded by a brilliant banner hung on the rail of the Maramount Three bar, directly outside the front gate of the base. One of our enterprising pilots had flown in early and arranged for the custom-made, 20-foot banner to be flown conspicuously from the second-floor balcony: "Welcome VA-145, Big Dick Warriors from Hell." The sign said it all, and set the tone for the several drunken days to follow.

I took one last aerial look at the point where East met West and turned back toward the ship, which was closing with the port of Subic. I had squadron duty tomorrow, so I would not have the opportunity to visit this island of intrigue for a bit longer. We came into the break over *Ranger* just a little faster than normal. There was nothing like an imminent port call to get the blood going. The ship continued to steam past the rugged Luzon shoreline toward Subic. The air wing would get the opportunity to finish the night flying schedule to keep her pilots current, and then *Ranger* would wait patiently outside the Philippine harbor so she could navigate to the carrier pier on the Cubi side of the base in the light of day. The word was that we would pass Grandé Island in midharbor at 0800, and then it was five days of pierside, cheap beer, and recre-

A message to Allied pilots written by the Kuwaiti resistance in 55-gallon oil drums in Mina Saud, south of Kuwait City. Photo taken by USS *Ranger* F-14 TARPS reconnaissance aircraft. (U.S. Navy)

The author (left) and Rivers Cleveland (right) in front of an A-6 bomb station loaded with 500-pound Rockeye cluster munitions prior to a strike against Republican Guards.

The author in his *Ranger* stateroom.

"Blood chit" carried by tactical aircrew during Desert Storm. The hope was that anyone finding a downed flyer would offer assistance in return for a reward instead of turning the pilot in.

Laundry set outside staterooms in the "alley" on the *Ranger*. Despite the massive size of the carrier, there was very little space to house the five thousand men who lived on board.

A-6 trapping as seen from the LSO platform. The goal of every pilot was to trap the number 3 wire, as this A-6 driver did.

Flight deck as seen from the bow prior to the first launch of the evening.

A-6 tanker crossing the fantail as seen from the LSO platform.

Flight deck as seen from the stern prior to the first launch of the evening.

Intruder preparing to launch off of Cat One. There were four steam-driven catapults on the USS *Ranger*, allowing for the rapid launch of its aircraft.

Less than three-quarters of a mile behind the *Ranger* "in the groove"— about thirty seconds from landing.

Rivers and the author in the Swordsmen ready room standing the Alert 15.

The ready room: "Greenie board" is high, left center; schedule board is to the right. The two aviators in flight gear are checking out .45s from the SDO (desk hidden behind them) prior to a combat mission.

Ordies manhandling 500-pound Rockeyes onto a multiple-ejector rack on A-6 station number one. Author's navigation bag is hanging on the landing-gear door uplock at left while he conducts the preflight walk-around inspection.

A-6 loaded with twelve (six per side) 500-pound general purpose bombs with snakeye fins for retarded (high drag, low altitude) delivery. The bombs painted on the side of the fuselage represent the number of Desert Storm combat sorties flown by this specific aircraft; the radar dishes represent the number of enemy radars attacked; the boats the number of vessels sunk.

Second section of lead division during a rare Air Wing Two daylight strike to Kuwait City. This was Rivers's first mission as an air wing strike lead during combat.

"Plugging" a tanker A-6. Unlike the air force, which uses a probe-type refueler, naval aircraft plug into a basket at the end of a long hose.

Rivers and the author after their final A-6 flight delivering a VA-52 Intruder to the Boeing Museum of Flight in Seattle.

Snax at his desk in a typical three-man stateroom. Space is always an issue on board a carrier, and everyone learns to live in close quarters.

Rivers at the back entrance to the ready room in the ordnance prepositioning area. In foreground are 2,000-pound bombs. Rivers is standing beside 500- and 1,000-pound laser-guided bombs.

Commemorative patch of the historic cruise by the USS *Ranger* and Air Wing Two during Operation Desert Storm.

ation. I managed to fall asleep that night despite a slight case of channel fever, that disease of the mind that grabs your thoughts and turns them to the delights of shore to the exclusion of sleep. The prospect of my 24-hour chain to *Ranger* as squadron duty officer, however, had dampened my enthusiasm sufficiently for a good night's rest.

The sun reflected brilliantly off the clear waters at the head of Subic Bay as *Ranger* steamed toward the huge dock adjacent to Cubi Point Naval Air Station. The large harbor was packed with American warships waiting to resupply before proceeding to the Persian Gulf. Lines were barely made secure before wave after wave of civilian-clad sailors piled off the ship for the first time in three weeks. The warm climate and penetrating rays of light had already affected those lucky enough to have flown in earlier, and each had the red tinge of a burn and the dull glow of a dehydrated hangover.

The highlight of my first 8 hours of squadron duty was the oversized mail call that flooded the ready room with all the letters that had been backlogged due to the limited flights out to the ship. I got only one letter, but it was from Laurie, and it was difficult not to get caught up in the pervasive euphoria that the port call brought with it. About a third of the ship and air wing complement were still on duty, busy onloading supplies and taking care of business that could be more easily accomplished with the greater accessibility of the shore-based communications and support facilities.

My only official business of relative importance that morning was to jot down a note for routing to the CO explaining the status of the khaki flight suits that had been ordered by the command months earlier. The squadron's request for camouflage flying apparel to blend in with the probable ejection environment of the Middle East desert was a small but concrete act of preparation we could make to avoid capture if we were unfortunate enough to be shot down.

All aviators of tactical aircraft were required to attend a 5-day advanced course in survival, evasion, resistance, and escape (SERE) prior to their first deployment, where the essentials of avoiding capture and proper POW conduct were taught. The fundamentals of survival revolved around simple things, and effective camouflage could not be overstated, unless, of course, you were a civilian bureaucrat working in the procurement process. If that was the case, then apparently spending 4 months finding the lowest bidder was the most important priority: so what if that would place the receipt of our survival gear two months after the anticipated start of hostilities. I made a mental note that I had better not eject, and live, for the sake of the "civil" servant who was probably getting commended by her boss for doing such a cost-effective job.

My destructive train of thought was disturbed by the petty officer who was assisting me in the duty. The first drunken sailor from our squadron had been escorted back to the ship, and we needed to set up a "drunk watch" to ensure that the poor bastard didn't puke and choke to death. Not bad—1745 and not even dark yet. I directed my able assistant to set up several of the ship's stretchers in the open space of the ordnance staging area and to get some help from the duty section in watching this first of what was certain to be many.

The first night in port was always the roughest, and this one proved to be no exception. The minor crises steadily poured in. I was just nodding off at 0230 when the phone rang. One of my chiefs was on the line with some grim news: He had been staying at a hotel in town with other sailors from the battle group to avoid being caught out on the street during curfew, when the flimsy structure caught fire and became engulfed in flames. There were definitely fatalities. The only personal knowledge he had of any VA-145 personnel was a petty officer from the airframes shop who had been severely burned and was in the base hospital. I got hold of the skipper and spent the rest of that sleepless night keeping him and the air wing honchos updated on the unfolding events. As it turned out, three sailors had been killed, none from *Ranger*.

Our single injured petty officer would remain behind for treatment when the ship continued its cruise west. Not a terribly pleasant way to end our first month deployed.

The bad news for the port call was definitely front-loaded with the hotel fire, and the remainder of the visit to the Philippines was peaceful. The threatened anti-American terrorist actions did not materialize. The 16,000 Marines who had stopped for a respite on their way to the Persian Gulf did not have any run-ins of significance with our battle group sailors, and the majority of the work that needed to be accomplished was completed in the first two days. On the docks the massive stockpiling of Marine equipment—tanks, APCs, LCACs—was almost sobering, which was no easy feat for the Philippines. We were clearly getting ready for war.

Everyone got an opportunity to burn off some steam in Olongapo or at one of the base clubs. I spent one day wandering the streets of Olongapo with Rivers, and headed out for a day of scuba diving with my Prowler friend Quiver on New Year's Eve day. We struck out for the naval communications facility at San Miguel, an hour or so jeepney ride north of Subic Bay. The jeepneys that littered the roads of the Philippines were open-air taxis that had been converted from jeeps left behind after World War II and now served as the principal vehicles for hire by the local populace. They were typically brightly colored and ordained with the trinkets and garnish befitting a Mardi Gras parade float, each a fast-moving carriage for the dozen drunken sailors who could be squeezed into one.

Quiver and I had never been to the San Miguel communications station before, and we had just a touch of apprehension as we took off into the countryside with our several thousand dollars of dive gear crammed into the back of the jeepney. What the hell, we would probably never get another chance at it again, and we had been told that we could rent tanks and a local bonka boat for passage to one of the coastal islands at the naval facility. Our superior ability to judge our driver's character—in other words, dumb luck—got us to San Miguel without incident. Following some minor frustration after finding the dive "store" closed, we ran across a dentist named Bill Wright, who offered to open up the store and steer us in the proper direction for hiring a boat. His advice and knowledge proved indispensable, and within the hour we were 100 feet below the surface of the South China Sea, enjoying the coral and hoping that the boat driver would not take off with our clothes and wallets.

The bonka boat operator proved to be reliable, and the only distraction to an otherwise peaceful interlude with the sea was the sound of explosions underwater from about a mile away. The local fishermen had set out to fill their nets with whatever types of fish floated after being finessed to the surface by skillfully tossed sticks of dynamite. The shock waves from this local fishing technique were not overly horrendous, but the noise got to be a tad much, and Quiver and I cut our dive short. We considered the day a success, particularly so because we had not been killed by an errant explosion weeks before arriving in the Persian Gulf.

It was a nice diversion to leave the confines of the ship, the base, and the town of Olongapo, which was teeming with sailors, and to be reminded that there was a world out there that did not revolve around flying and bombing. I savored the few hours, knowing this would be my last look at civilian society for quite a while, and possibly my final impressions of the outside world unjaded by the events that were to unfold in the months to follow. The navy offered a life of contradictions and contrasts, weeks and months with the singular focus of mission and squadron, and days of bizarre and singularly unique experiences that would be impossible to reproduce in the United States. Quiver and I jumped on a navy bus that ran back to Subic, and we made it to the Cubi club in time for the start of the New Year's Eve festivities.

Our remaining two days in port were spent recuperating around the pool, and feeling compelled to participate in the daily run to the base hospital to work off the bitters as the local monkeys nipped at our heels. The surreal impact that the 5 days ashore in this tropical oasis had on my mind was an appropriate primer for the changes I could expect to encounter the next time I would see land, once we entered the Strait of Hormuz 2 weeks in the future. USS *Ranger* and her escorts pulled out of Subic Bay at 0900 on 3 January 1991 and started what most of us had come to realize was the beginning of the "real" part of the cruise. What remained of our casual attitudes disappeared completely with the last distraction and obstacle between us and our destiny in the Middle East.

# Chapter Ten

# . . . in dread silence reposes . . .

3-14 January 1991,
the South China Sea and the Indian Ocean

I studied the Department of Defense topographical chart of the Persian Gulf that Tony had taped to the side of our stateroom lockers until I found the name that consumed my focus: Umm Qasr. Immediately after *Ranger* raised her dockside lines, the strike planning resumed in earnest. I still was not officially "read into" the plan, but I now knew what the target for *Ranger*'s first strike into Iraq would be: the Iraqi naval base of Umm Qasr. Umm Qasr was north of Būbiyān Island on the Khawr Abd Allah waterway en route to the city of Basra, and contained the aim points for our initial mission tasking. Rivers and I were officially designated the alternate lead aircraft for the Jakal skipper's strike, and as such it was time on this second day out from the Philippines to become involved in planning the attack.

We did not yet know the full complement of classified information, but we now had the basics of the mission's objectives to review: to sink or disable as much of the Iraqi fleet of antiship missile patrol boats as possible. The Iraqi navy fielded Soviet-made Osa and TNC vessels. Each was capable of firing missiles that could sink or cause serious damage to the myriad of Allied warships that would be operating in the Persian Gulf and that would be providing the supply lines to the troops in the field. The Iraqis had a variety of other smaller boats that could be utilized to lay mines, and these, too, would need to be neutralized. The danger of an Iraqi amphibious assault in an end run around Kuwait had to be dispelled as quickly as possible. Additionally, we needed to control the gulf so our forces could pose a realistic amphibious threat of our own and draw a sizable portion of Saddam's forces away from the Saudi border. If the Allies were to provide an effective forward presence and launch strikes from off the southern coast of occupied Kuwait, then the Iraqi navy would have to be eliminated as a viable force. The *Ranger* battle group had the collateral mission assignment of overall commander of the naval order of battle. It would be our job to ensure that the Allied fleets could operate with impunity in the shallow gulf waters.

I was still in the dark as to the specific aimpoints at the Umm Qasr quays, but we had enough information to assist Stilts and his CO in their logistical challenge of getting six bomb-laden Intruders through the enemy defenses and safely returned to *Ranger*'s decks. The seemingly endless assembly line of 500-pound rockeye cluster bombs that *Ranger* had onloaded in Subic Bay fit our strike purposes perfectly. Our challenge was to determine the most effective manner of delivering the Intruders and their rockeyes to Umm Qasr without being shot down.

Stilts and I worked on the aspects of the strike plan that were pilot-oriented: the timing of jets over the target, the fuel and logistics requirements, and the support package of jammers and HARM shooters that would be necessary to make our ingress more survivable. Designated Tomcat crews developed the fighter plan, where and how the F-14s would engage any possible MiGs sent out to intercept our Intruders. Rivers was fully read into the strike, and he set to work on refining the radar and forward-looking infrared aim points, a critical task specifically reserved for an experienced B/N. The big-picture design of routing to and from the target, the definition of specific aim points and assignments to individual bombers, and the development of an overall tactic for attack was the job of the air wing strike lead, the Jakal commanding officer.

The newly found enthusiasm of being in the know dominated our days in the carrier's Intelligence Center, making us virtually unaware of the battle group's progress westward. With the end of the Cold War the ordinarily prolific visits from Russian "Bear" multiprop bombers were whittled down to just one as we passed the coast of Vietnam. *Ranger* steamed to the west of the controversial Spratly Islands, barren pieces of rock in the South China Sea that were the source of constant diplomatic confrontation, and occasional military action, by every country in the region that desired her promise of potential oil riches.

The air wing endured three consecutive no-fly days while *Ranger* and her entourage attempted to blend in with the hundreds of massive merchant ships steaming past Singapore, and then waited for the cover of darkness to transit the choke point of the Strait of Malacca. Having successfully passed into the open waters of the Indian Ocean on 7 January, the air wing had a last safety stand-down. A "steel beach picnic" was to follow—a carrier deck barbecue of hot dogs and hamburgers organized to break the monotony of the average sailor's existence living in the depths of the ship.

We marked our progress across the Indian Ocean by watching events unfold in Iraq; Washington, D.C.; and the United Nations in New York. The few old newspapers that migrated their way out to the ship were dominated by headlines of impending war with Iraq. CNN seemed to rotate through the same stories, over and over, trying to find a new twist to the waiting we were all enduring as President Bush's 15 January deadline for Saddam to leave Kuwait inched closer. Pete Rose was released from prison after finishing a sentence for income tax cheating; Pan Am filed for bankruptcy; the rest of the national news paled in comparison to the buildup in the gulf.

I spent the first five days out of port in the repetitious cycle of strike planning, aircraft divisional duties, shipboard general quarters (GQ) training, and at the gym working off the pent-up frustration of the no-fly days. There was plenty that needed to be done, and GQ drills were a daily hurdle, but a grudgingly accepted necessity, to the smooth flow of planned events of a naval combatant. General quarters would occasionally be a scheduled exercise, but as we neared the gulf they became more random and unannounced. Regardless, they entailed 60 to 90 minutes of sucking rubber with our gas masks and fire-retardant flash hoods on, reluctant prisoners in the squadron ready room. All of *Ranger*'s watertight doors would be secured shut for the evolution, and elaborate and specific routing to the flight deck had to be adhered to, to get to our jets to fly.

During GQ, ship's company and air wing ground pounders manned damage control teams, fought simulated fires, and controlled flooding from feigned missile hits to *Ranger*'s waterline. Aviators had no specific duty assignments other than to stay out of the way and be prepared to fly missions. A trained aviator was difficult to replace on the cruise, and the risk posed to us by exposure to an at-sea calamity ordinarily exempted us from shipboard fire or damage control parties. But there were exceptions. Ever since the carrier *Forrestal*'s disastrous blaze of 1967 off the coast of Vietnam with the loss of 134 lives, all hands were trained in fire fighting in the event of a catastrophe. Virtually all of *Forrestal*'s dedicated fire-fighters were killed in the first 5 minutes of their flight deck inferno, leaving only untrained personnel to man the hose teams. For us, general quarters was a physical disruption to accomplishing our everyday workload, but it also was a drill that clearly needed to be practiced until it was firmly entrenched in the minds of all of *Ranger*'s sailors.

The A-6 community received unwelcome news on 8 January that proved a minor temporary distraction, but a major blow to the potential naval careers of Intruder aviators. Due to cost overruns, the A-12 project had been canceled. Suddenly the A-6 community was left in limbo as to which direction our professional lives would take. I felt severely conflicting emotions. Screw the defense contractors who routinely went over budget and expected the taxpayers to make up the difference, I thought, but I continued to hope that Secretary of Defense Cheney had another plan in mind to sustain the life of the medium attack mission in naval aviation. Our long-term goals and plans were thrown into the same murky uncertainty as that of our lives in the months to follow, and I became ever more dependent on the routine I had developed on the ship.

Our skipper had completed the initial planning for his strike package into Iraq scheduled for the first day hostilities commenced, and Rivers and I flew on the mirror image exercise. It started to look like a busy first day if it came to blows with Iraq; we would be participating in two strikes in the first 12 hours of the war. Our CO was assigned to destroy several Chinese-made Silkworm antiship missile sites at the most southern tip of the Al Faw peninsula, adjacent to the border with Iran. The daylight raid did not optimize the capabilities of the Intruder, and made the players on the skipper's strike quite vulnerable to enemy fighters. Fortunately, the missile site was at the far perimeter of range of the defending SAM batteries, and they posed a lessened risk to the A-6s. Our CO had decided to conduct his attack from high altitude to avoid the bulk of the antiaircraft artillery that would be particularly deadly in the light of day. The mirror image practice runs went smoothly and validated the coordinated planning of the strikers and their fighter cover.

Secretary of State Baker finished a summit with Iraqi foreign minister Tariq Aziz in Geneva on 9 January, initially inspiring hopes for peace, hopes that fell quickly into disarray. From our warship in the middle of the Bay of Bengal, insulated from the news except for what CNN deemed was the important point of focus for the day, it was exceedingly difficult to gauge the mood in the United States. I seesawed daily between feeling that this tremendous buildup was for naught, and a fixed conviction that war was inevitable. I vacillated between a desire to test my mettle in battle, and the hope that this all would pass and we could retreat into the boredom and solitude of the cruises we had become accustomed to.

Subtle questions took a tenuous hold in the back of my mind while we continued work on our strike. Now that I had a glimpse of our skipper's plan of attack, I began to wonder why the basic tactics differed so greatly from the profile of the Jakal CO. The Jakal CO was conducting a strike in the traditional mission style that the A-6 community had trained and prepared for since the Intruder was introduced into service. To defeat what our strike had determined was the primary threat—surface-to-air missiles—we would fly to the target low and fast, utilizing the cover of darkness and what little terrain we could muster to cover our ingress. The hornet's nest we would inevitably stir up would theoretically be mostly behind us as we dropped our bombs and egressed at 300 feet over the marshy lowlands.

The skipper and Snax had approached their problem from a different perspective. Granted, their strike would be conducted in broad daylight, which would make them much more susceptible to antiaircraft artillery, although the SAM threat was diminished in the area of their target. Even so, a high-altitude run-in was not what we in the Intruder community had prepared ourselves for over the past 30 years of our cumulative training. Initially I convinced myself that the differing circumstances dictated different tactics, but after talking to Tony about the planning of *Ranger's* third proposed strike, I began to have doubts.

Tony was on our executive officer's planning team. The XO would be leading the air wing's third set of sorties into enemy territory, this time to attack Silkworm missile sites on the Kuwaiti coast during the early-morning hours of the second day of the conflict. This strike would be conducted under cover of darkness, in what was a substantial SA-8 missile threat environment, and they were going to fly in at high altitude. What were the XO's motivations for dismissing the low-level option when there existed a viable SAM defense and the strike was going in at night?

It took a while for the inside scoop to come down to us lieutenants, and when the reasoning behind the break from our training tradition surfaced fully, it confirmed most of our worst fears. The emphasis by the senior strike planners on what would be the most dangerous and effective threat to the inbound bombers differed fundamentally, and was shifting decisively from SAMs to AAA. The problem was that this was not the result of a lessening in capability of the SAM batteries, but rather an initial underestimation of the Iraqi anti-aircraft artillery defenses.

The Iraqis had a lot of guns, and hundreds of thousands of men to point them into the air and shoot. Some of the guns were big, some were huge, but all had one thing in common: They propelled hot metal into the air in a barrage of flak capable of obliterating an ingressing A-6. Antiaircraft artillery did not need to be sophisticated, it did not require a radar system to guide it, or even daylight or good weather to make it effective. Barrage AAA as a tactic utilized the odds that a low-flying jet would run into a solid wall if enough shooting metal was propelled into the air. For barrage AAA to work you needed a lot of guns, a lot of ammunition, and somewhat willing targets that would expose themselves by flying low. The Iraqis had plenty of the first two; now the question was: Were we setting ourselves up by providing the last?

I just didn't know the answer. Umm Qasr was smack in the center of the effective coverage of SA-6 and SA-2 missile systems, two Soviet SAMs that complemented each other well in covering the entire altitude spectrum from high to low. We had limited real-world experience with the true effectiveness of the newer SA-6 system, and probably overestimated the missile's capabilities. It had become a "death ray" of sorts. During air wing training at the sophisticated target complex in Fallon, Nevada, we took every step possible to avoid flying into a simulated SA-6 coverage. When we did, our fears were reinforced by the computer system consistently shooting us down for the exercise. A general feeling had developed that the SA-6 was invulnerable to radar jamming. We were of the mind that the only survivable tactic when transiting its envelope was to fly low and rain down HARM missiles in an attempt to shut down the SAM radar for the entire time the strike package was within optimum range.

It was a tough question. Historically, AAA had shot down more planes than anything else. But this was in many respects the new age of modern air combat. There had not been a sustained campaign of the magnitude being proposed since Vietnam, and the SA-6 had been used only in relatively limited and isolated instances. Although I was wary, I justified in my mind that the SA-6 threat made the difference between *Ranger*'s first strike and her two to immediately follow. In the end it was not my decision to make; it was the Jakal CO's plan. I felt relieved that the question of high versus low would be resolved by someone else, a commander who was a bombardier/navigator from our sister A-6 squadron, an aviator with more experience and resources than a lieutenant. The hesitancy of commitment to the argument did not disappear from my mind, but I was able to banish it to a common plane with the emotions of fear, exhilaration, and anticipation that the process of preparing for war had produced.

The few hours between the first two strikes was deemed too short to utilize the same aircrew, and we were switched from our skipper's daylight attack to the role of a HARM shooter on our XO's mission. Rivers went over the "switchology" drill of shooting multiple HARM missiles, working to avoid flipping the wrong toggle, or inputting the incorrect targeting parameters into the missile computer. Either would knock us off of our shooting timeline or turn our missile into a dud. Different settings were required for each missile, and a single out-of-place switch would make it impossible to hit the target.

Suddenly we missed the old days of the cruise, where there was nothing but time. It was a race against the clock to check and recheck our plans, our individual tactics and knowledge, our evasion and escape routes if shot down, to continue to hone our physical and mental states. The work of the squadron troops went on, and in the midst of our heightened frenzy of preparation for war the organization of the maintenance department needed to be maintained. My new division chief petty officer was not working out; I replaced him and tried to smooth things out between hourly visits to the Intelligence Center and general quarters. We did not need any pissed-off wrench turners fixing jets when things began to get heated. The same day, 12 January 1991, the Senate and the House passed resolutions supporting use of force in the Persian Gulf.

I barely was able to make time to write a quick note to Laurie:

*12 Jan 91*

*Hi Babe,*

*We're 3 days out from the Gulf and we don't know much more than you guys. By the time you get this things will probably have happened one way or another. Rivers and I have been planning and practicing a lot, I think we're ready for whatever happens.*

*Sorry the writing's a little rough but we are at a practice general quarters and it's tough to write with all the protective gear on. I haven't had a chance to get bored (yet) which is good, but it would be nice to take it easy for a couple days.*

*Everyone (Snax, Tony, Rivs, etc. . . .) are all fine, we're not getting on each others' nerves too much. Interesting times to live. I worry about my folks, but you guys too. Laurie, if war breaks out stay the hell away from the air-*

*lines for at least a week. Common sense, but there could
be terrorists anywhere.*

*As usual there's not much to write about—I miss you,
look forward to the future, but I try not to think about it too
much so I can concentrate on the task at hand.*

*I love you,
Send me stuff!*
*Pete*

The realization came to Rivers and me that we would be
the first of the VA-145 Swordsmen to cross the beach if hostilities erupted. I felt some pressure, but mostly pride that,
however inadvertently, we would have the honor of being the
first to go. I also heard the words of Tug, our rotund, cherub-
like tactics officer, in admonishment to the junior officers
after every one of his ready room flight briefs: "Don't fuck it
up." There was lots of potential for that here.

The detection of the SA-2 site in the vicinity of Umm Qasr
by our intelligence folks had come about only in the past few
days, and it presented a problem as to how we would allocate
an A-6 to shoot a HARM missile at it. The Prowler's radar
jamming was a known success against the older SA-2 missile
system, but it was the consensus of the planners on the Jakal
strike team that at least one HARM should be designated for
it. The difficulty was that the two A-6s that were to augment
the Prowler by shooting HARM missiles were barely able to
provide continuous coverage for the five bombers while they
were in the heart of the SA-6 envelope. They could not spare
any of their total of ten HARMs to target the SA-2. Rivers immediately came forward with the proposal that we carry a
HARM on our Intruder, shoot it on our way to the target, and
then switch back to a bombing run to drop our rockeyes.

The challenge posed by this was that the upgrade to the
A-6 weapons system, and the "maturity" of the Intruder, required thirteen steps to switch from a HARM missile shot
back to a rockeye attack, and this would have to occur while

smack in the middle of the threat envelope. While conducting these thirteen steps, Rivers' attention also would be required for navigation, lookout for AAA and missiles, and the initial acquisition of the boats at Umm Qasr for our bombing run. Loading a HARM on an A-6 bomber had never been tried before in combat, and the experts at our Medium Attack Weapons School back at Whidbey had strongly discouraged it due to its complexity and division of attention in the heat of battle. On the other hand, Rivers and I had been practicing this exact procedure, as a "just in case."

Rivers knew I was game, and he sold the strike team leader on his idea without bothering to give me a glance. The complexity of our mission went up significantly.

*Ranger*'s trek westward took a decided turn to the north, and we found ourselves looking out at the same patch of water in the Gulf of Oman where we had steamed circles for 3 months on our last cruise. The water in the northern Indian Ocean looked the same, but a brief glance at the wall chart marked our nonchalant progress toward our old nemesis, Iran. By 14 January *Ranger* was just outside the Strait of Hormuz and the Persian Gulf. We were now steaming in territory virtually unknown to U.S. aircraft carriers until only a few short months ago. We would join *Midway* on station in the gulf, and could expect *Roosevelt* and *America* to fill out the remainder of the four carrier battle groups destined to operate in the confines of the gulf's cramped basin.

Time was running out. Fear was a compartmentalized emotion in the world of naval aviation, one that was normally overshadowed by competition, ego, and the pressure not to let down your peers. The casual ready room joke was that it was better to die than to look bad, and while outwardly no one paid the phrase more than lip service, there was an underlying truth to the saying that struck close to home. Letting down your buddies, your service, or your country was definitely looking bad, and there were few aviators who would not at least approach the threshold of the ultimate sacrifice to avoid the personal stigma of falling short of the expectations of their comrades.

We would joke about anything and everything. The endless banter and prattle of wit and halfwit obscured the threat of dwelling too deeply on the danger that perpetually lay in wait around the corner. If you attempted to view carrier operations analytically, the potential for disaster was simply too frightening—the daily risk could appear to be too great to consciously make it a routine part of your life. A touch of a flippant "What are they going to do, shave my head and stick me on a boat for 6 months?" attitude was required to bounce up to the flight deck all happy-faced to do your job. A constant flow of easygoing sarcasm provided consistent, albeit small, relief from the pressure.

I thought more and more about how I would react in combat. I had been physically afraid to varying degrees many times in my life, but usually that fear had been overwhelmed by Tug's sage advice not to "fuck it up." The internal pressure to succeed was a tremendous impetus to the energy level the carrier aviator enjoyed over long stretches at sea. I tried to think of when I had been the most scared before. My most intense navy flying experiences were overshadowed by the fear of not making the grade, or letting down my squadronmates, or the plain old harassment I might receive from my buddies at a bar one night for some knuckleheaded stunt. The actual physical, soul-revealing, and belly-churning emotion of fear was intense but fleeting in naval aviation. Granted, I left the cockpit after virtually every night trap dry-mouthed and shaking with an eternal gratitude that I was no longer airborne, but that was different from the "look in the eye of the Reaper" kind of fear.

I had to reflect back to civilian days to dredge up a bone-deep, "I'm going to die" exposure to fright. The most vivid experience I could recall was during a dive on the wreck of *Andrea Doria* in the early 1980s. I was in college, and during the summers I would work on the charter dive boat *Wahoo* for free passage on various trips off the southern shore of Long Island. *Andrea Doria* had sunk in a collision in 1956 about 100 miles from Montauk Point, New York, and it was a challenging dive to say the least. Draped in nets amid the swift currents that were at the edge of the Gulf Stream on its northern run, *Andrea Doria* rested on her starboard side in sand, at a depth of 240 feet. In 1981 Peter Gimbel of department store fame had hired a multimillion-dollar salvage operation to find the purser's safe deep in the interior of the sunken ship. Although he was only partially successful, the operation did use torches to cut through a portion of *Doria*'s port hull at a depth of about 170 feet, giving sport divers great access to the wreck's interior.

Gimbel had provided an avenue to a treasure trove in the form of the pantry that led to the first-class dining room. This dark passage, with cables strewn across it and its sinks on the "ceiling," was a gold mine of handpainted first-class china buried in several feet of silt. Two dive buddies and I had dropped down through Gimbel's hole to the passage at 205 feet, and proceeded inward to retrieve as much china as we could put into our mesh bags within our brief 20 minutes of bottom time before we had to ascend and decompress. My friends stopped and dropped their knees onto the mud after about a 30-foot swim into the eerie passageway. I continued on just a bit farther out of curiosity, and was soon shining my powerful dive light into the inky darkness of the vast first-class dining room. I swam out, suspended in neutral buoyancy only about 5 feet from the hole from which I had entered, and took a quick look around for anything recognizable. I was evidently too far from any other bulkheads, and after realizing that I was not going to catch a glimpse of anything recognizable, I turned back to join my friends.

When my body rotated with the flip of my fins, my mask was suddenly engulfed in total blackness. I raised my light up but could not see more than a few inches through the silt that had been stirred up by my digging dive buddies 50 feet away.

The current had gently wafted the fine particles into the dining room and reduced visibility to virtually nothing while I was still suspended in midwater with no reference point to hold on to. I immediately swam into the silt, knowing it was the correct direction to regain contact with the entrance of the 8-foot hole. In the subtle glow of euphoria generated from the nitrogen narcosis of the depth I began to feel a twinge of panic as my hands ran into a solid wall. All right, I thought, I must have sunk down a few feet; just follow the wall up and the hole will be there.

The bulkhead started to recede after only a few feet, and I began to regain my confidence. I swam into the wall as it arched away from me for about 10 feet, and then felt a renewed and intensified flutter of my heart when the "passage" abruptly stopped in a narrow V. Where the hell was I? How was I going to get out of here? I stopped and tried to control my breathing: Was I going to die here? Many divers had died on this wreck over the years, but I never thought it could happen to me. Shit, what did I do? There was one possibility: Perhaps I had drifted too high when the silt hit me in the face, and the elusive hole to the outside ocean and safety was actually farther below me. Slowly I backed out of the V and started to work my way down, careful not to lose my grip on the bulkhead in front of me in the blackness, or my tenuous grasp of mental control.

Twenty feet into my descent I felt an opening. I cautiously entered the passageway; the size seemed about right. After a 30-foot swim down its length with my mind racing in the hope of salvation, I saw a dim flicker of light through the silt. I had found my buddies and my way out. The whole episode could not have taken more than 3 minutes, but it had an enduring impact on me. I learned several things: I was not invincible, true terror is really bad, and I had better straighten up and live right. The first two lessons stuck with me, and I managed to hold on to the third until *Wahoo* weighed anchor and the beer started flowing. Two out of three wasn't bad, I thought, at least for a college kid.

The experience of being lost in *Andrea Doria* had a strong enough impact that I knew that whatever happened to me in combat, it would be intense and powerful, and I could only hope I would live up to the challenge. It was enough to temper my excitement with a touch of the true gravity of the situation, and the profound effect it would have on me and those around me. But I entertained these thoughts mostly at night, in the few fleeting moments of private reflection afforded a sailor before falling asleep. By addressing the possibilities I hoped I would be able to concentrate more easily when the time came to put my training to the test.

*Ranger*'s final two days outside the Persian Gulf were filled with reminders of the unique circumstances surrounding our final destination. I walked up to the hangar bay on one particularly sunny morning and found that a helmeted Marine in a flak jacket, toting an M-16, blocked my access. He would not say a word, but it was clear it would be an extraordinarily bad idea for me to try to duck under the rope that cordoned off a path to the open hangar bay door. Finally, a chief in khakis walked over to where I was standing and directed me through a maze of crates and pallets until I was in the open space on the opposite side of the roped-off area. I turned back at my now-unobstructed view to see what all the fuss was about.

In typical at-sea fashion, a supply ship was cruising close alongside *Ranger* at an identical speed and course, and several taut lines were strung between the two ships to pass cargo back and forth. Nothing unusual about that, but then I got a glimpse of the cargo—what looked like dozens of "special weapons" being gingerly hoisted out of one of *Ranger*'s thirteen weapons elevators and transferred to the supply ship alongside. Evidently it had been decided that it was unwise to bring the sensitive material into the shallow waters of the Persian Gulf in the event *Ranger* was sunk during enemy action.

All of the ship's "special weapons" were unloaded and stock-piled at a location where security could be better guaranteed. With the end of the Cold War, and President Bush's impending change in official policy, none of the off-loaded weapons would ever make it back on board *Ranger* again.

*Ranger* went to a higher level of preparedness for the possi-bilities of a chemical or biological attack, and her entire com-plement was required to carry gas masks on their persons at all times. The bagged masks tied close to our sides soon be-came second nature, and I felt more than naked and vulnerable when I forgot it once on my way to the shower. The aviators were issued chemical warfare shot kits consisting of atropine and a chemical accelerator for the "medicine," and were given simple but distressing instructions on how to use them if in-fected with a nerve agent. We were to grasp each of the two cylindrical containers firmly in our fists and jam them down forcefully into our thighs. A needle would shoot out and pene-trate our G suit and flight coveralls, injecting us with solutions that might save our life. Of course, we were expected to do this while flying if we suspected we had gone through a chemical cloud, and then there was the additional warning to try to miss your thighbone or you would not be walking for a while.

Forty-five-caliber automatics fresh from their boxes were stocked in the various ready room safes, waiting to be issued for our first flights over hostile territory. One day out from the Strait of Hormuz, and the live ordnance began coming up at a steady pace to the flight deck. Rockeyes with their hun-dreds of tank-busting cluster bomblets littered the bomb farm. Mark 82 500-pounders, with "VT" fuses set to go off while still airborne to shroud a target in shrapnel, came up next, fol-lowed by laser-guided skippers. Skippers were 1,000-pound bombs, each rigged with a rocket motor to enable the A-6 to shoot it outside the range of small-arms fire. The familiar blue band to denote practice ordnance was conspicuously missing from the bomb farm and all of the prestaged weapons hanging on the Intruders. Instantly the bombs were marked with such pithy statements as "To Saddam with love" and "Eat this, Saddam."

Although our minds were on combat, the very real dangers of carrier operations were still all around us. The day before we entered the Persian Gulf, word spread through the air wing that there had been a fatal accident involving one of the carrier *America*'s F/A-18 Hornet squadrons. It was a passing point of conversation for most, but I paid particularly close attention to any details forthcoming. I went to flight school with Laurie's brother Tom, and was actually introduced to Laurie through Tom on the day we both got our navy wings in Kingsville, Texas. Tom was now flying Hornets off *America*, and I started feeling that absurd mix of emotions wishing that the dead pilot not be Tom. Absurd because if not Tom, then whose brother or friend would that pilot be? Hope and guilt became easily melded into one emotion of constant discomfort.

I would find out several weeks later that while Tom was fine, his roommate on the ship was the unlucky aviator who had been killed. Only days away from combat, and Murphy's Law wouldn't let up for a minute. What a waste.

On 14 January, Jakal 1 had a final opportunity to exercise the game plan for *Ranger*'s first strike of the war. The mirror image took place over the remaining vestiges of open water in the North Arabian Sea before we made the transit into the Persian Gulf, and we briefed and flew it like it was the real thing. The plan was to utilize air force tankers to top our jets off with gas before the six A-6s and their various fighter, jammer, and HARM shooting escorts pressed on to the target area. In an effort to simulate the confines of the gulf, the three KC-135 tankers were stacked at 15,000, 16,000, and 17,000 feet directly overhead *Ranger*, where they waited for four to five jets to join on each of them for fuel. The three tankers were situated close together to expedite the rendezvous of the strike package after tanking, so the entire fourteen-plane gaggle could head en masse through the night sky to the target.

What looks good on paper does not always pan out so well, which was why we flew mirror image exercises. The light show of three huge KC-135's and fourteen Intruders, Tomcats, and Prowlers all within 3,000 feet and 2 miles of one another in the dark sky was a bit confusing to say the least. By the time we had completed tanking, it became apparent that it was taking far too long, and the first strikers to tank would find themselves perilously close to not having enough gas to complete their mission by the time they were done waiting for their comrades.

The second half of the mirror image went much better, and the six Intruder crews were all afforded an opportunity to practice low-level flying and high-G turns, albeit over the flat ocean. It was nerve-racking to put four Gs on the jet in the pitch black at the 500-foot target altitude at which we had decided to practice. We could certainly fly lower, much lower, but I began to doubt how much maneuvering we would be able to accomplish in the dark of night at extremely low altitudes. The ingress to Umm Qasr was mostly flat, but even the mild, rolling terrain of 25-mile-long Būbiyān Island posed a hazard if the jet's altitude began to deviate in a high-G turn. Oh, well, I thought, it's too late now. Maybe we could have practiced harder, or smarter, but I doubted it. Aggressive maneuvering on the instruments at night below 500 feet was scary shit; it was as simple as that.

Later that night I could not shake my discomfort with the confusion surrounding the tanking during the mirror image exercise. The formation flying and tanking plan seemed to be major problems, and primarily out of the raw fear that I would have a midair collision with one of our own guys before ever encountering the enemy, I came up with an alternative that in retrospect was the obvious solution. I approached Stilts with the idea of eliminating the strike package's join-up in formation, and instead assign each individual aircraft a strict timeline for its respective mission. Once an aircraft was catapulted from the deck it would be on its own to put forth all of the crew's efforts into flying the mission, with each aircraft maintaining separate altitudes to help deconflict jets in the same piece of the sky. We were not sacrificing any tactical advantage by forgoing formation flying. Without the benefit of air-to-air radar, the Intruders could not provide formation flying's advantage of mutual lookout support to each other in the dark.

Stilts broke out the planning charts and manuals, and soon it became clear that by avoiding flying formation none of the six Intruder bombers, or two Intruder HARM shooters, would need any extra fuel. The Tomcats and Prowlers could now utilize the organic tanking *Ranger*'s A-6s and S-3s had to offer, and we could all effectively meet up at specific points in the sky, separated by the buffer of different altitudes, well outside the threat envelopes of the target area. Stilts sold the plan to his B/N, and I felt a great sense of relief that at least the precursor to our entrance to hostilities had been greatly simplified. The applicability of the acronym "KISS" was greater to strike planning than to any other evolution in naval aviation: "Keep It Simple, Stupid."

It had been a long and drawn-out process, but the nuts and bolts of the Umm Qasr strike were in place, and all that remained was the pinpoint targeting and refinement to the final timeline for coordinating the attack. The general plan was simple and direct and therefore had a decent chance of succeeding. Five Intruders would drop twelve rockeyes each on various Osas and TNC guided missile patrol boats at the Umm Qasr boat basin, 25 miles up the Khawr Abd Allah waterway, while a sixth would string twelve rockeyes across the Mina al Bakr oil platform off the coast of Kuwait and put it out of production.

To provide air cover for the strikers, four Tomcats would supplement the existing combat air patrol that maintained an orbit to the east of Kuwait. The F-14s would stay feet wet, but would be ready at the first indication from the early-warning E-2 Hawkeye to enter the target area and shoot down any interceptors launched in response to our attack. Discerning between friend and foe would be accomplished by the bombers selecting specific codes for their transponders, and flying predictable and prebriefed altitudes and airspeeds once they were safely feet wet over the gulf. As a last resort, code words were assigned to be transmitted to avoid a "blue on blue" situation where our own F-14s shot us down, thinking we were Iraqi fighters coming out to play.

Two EA-6B Prowlers would continuously circle south of Būbiyān Island in an opposing pattern. This would maintain at least one of their jamming systems on axis with the SAM radars at all times, and would degrade their ability to acquire the Intruders on our ingress to the target. Prowlers also would fire HARM missiles at specific times to shut down the enemy radars permanently as the Intruders entered the "vulnerability window," where the A-6s were too close to the SAMs for jamming to be effective. The combination of "soft kill" via jamming, and "hard kill" utilizing HARM, was a comprehensive tactic that attempted to cover all of the bases and protect the Intruders in the target area when they became dangerously exposed to the enemy's defenses.

To augment the Prowlers, two additional A-6s would be orbiting high over the water, each shooting four HARMs at prearranged times that would sustain a steady impacting of the radar-seeking missiles while the bombers were most vulnerable. If the Iraqis decided to husband their resources and leave their radars off, there would be a lot of missiles flying ballistically with no signal to home in on. Although the SAMs would live to fight another day, they would effectively have been "soft-killed" for the duration of our strike.

The planning required to shoot four HARMs, and have them impact at exactly the right moment, was as arduous a challenge as the timing problem required for the strikers attacking Umm Qasr. The bombers were attempting to drop their rockeyes on target at precisely the correct instant to avoid running into any of the other Intruders trying to do the same thing, and to take advantage of the prearranged protection to be provided by the HARM shooters. The HARM shooters would be required to fly a tight pattern to be at a pre-planned point in the sky. The fly-out time of each missile would be computed to provide a steady and consistent pattern of HARMs impacting the radar sites while the bombers were in the final phase of their attack run. During a coordinated strike the world revolved around the clock, and being more than 10 seconds off of your designated timeline could have catastrophic results.

The most worrisome gap in the strategy was the effect the heavy antiaircraft artillery in the area would have on the Intruders. Flying low meant being extremely vulnerable to AAA, depending only on the cover of darkness and the maneuverability of each individual A-6 to counter the threat of running headlong into a mass of airborne metal.

It was a big game of chicken—the Iraqis did not have to shoot us down to win, just make our flight path so erratic that a targeting solution was not possible. For the Iraqis a downed U.S. jet was a bonus; having the attacker's bombs miss the target was the goal. The bombers had a similarly simple set of goals: first to hit the target on time. This ideally meant five loads of rockeyes on five separate vessels, but as with any mobile target, a backup plan also was required. If the boats were not where our intelligence had said they would be, then we would need to flex to an alternate target, in this case the wharf storage buildings and support facilities on the quay at Umm Qasr. Our second goal after hitting the target was returning all assets and aircrew safely to *Ranger*.

## 15 January 1991, Entering the Persian Gulf

*Ranger* transited the Strait of Hormuz and entered the Persian Gulf in the early morning hours of 15 January, a far different naval combatant than the first U.S. vessel to enter these waters more than 100 years earlier. U.S. involvement in the Persian Gulf was sporadic in the nineteenth century, but it steadily grew. In December 1879, Commodore Robert Wilson Shufeldt and the man-of-war *Ticonderoga* enjoyed the distinction of being the first American warship to transit the Strait of Hormuz. The only significant American presence in the Persian Gulf to this point had been persistent Protestant missionaries, who garnered a small but firm foothold, primarily in Persia. Commercial interests were isolated and far overshadowed by the British, but Commodore Shufeldt sought to change that, and in his travels went as far as 70 miles up the Shatt al Arab waterway, the confluence of the ancient Tigris and Euphrates rivers, and to the city of Basra.

Commodore Shufeldt was prophetic in his understanding of the potential importance of the gulf's strategic geography, and his entreaties to the Persians, Arabs, and Turks were met with enthusiasm as a possible offset to the dominant British Empire. The Persians in particular were anxious to win an alliance with an outside power, one that might hold at bay the mighty pincer of pressure of the British to the south and the Russians to the north. The seed that Commodore Shufeldt had sown would eventually grow into a long-lasting relationship between the shah of Persia and the United States, one that was officially begun in June 1883 with the arrival of an American minister in Tehran. This relationship offered the United States greater opportunities for trade and the Persians a formal diplomatic channel to act as a future wedge between the competing imperial giants of the day, Britain and Russia.

America's first overtures to the region had been conducted by a naval vessel, and the U.S. Navy had sustained a gradually growing force in the gulf ever since. The first permanent U.S. naval presence in the Persian Gulf was established in 1948, and would eventually become the "Middle East Force," a flotilla of several vessels and a command ship headquartered at Bahrain, the major British base in the Persian Gulf at the time. In that same year a U.S. carrier task force visited the gulf, a modest showing compared to the aerial armament that was positioning itself in the confined gulf waters in 1990 and early 1991. The inseparable connection had been made by the 1940s, however, between America's policy to accept dependence on Middle Eastern oil is a fact of life, even a desirable truism, and the requirement of the U.S. Navy's presence in the region to guarantee the continuity and stability of that policy.

The tumultuous 1980s in the gulf region saw a gradual buildup of American naval power, starting with the Iranian hostage crisis and continuing throughout the Iran-Iraq war. Combat strikes against Iran were undertaken on several occasions in retaliation to the aggressive actions of the Iranian navy. American aircraft launching from carriers positioned hundreds of miles away in the Gulf of Oman escorted reflagged Kuwaiti tankers waving the U.S. banner. The threat of American firepower was an attempt to deter attacks on tankers plying international waters with their lifeblood of oil and was not always successful. An Iranian Silkworm missile hit the tanker *Sea Isle City* in 1988, and an accidental casualty was the USS *Stark*, attacked by two Iraqi Exocet missiles in 1987.

Given the steady acceleration of the U.S. military presence in the Persian Gulf over the past hundred years, the vast armada of carrier battle groups entering the gulf in 1991 should not have seemed surprising. There was no escaping it, though; it was a dramatic and unexpected unfolding of events, if for no other reason than due to the massive concentration of firepower.

Rivers and the rest of the strike's B/Ns were camped out in the vault in CVIC, the Intelligence Center, studying satellite photography of the Umm Qasr quays and crunching numbers to obtain offset aim-point data for the Intruder radars. Stilts and I put the finishing touches on the condensed information packages, then cut them up into cards to be copied and issued to each strike participant at the beginning of the brief. The package would be clipped onto the aviator's knee clipboard during the flight for quick reference. For the pilots, the card that would sit on the top of the six-page package would have navigation way points, headings, distances, and times to be at each checkpoint. I wrote notes in the margin of the top card, parts of my combat checklist that were time critical in their completion. The B/Ns had a similar primary reference card, but it was much more cluttered; it contained exact latitudes and longitudes for each way point and vital targeting information.

Piled beneath our navigation cards, in no particular order, was a wealth of information we needed at our fingertips. Aircraft call signs, planned fuel necessary to complete the mission at each checkpoint, transponder codes, assigned altitudes and airspeeds, radio frequencies, and various code words were crammed into every card in the stack. Each aviator organized his particular set of kneeboard cards in the system of order he had developed during numerous practice strikes. In addition to the kneeboard cards designed specifically for our strike was a twenty-five-page package of generic codes, radio frequencies, and flight profiles for all Allied aircraft operating in the Kuwaiti Theater of Operations, the "KTO." Then, of course, we had all of the standard numbers required for a "normal" launch and recovery off the aircraft carrier. Effective organization was critical, and most pilots and B/Ns found a way to condense the absolutely essential information onto the top two cards, leaving the rest for reference once the Intruder was safely off target and feet wet.

I finished up work on the cards and headed for the alley.

It was 2130, and the day's flight schedule posted on the alley door had red ink on it. Not good. I read it and found out I was scheduled for an alert surface combat air patrol, or SUCAP, at 0200. That meant we would be circling the ship with live weapons ready to be called in for an attack on any vessels the battle group found threatening. With the limited warning available in the confines of the Persian Gulf, common sense dictated that we have our defensive assets airborne; the normal 15 minutes to launch an alert bomber might be too long. Brief time was at 0100. I ran back to the Intelligence Center to let Rivers know, then I headed to the rack to try to get 2 hours' sleep before we spent the rest of the night flying circles around *Ranger*.

We landed the next morning, 16 January, just before sunrise, a little disappointed that we did not get an airborne view of the inside of the gulf. The ship was humming when Rivers and I walked into the dirty shirt for breakfast at 0530. We sat down next to Bluto, who looked as tired as I felt.

"Well, smart guy, what's the word? Is it safe for me and Rivs to get some sleep?" I asked, hoping to pry some privileged information out of the intelligence officer.

"Seeing as how the two of you are both on the first strike, and seeing as how today is President Bush's Stateside deadline to Saddam, I think it an extraordinarily good idea that you catch up on your sleep immediately." I scanned his eyes for a hint of the direction the political situation was taking.

"Does that mean that Rivers and I might be flying in the wee hours of the morning?" Tell us just a bit more, Bluto.

"Let's just say that I do believe that our president is a man of his word." And with that, Bluto got up and left the wardroom.

"What do you think, Rivers?" I asked after Bluto left.

"I think that we're going to war."

My heart pounded. Would somebody just tell us what the hell is going down? I thought. The mood on the ship, Bluto's hints, and Bush's intractable position on a 15 January deadline Washington time for Saddam to withdraw his troops from Kuwait seemed to point to a singular conclusion. But with less than 24 hours until the commencement of hostilities, I began to doubt that they would let us wait until the absolute last minute before telling us it was a go. Or was it just the wishful-thinking side of me hoping temporarily for the known quantity of the boring 6-month cruise with no big surprises? Shit.

"You really think so? You think Bluto is bullshitting us?"

"No, I don't." Rivers squared his face with an unusually serious expression. "I think that this time tomorrow we're going to be at war."

Damn. It was tough discounting Rivers' opinion, especially when I looked at all that gray hair. This must be stage fright, last-minute jitters, hoping simultaneously that we would be afforded the opportunity to test our training and ability, and that the whole thing would just go away. Damn.

"I'm hitting the rack. I'm going to meet Stilts at 1000 to copy the kneeboard cards. What are you up to?"

Rivers answered with slow determination. "Heading up to CVIC. Let's meet later and go over the switchology for HARM to rockeyes. How about 1300?"

"Yeah, all right. We can go over the entire flight again while we're at it. Get some sleep sometime, will you?" Rivers was purposely sacrificing sleep to make absolutely certain he had planned his attack in the best manner possible. I didn't want him falling over just prior to bomb release.

"Don't worry. See you." He disappeared around the corner, and I headed down the ladder to my stateroom and hopefully a few hours of oblivion.

I woke up at 0900 and couldn't get back to sleep. This was going to be a long day. I went up to the Intelligence Center to take another look at the ship's position and the threats surrounding Umm Qasr. *Ranger* was now steaming a set of circles within a 20-square-mile area that had been allotted to her to avoid conflicting with *Midway* and her air wing. This was an extremely unusual situation for the carrier to be in. To the east was our old nemesis Iran, to the north was Iraq and occupied Kuwait, and to the south was the choke point of the Strait of Hormuz. Saudi Arabia, to the west, was the closest thing to a friendly area we had, and *Ranger* looked vulnerable depicted as it was on the chart, deprived of its normal open ocean to maneuver in. I moved over to the chart of Kuwait and southern Iraq.

Three small red rings and one large yellow one circled
Umm Qasr. Only one of the red SA-6s was a serious threat;
the other two were at the maximum missile range from our attack course. We would have to traverse the entire spectrum of
the yellow SA-2 coverage to reach the target. To the south of
Umm Qasr was Būbiyān Island, 25 miles of barren sand and
gun emplacements. To the east and southeast were Warba Island and the vast marshes that separated Iraq from Iran. Inhospitable, but habitable for a time, and certainly firm enough
for AAA sites. This did not look like much fun.

To the north, west, and southwest were markers indicating
Iraqi army divisions in Iraq and occupied Kuwait. They meant
AAA and very bad places to land if one had to eject. In fact,
the best place to punch out seemed to be over the marshes if
we could not make it feet wet. We might possibly avoid capture for a few days by mixing in with the snakes and mosqui-
toes. I came to the conclusion that getting shot down would
not be a great idea.

I went looking for Rivers and found him in the ready room,
which was unusually quiet. Everyone else was either flying or
in Intelligence Center planning. Rivers was sitting at the part
task missile trainer gazing at the screen's image of the A-6 armament panel.

"Practicing your button pushing?" I asked. "Looks like
good work for a monkey to me."

Nothing was as simple on paper as following a checklist
and flipping switches—that is, unless you were getting shot
at and trying to do five other things at the same time. One
switch out of position and the HARM would not fire or the
rockeyes would not drop. That's all right, I thought; there
were only thirteen steps to screw up.

"Watch it or this monkey's going to lose the pilot candy.
Let's go through this a couple of times."

Rivers touched each of the thirteen toggles depicted on the
screen that would be required to go from missiles to bombs.

He continued over and over again until he was virtually looking away as he reached for the buttons. The flattened images on the screen changed position with each of Rivers' correct motions. Finally, satisfied with the flow pattern he had developed, he looked up at me standing next to his shoulder.

"Okay, let's go over the whole thing one more time. Let's fly the mission from start to finish."

We talked our way through the entire strike as we envisioned it going successfully, but most of all we talked about the target. How we would find it, the offsets we would use, what altitude and airspeed I would need to fly to get the best aspect on radar. How the target should look on the black-and-white forward-looking infrared TV display, and what we would do if the boats were not there. Over and over again until we had raised and answered every question we could think of.

Rivers and I spent hours mentally preparing, attempting to turn thought into reflex, written tactics into action. The afternoon slipped by. I went up to the hangar deck to look out at the water, to see if any land was visible, but the massive hangar bay doors were shut tight to avoid interior damage if we were attacked by a missile. Welcome routine was restored when the wardroom opened for dinner, and we ate sparingly what a few of us must have considered might be our last meal. I went to my stateroom to sit down, get my thoughts together, and write what might possibly be "good-byes" in my journal. At 1930 I heard a knock on the door, and opened it to find Bluto with an uncommonly serious expression on his face.

"It's a go. The brief's at 0100, launch at 0400. Good luck." Overwhelming relief. No more BS, time to get to work.

"Thanks."

What else could I say? I realized that if I got in the rack now I might be able to sleep 4 hours before the brief. I pulled the covers over me tightly in what I was certain would be the last vestige of security I would feel for quite a while. It was all mental conditioning because I knew I needed sleep; it took me an hour and a half, but I finally drifted off into a semiconscious state of near-relaxation. From here on out worry and stress were counterproductive: focus and strength, focus and strength.

# Chapter Eleven

# The havoc of war

California, 16 January 1991

Laurie threw her head back in the parked Mustang rental, savoring the cool ocean breeze. The flight out to Los Angeles had been comfortable, even pleasant, and the second day of her business trip had been short. Time to relax.

She reached up to turn on the radio. The music wafted through the salt-tinged air, naturally mixing with the sounds of the skateboards and Rollerblades on the Manhattan Beach sidewalk. The music suddenly stopped.

"Bombs are dropping in Baghdad. Bombs are dropping in Baghdad. We are at war with Iraq. There will be American casualties, nobody knows how many. But there will be casualties. We are at war with Iraq."

Laurie went rigid in her seat; her mind guiltily snapped from a calm wandering to focus on her fiancé and brother in the Middle East. Her hands shook slightly as she reached for the car keys, started the Mustang, and pulled away from the curb.

She stopped at the first bar with a TV she came to, and walked in with cautious fear. The only noise in the happy hour crowded room came from the television. She ordered a drink and sat down, glued to the corner TV. Laurie, like millions of other Americans, watched the news quietly as events thousands of miles away in the Middle East began to unfold. How, she thought, could this be happening?

## On Board USS *Ranger* in the Persian Gulf: Operation Desert Storm

The previous 8 hours were a blurred whirlwind of images in my mind: the mission brief, our first strike into Iraq, the AAA, getting back aboard the ship. We had survived. I felt practically giddy with fatigue and residual adrenaline by the time Rivers and I debriefed the intelligence officers in CVIC and made our way to the ready room. In the familiar surroundings of the squadron emblems and ready room chairs I questioned whether we had actually dropped bombs in combat mere hours ago. The room, the people, the boat were all the same, but I was no longer certain I was.

It had been the closest I had ever come to losing my life. Within a few brief minutes my cavalier "can't hurt me" attitude had been shattered. The facade remained; the military bearing would stay intact. My actions would hold true to the course I decided I would follow when I joined the navy. But my mind was no longer a slave to the self-image I had created over the years, an image of calculated toughness, the sense of being bulletproof. My body would still act the role, but my mind had received a jolt.

This was not some sort of political or spiritual awakening, but rather the acknowledgment of the full brunt of an intense emotion. My father had taught me rationalization to a fault, and it made it possible for me to separate my emotions from my intellect, my thoughts from my actions. For the first time in my life I had been scared shitless.

The duty officer was standing at the greaseboard, writing furiously in red ink, changing the changes he had put up only moments before. Things really were the same, I concluded. We checked in our handguns and waited for the SDO to pause for a breath so we could crane our necks over his shoulder to see what our next most immediate field of concern would be.

We were scheduled for a 1230 brief for an airborne surface combat patrol. The weapons loadout consisted of two rock-eyes and two VT-fused 500-pound bombs, designed to airburst over a speeding vessel. With 2,000 pounds of total ordnance, it would not be a problem trapping aboard the ship with the bombs if we could not track down any missile patrol boats before the end of our scheduled airborne cycle. We were in the lead jet of the two Intruders, and I was assigned to brief the flight. I made a mental note to be down in the ready room at noon for some quick preparation for the brief.

Rivers and I headed up to the dirty shirt, where we were informed that chow hours had been extended to serve food as long as flight operations were under way. That told me the wardroom would be open for 24 hours from here on out. We didn't talk much, just ate our eggs and toast and thought a lot. It had become patently obvious that several of the Umm Qasr mission's targets had utilized their advantage of mobility to shoot at us as we overflew them at the initial point on the way to the pier. At least they had not scored any hits—how embarrassing, to be shot down by your own target. The frustration of not knowing exactly what we had hit was offset only by the fact that it had exploded. We finished breakfast and went to our respective staterooms to try to catch an hour or two of sleep before the 1230 brief.

It seemed as if I had just lowered my head to the pillow when the chirp! chirp! of the alarm on my watch shattered my oblivion. The ship was so noisy all of the time that each individual learned to subconsciously drown out certain sounds and focus on the important ones. I had just slept through 2 hours of gut-thunking catapult shots and spine-screeching arrestments as thick, coiled cable was paid out from battery, but all it took was the almost imperceptible squeak from my Casio G-shock to instantly bring me awake. In the shipboard routine that had become rote, I rolled out of my middle rack without pause and began moving to the sink as my mind slowly caught up with my body. I splashed water on my face and rested my hands heavily on the porcelain sink, trying to rewind my thoughts to the present and concentrate on the most pressing matter before me.

I pulled the single dog tag around my neck back from its migration over my shoulder to the center of my chest, grabbed my flight suit off the hook where I had hung it, and picked up my flight boots. The socks draped over the ankle-high leather were still wet with the previous night's sweat, and in a rare moment of self-charity I decided to treat myself to a fresh pair. Dry, warm socks were a surprisingly effective way of giving yourself a shot of energy in the illusion that you were clean, dry, and well rested. I got my boots on and headed to the ready room.

Rivers was already at the front of the high-backed chairs, writing information down on a kneeboard card and referencing a tactical weapons manual.

"Did you sleep, Rivs? It's only 1205."

"Yeah, I got about an hour's rest. I wanted to make sure we had the ACU settings all squared away for the VT Mark 82s. How about you?" The armament control unit settings were different for each type of ordnance.

"Two hours; I guess that means you get to sleep in the jet." At least he had the radar boot to rest his head. Yeah, right. "What's the story with the SUCAP? Do they have any specific tasking for us before launch?" I asked.

"No," Rivers replied, "they're supposed to vector us out of a holding pattern over the northern gulf if any surface combatants are identified. Other than that, we just drill circles and check out contacts after the E-2 identifies them." Rivers rolled his shoulders in a resigned shrug.

"Have you cycled through CVIC? Is that what they're putting out?" I anticipated that Rivers, as usual, had been doing my job for me and had asked all the pertinent briefing questions before I had even arrived in the ready room.

"Yep, that's all they're saying. I think it's a max flex drill at this point, nobody really knows what to expect, so they want to make certain there are bombers airborne all the time to take care of any stray boats." No need for me to go up to the intel spaces.

Time was flying. We briefed, geared up, and headed to the flight deck. I could tell that something was not right the moment we stepped out onto the catwalk into the bright sunshine. Our assigned jet was directly in front of us, but its bomb racks were empty, and there were no ordies to be seen. I hailed the plane captain, the sailor in charge of servicing our jet.

"Where's our bombs?" I yelled into the salt-tinged wind that swept over the flight deck.

"Sorry, sir, the airframers are trying to fix a hydraulic leak. Flight deck's not going to let us load it until it's an up jet," the 20-year-old sailor yelled back into where my ear should be beneath my helmet. At least the decision-making process was easy—the XO was in the spare A-6, so kicking him out and taking his jet was not an option. Nothing to do but wait and hope they fixed it.

Forty-five minutes later, Rivers and I were burning the last vestiges of caffeine out of our systems as we watched the XO launch in our place. Occasionally, manning the spare could be a good deal. I trudged after Rivers, following the heels I had grown to know so well, along the catwalk, through the hatch, and down three ladders. Rivs did not wait to take off his flight gear but headed directly for the coffeepot, and then to the SDO desk to see if there was a hole we could fill in the flight schedule. Dutifully I paced after him, only to find out that we were, once again, all dressed up with no place to go. We went to the pararigger shop and got out of our damp gear for the second time that morning.

There was only one other place to be besides the ready room in such interesting times as these, and that was in the Intelligence Center, gathering as much information as possible

on what was transpiring in Kuwait and Iraq, and planning for
our next strike. The long schoolroom tables were covered
with charts, and every seat was taken either by aviators getting debriefed by the intel officers or by aircrew plotting out
threats to avoid on future strikes. I looked at Rivers.

"You want to hang around a few minutes, listen in on
what's up?"

"Sure; let's get a feel for the rest of the theater and then go
do some work on our HARM shots for the XO's strike,"
Rivers answered and struck out for the noisiest corner of the
room to spend some time absorbing information.

The initial word filtering through the ship was that so far
one Marine F/A-18 and one British Tornado attack jet had
been shot down in the fighting. Not too bad, I thought, given
the strength of the enemy defenses, if those were the only actual losses to date.[1]

We were quickly satisfied that we had all the information
forthcoming, and Rivers and I moved down to the ready room
to set up shop in our chairs and begin to plan the HARM
shots for the XO's strike scheduled to launch early the next
morning. I looked at my watch: 1736, almost exactly 12 hours
since we had released our rockeyes at Umm Qasr. About 7
hours until the XO's group brief. I detected the beginning of a
routine.

Our role in the morning strike would entail standing off
from the target at high altitude and firing four HARM missiles
spaced approximately a minute and a half apart. Each HARM
would target one of the four SA-8 or SA-2 SAM sites that
encircled a Silkworm antishipping missile emplacement. It
was not a particularly hazardous mission for us, but it did require a good deal of coordination to ensure that we launched
each of our HARMs at exactly the correct time, from a pre-

1. The actual Allied air losses on 17 January were an A-6 and an F/A-18 from
the carrier *Saratoga,* a Kuwaiti A-4, a French Jaguar, two British Tornadoes,
and one Italian Tornado.

cise geographic location, targeting a specific SAM. If we screwed up our timeline we would potentially be leaving the Intruder bombers hanging out to dry, high above most of the AAA but vulnerable to the SAMs.

Rivers and I first made certain that our maneuvering plan was valid to get from one "shot" point to the next. Then we headed over to the part task trainer to work the switchology drill again and again. During the minute and a half between HARM shots I would be pulling the A-6 around in a 4-G turn to get us to the exact position, at the correct time, for the follow-on launches. Rivers would need to cycle his target steering in the navigation computer, reprogram the missile computer, and change the ACU settings while we were in this constant 4-G turn. If he screwed it up the shot would be late, and a window of vulnerability might be opened for the SAM batteries. We practiced until Rivers could move the various switches with his eyes closed and he was satisfied that I could back him up on each step he took. We called it quits after a while and headed up to the dirty shirt for chow and then a feeble attempt at a catnap.

Snax walked into the stateroom at 2300, and it was good to hear that our skipper's dusk strike had gone well and that all of Air Wing 2's aircraft had returned safely. The Silkworm missiles they had attacked were on Al Faw Peninsula, not very far from Umm Qasr, and within the same SA-2 threat envelope we had targeted with a HARM in the early-morning hours. Snax's thin frame exuded the electricity of the strike. The SA-2 had not illuminated any of the attackers; it was beginning to look like we actually may have shut it down with a hard kill.

Rivers and I took a back-row seat during the strike briefing, giving up the closer chairs to the bomber crews who would be flying with the XO into the thick of things. The XO's stern expression conveyed the gravity of the decision he had made regarding the general tactics of his attack. There were three SA-8 sites and one SA-2 site protecting his aim point, and by flying his bombers in high he was optimizing the SAM's targeting solution. Of course, he had known this all along, but it must have continued to nag him with a touch of doubt—all of the bombers on the first strike had flown in low and survived, but from the debriefs it must have been clear to him just how great a threat the AAA was. He attacked the challenge with tenacity, his compact frame shifting back and forth in emphasis at the front of the ready room.

Tony was slated to fly one of the bombers, and after the briefing concluded I grabbed his elbow to wish him luck. He mumbled thanks, clearly intent on maintaining his focus on the job at hand, but equally clear in his unease with his first combat mission. I wished him luck again, and thought of his two small boys back home at Whidbey. We struck out for the pararigger shop to get geared up for the mission.

The HARM shooters were at the front of the pack to launch; ours would not be a fuel-intensive mission, loitering high and out over the water, away from the danger as long as the Iraqi fighters did not come out to meet us. The skies were clear between the sporadic clouds, and we were afforded an unobstructed view of the coast of Kuwait and the most southeastern tip of Iraq.

Suddenly the tranquillity of the distant horizon was disrupted by the sheer enormity of instant destruction. Beneath one of the cloud layers an entire section of the landscape illuminated in lightninglike fury. At first glance it appeared to be one massive explosion, but on closer inspection I could see that there were dozens of large detonations. B-52s carpet bombing an area target, I thought, an airfield or troop emplacements, each bomber dropping countless 500-pound weapons. The scope of the single strike so many miles in the distance was impressive in its magnitude. Enough sight-seeing; the XO's strike package was nearing the coast.

The bombers ingressed at 15,000 feet and then began a 20-degree dive to reach their release point with max knots at about 8,000 feet, still above the bulk of the AAA. I pulled our

Intruder around in the dark sky, steadying up only long enough to center steering, squeeze the commit trigger on the control stick, and hear and feel the release of another HARM streaking in a brilliant flash toward its target. There was no time to look at the coastline during our maneuvering, but once our last HARM was away I set up a steady orbit so Rivers and I could better monitor the strike's progress. From our vantage point it appeared that there was only a modest amount of AAA in the air, but missiles were flying everywhere. There had been some question regarding the effectiveness of the SA-8 missile system, and either due to their own failings, the Prowler's jamming, or the multitude of HARMs that rained down on them that night, none of them intercepted an Intruder. But it sure wasn't from lack of trying. From 25 miles away we could see missile after missile get airborne, but with the bomber's lights extinguished we had no way of knowing whether or not they were tracking an Intruder. When the final A-6 called feet wet, Rivers and I let out a sigh of relief—three *Ranger* missions down, and so far some close calls but no losses.

It was after 0600 when we entered the dawn Case 2 pattern back at the ship. The carrier landing had once been the focus of stress and achievement during a hop; it was now rapidly turning into merely the final hurdle of an action-filled sortie. I used to begin thinking about a flight's landing in subtle preparation from the moment the flight briefing began. Now the trap was completely pushed from my mind until the last moments of the flight, those 10 to 15 minutes when our final reserves of concentration and alertness needed to be rallied to get our Intruder safely on board. I suppose that all that training had paid off; carrier landings needed to be second nature now, there were too many other aspects of the mission that required our undivided attention.

During the next 12 hours we were treated to the frustrating monotony of manning jets on three separate occasions and having each of them go down for mechanical problems. The missions were not particularly significant, but by the early evening of 18 January 1991, I realized that in the past 36 hours I had been briefed, gotten geared up, and made the trek to the flight deck six times, only to launch twice. Fortunately for the squadron, these three mechanical incidents were the only grounded jets from the Swordsmen during the first two days of the war. But unfortunately for Rivers and me, we happened to be in each of the mechanically flawed aircraft. It was of little real consequence, we had flown on the strikes that were important, and Rivers had bartered our way into most of the added-on sorties anyway. But it was frustrating to put in the extra effort and then not get airborne. Besides, it was tiring.

Spending the entire day cycling back and forth between the ready room and the flight deck gave me an opportunity to catch up on some of the news of the conflict as reported by CNN, and to pen a quick note to Laurie:

*18 Jan 91*

*Baby,*
    *Not much time to write—obviously we're pretty busy. We are in the Gulf flying combat sorties around the clock. So far I've flown two and I'm getting ready for my third. I was in our 1st strike (the carrier's) across the beach (was it only one and a half days ago?) and it was "interesting" to say the least.*
    *I'm doing great and I'm confident all will go well. Please give my family a call and tell them I'm all right. I know Tom's squadron lost a jet last week but I don't know who was flying in it. I hope and pray it wasn't Tom. If you haven't heard anything by now then it definitely wasn't.*
    *Gotta go, don't worry—child's play,*
        *Love,*
        *Pete*

Apparently Scud missiles were being launched into Israel and Dhahran, Saudi Arabia. The inherent inaccuracy of the Scuds was reassuring from the tactical perspective, but strategically I wondered if they would escalate the conflict further, in the worst case baiting Israel into an offensive action against the Iraqis, which could dissolve the Arab coalition in a heartbeat. I also wondered if there were chemical warheads on the Scuds, and if this would be a precursor to what we could expect in a long and ugly biochemical warfare scenario.

Rumors spread briefly of an Israeli counterattack, with as many as fifty-six aircraft inbound to Iraq. Immediately I thought of my parents in Syria; it was probably too late to get out now, but if the Israelis bombed Iraq, who could tell what rifts and cracks might be introduced into the incredible patchwork of an alliance that President Bush had put together. What role was my uncle at the United Nations playing now that the action had begun? Had there been time to contact my parents? A sense of profound dread settled in my gut. I could only hope my folks had left the country before hostilities began. I pushed them from my mind and got back to concentrating on the small role I had in this war.

Evidently the Israeli jets were recalled, or it had all been BS. Regardless, for the time being, the Israelis were acting the role of the docile martyr, the only role they could play in the hope of keeping a united front against Saddam Hussein's military machine.

I was taking my perpetually wet flight gear off for the last time that night when Snax entered the pararigger shop, just back from a flight. I hung up my helmet and walked by him on the way out the door.

"How'd it go?" I asked. I wasn't even sure what mission he had been on.

"Pretty good; we put some kind of armed patrol boat dead in the water. Damn idiots shot at us first!"

"What happened? What did you guys drop on them?" I pressed.

"We were on a SUCAP going by this guy, just checking him out to see what he was, and we see tracers starting to come up! We probably would have left the dumb son of a bitch alone, but he starts shooting at us!" Snax went on. "So the skipper pulls off high, and we set up for a roll-in with a VT 82."

"Did you get 'im?" I asked.

"All that we could tell was that he was maneuvering around pretty good when we first saw him, and after the run he's just sitting there, dead in the water. So we climb again to set up to drop our rockeye on him, we're going down the chute, master arm's on, and the skipper sees that they're putting lifeboats over the side. Skipper decided not to drop. I guess lifeboats are pretty much the same thing as surrendering." Snax finished with a sharp chop of his hand, obviously still a little pumped up by the action.

"Was this up by Al Faw?" I questioned him.

"Yeah, same spot where most of these guys have been moving in and out. I think they're hiding out under the oil platforms, maybe acting as early warning or something," Snax replied.

"That makes sense. The other morning the bastards were shooting before the first striker crossed the beach. If they've got guys out there in the oil rigs, that would be a helluva heads-up for the gunners ashore; just wait until they hear or see jets fly overhead and radio back to land." One less minor mystery for me to ponder. "I assume the skipper knows about the possible early-warning thing?" I continued.

"Yeah, he's going to mention it to CAG. From the sounds of it the coastal oil rigs are fair game as targets as it is." Snax hung the last of his gear on his metal hook and caught up with me as I opened the door and we headed back to the ready room.

I opened the ready room door and held it briefly until Snax got his hand up to catch it. Immediately I knew something was wrong.

The dark mood poured out of the ready room door like a dull, ominous fog. It was unusually quiet, CNN was off, and the sound was turned down all the way on the plat camera. The duty officer had a couple of pilots and B/Ns cluttered around the desk, and they were all speaking in hushed voices. I inched my way up, sensing enough of the mood to know to keep my mouth shut for just a moment. Five seconds of standing at the perimeter and not figuring it out was enough for me.

"Hey, Roscoe," I directed to the SDO in a soft voice, "what's going on?"

"They just called in the BDA from the last strike; it looks like one of the Jakals didn't call feet wet." The mission had been to mine the waterway at the mouth of the estuary to Umm Qasr. They had gone in low to more accurately place their mines along the channel.

"Do they know what happened?" I asked, knowing instantly, of course, that nobody had a clue. On a low-level mission at night you flew solo, purposefully below radar coverage. Radio transmissions were the only indication that the E-2 would have of the return of a bomber from the target to the relative safety of over water. The omission of the "feet wet" report was very bad news.

"No; TC and Tuna are the crew. They are definitely missing," Roscoe said sternly.

TC and Tuna. I didn't know either one well; I knew that TC was single; Tuna was married. I thought back to our last night on the beach in San Diego before the ship pulled out. Tuna, Snax, and I had gone into Coronado to eat Italian. Tuna was a likable B/N with a boyish face and a bushy mustache. That dinner in San Diego was the most I had ever spoken to him. Nice guy. Damn, why couldn't I remember how many kids he had? I looked at the SDO for a moment longer, but there was nothing else to say. I got a cup of coffee and waited.

Thirty minutes later, everyone on *Ranger* had all the information we would get that night regarding Jakal 404. There were solid clouds over the target area, even at the low altitude where the strikers were ingressing. The drop zone was not quite all the way up to Umm Qasr, but the AAA was frighteningly thick. It seemed self-evident to me—what the aircrew could not see they could not avoid. They flew smack into the ideal scenario for effective barrage AAA—a low-altitude ingress in the clouds with no reference as to where the threat was or how to avoid it.

Initial word around the ship was that one of the crew had been able to make a transmission on his PRC-90 survival radio, presumably after a high-speed ejection. The rumor continued that the downed crew member had identified himself by his Jakal call sign, and placed his position as north of Būbiyān Island. In the clouds, at night, with this tenuous communications link, a reasonable attempt at a combat search-and-rescue mission did not seem likely. I held out hope that whoever had made the transmission could evade enemy capture, at least until the following day, when there was a more realistic possibility of authenticating the survivor and launching a rescue mission. Hopefully he could work his way to the inhospitable marshes to the east, and then south to the coastline. Hopefully there really was a survivor, and it was not simply an Iraqi trick to get a helicopter close enough to shoot it down.

There was a rough copy of the next day's flight schedule on the bulletin board, and I slouched over to look at it. First thing in the morning I was leading a section of two A-6s on a surface combat patrol. If any real-time information came into the Intelligence Center regarding patrol boat positions, we would be the ones to launch and attack them. I straightened my shoulders and took some satisfaction that at first light I would be able to take some action, to chart a course other than the racetrack I had been circling between the flight deck and the ready room. I saw Bluto across the green-backed chairs and decided to bend his ear a bit, to find out what he might know about Jakal 404, and whether he had any insight as to where the elusive missile patrol boats had last been imaged. He could add no information to either question, but he did have more bad news from the war effort in general—the carrier *Saratoga* had lost a low-level A-6 as well. I let my frustration and pain evolve into anger, a far more effective emotion for the days ahead. I went up to my stateroom and got the first string of more than 2 hours of sleep in 2 days.[2]

Refreshed and with a newfound clearheadedness, I grabbed some quick chow and headed down to the ready room to prepare for the SUCAP. I took a few extra minutes to familiarize myself with the terrain of where Iraq met the sea, and looked up from the wall chart in the ready room in an attempt to visualize what the marshland would look like in the light of day. The ancient swamps were an apparent anomaly adjacent to the vast desert, a land where the only commodities in abundance were "sunshine, water, and mud."[3]

The fringes of the marshland had been inhabited for thousands of years by an Arab culture that had learned long ago how to survive, and even thrive, in the harsh environment of the perpetually flooded delta. It was only in quite recent history, with the advent of the Iraq-Iran war, that their lifestyle had been seriously invaded by the outside world. The location of the marsh, adjacent to the international border of the Shatt al Arab waterway, had altered the path its people would take forever, placing them in the midst of a war between the Iraqis and the Iranians and turning their backyard into a battlefield.

The cessation of hostilities between Iraq and Iran in 1988 had not appreciably improved the stability of the region. Rebels to the Iraqi regime had discovered the delta as a last refuge from the oppressive crackdowns of Saddam Hussein and his minions, and the eventual victim of the ongoing battle would be the sanctuary of the marsh itself. The brackish waters were destined to be drained by the Iraqi government in an attempt

2. One A-6, one Tornado, one F-15, and an OV-10 were shot down on 18 January, bringing the total to eleven Allied combat losses by the end of the second night of the war.
3. H.W.F. Saggs, *Babylonia and Assyria*.

to remove the last vestiges of cover the rebels possessed, but this radical tactic would not come to pass for several years.

I wondered how much of the topography had changed over the centuries, since the rise of the ancient Sumer culture on the edges of just such a southern marsh more than 7,000 years ago. The floods of the swollen Euphrates and Tigris rivers combined with subtle shifts in the tectonic plates from the nearby Zagreb mountain range to produce a terrain that had continuously changed over the aeons. The ancient sites of one of the world's first civilizations were now scattered in the desert and quite possibly underwater.

The land of Mesopotamia, from the Greek "land between the rivers," had been a crossroads of trade and peoples of varying ethnicity and cultures for thousands of years. And a land of continual war and conquest—from earliest times the Babylonians, Assyrians, Medes, and Chaldeans vied for supremacy in the fertile alluvial planes of the Tigris and the Euphrates. Much later, and in some of the first documented histories, the Persians utilized the land to launch attacks on the Greeks, and eventually Alexander the Great conquered the region under the banner of Macedonia.

The position of the marshes had changed over the past several thousand years, but the timeless strife that surrounded their fringes went on. It was humbling to place modern man into his tiny niche in historical perspective when considering the impact, quite literally, that our bombs were having on the ancient countryside. As one of our intel officers would later coin in a catchy phrase, we were "Bombin' Babylonia." The cavalier callousness of the phrase captured perfectly the scope, and lack of scope, of what we were doing: the historical inevitability of man to act like man, and to maintain the hubris over the centuries to believe that he was doing anything more than merely that. I walked up to the flight deck to man our jet.

\* \* \*

The 502 strained against her holdback fitting while our Intruder's engines screamed at full power. The flight instruments vibrated in their frustration to defy nature and fly. I took one last look around the flight deck, absorbing the features that had been hidden on my previous Persian Gulf sorties by the darkness. I let fly a salute, hunched my shoulders, and planted my head firmly into the ejection seat headrest.

My vision tunneled briefly as the cat stroke pressured the blood to my feet. The familiar rat-tat-tat of the accelerating nose gear shuttle reverberated in my ears and culminated in a distinct, airframe-shaking thunk with the slam of the shuttle in its stops 20 feet shy of the deck edge. Less than a second later we were airborne in a clearing turn to the right, enveloped in the relative silence of the aftermath of the violent slingshot into the air.

I craned my neck over to the left to see our wingman, who had launched off cat 2, and saw that he was about 100 yards behind us. I could barely make out Tony's helmet glued to our jet as he closed in on the rendezvous. His B/N, the air wing's deputy air wing commander, was head-down in the radar boot, not a very smart place to be, I thought, only 500 feet above the water after a cat shot. The deputy, a dark-haired man of medium height, always seemed to have his flight suit waist straps stretched just beyond where they should be. He had previously been the CO of VA-155, and he had made the transition to working full-time for CAG at a certain expense to his expertise as a B/N. His position made it difficult for him to allot time for flight planning, and he had a reputation for relying on the junior officers to get him up to speed on the mission of the day.

Rivers was patiently waiting until our climb at 7 miles in front of the ship before he began to transmit on the radio. He didn't wait a second longer than he had to.

"Sun King, Rustler 502, flight of two Intruders up for your control, SUCAP."

"Rustler 502, King, your vector 310 for 75 miles. Top off from air force tanker at angels 15 and report back up," the E-2 answered while they flew at their top speed from *Ranger* to the combat air patrol (CAP) station at the far northern end of the gulf. I figured we could tank and still get to the CAP station at about the same time as the E-2 if we hustled.

"Something must be going on if they want us to top off this early," Rivers muttered under his breath. "We're only going to be able to squeeze in a couple thousand pounds."

I made a hitchhiking signal with my thumb over my shoulder, putting Tony and the deputy into cruise formation, and pulled 502 into a 300-knot climb. I did my best to avoid the clouds—they seemed to be at virtually every altitude—and finally managed to find a path through the big puffies at 15,000 feet. We didn't know what kind of air force tanker we were going to, but it had to be a big one with lots of gas, which meant that there was sure to be a flock of fighter guys surrounding it, begging for a few extra thousand pounds. Without benefit of air-to-air radar, we needed to stay visual to ensure that we didn't run into any other jets on our way to the tanker's orbit.

I maneuvered aggressively, trying to stay clear of the clouds, and it took two more vectors and a touch of G before we popped out into a hole and saw the tanker. It was a KC-135, with its steel-rimmed probe-buster. What the hell, why make any of this easy? I saw that Tony was holding on tight, and I stood our Intruder up on its wing to get to the inside of the KC-135's turn without losing sight of him in the clouds. We punched through a thin line of stratus just as we were getting on the tanker's bearing line. When we regained sight of the big four-engine gas passer it became immediately apparent that we were much too fast. Such were the hazards of doing a zip lip rendezvous: no radio calls, no traffic advisories, and no idea at what speed the giant KC-135 was flying.

I cracked our speed brakes out for a second to give Tony a heads-up, and then held back on the throttle button until they were fully extended. Tony got the picture, and his speed brakes opened in a streamlined clamshell at his wingtips in perfect synch with ours. I kept the throttles just off the idle stops to give Tony some room to play with on the power, but even so, I could see he was having difficulty staying behind us on our Intruder's bearing line. Judging from our closure rate with the tanker I didn't think I could afford to bump up the power any more. I was just about to knock it off, go under the KC-135, and try again, when I saw Tony's jet turn into an abnormal, slightly cocked angle and slowly move backward into position. Excellent, I thought. He had cross-controlled the flaperons and the rudder in a slip. The increased drag killed enough of his A-6's energy to slow it down and put him back into position. I turned my attention back forward to the looming tanker and the pair of Hornets that were currently vying for her basket.

We waited patiently for about 10 minutes, matching the KC-135's erratic, cloud-avoiding flight path while the Hornets filled up, and then cleared out to the right side of the air force tanker. As soon as they had vacated the patch of sky behind the 135 we broke away from Tony and worked our way to a position about 10 feet directly behind the heavy metal basket. I hesitated for a moment while the Intruder stabilized, and then added power and took a stab at getting into the steel-rimmed target. I made a last-second play with a rapid wing dip and entered the refueling zone, the point where the 135's hose made a 90-degree loop as our A-6's probe pushed the basket in far enough to make a seal. Too close and we might impact the long metal boom that hung down from the tanker to secure the hose in place; too far and the tanker would not be able to transfer fuel. We went in and out of the clouds, and I struggled to stay in position, asking Rivers frequently how much gas we had left to go. Finally Rivs assured me that we were full, and I backed out as straight as I could so the 50-pound metal hoop did not tug on the Intruder's refueling probe at an angle and prang it off.

I cleared out to the right side of the 135 and waited for Tony to take his turn at the fun. I lost sight momentarily in the clouds, but apparently Tony got into the basket on his first attempt as well. He took his gas, flew out beneath us, and picked up a parade formation position on our right-hand side. Glad that this administrative exercise was over, I broke away slowly but deliberately, and descended down through a hole in the clouds to guarantee that we did not inadvertently run back into the 135. Rivers punched up steering to the CAP station and hailed the E-2 again on the air wing's strike common frequency.

The E-2 answered immediately: "Rustler 502 and flight, go secure."

Rivers turned the Intruder's radio encrypting gear on, and the familiar background hum came over the headset. "King, Rustler 502's up secure, awaiting your control."

"Rustler 502, King, your mission is CSAR [combat search and rescue]. We have a radio hit on downed Jakal crewmen on the Al Faw Peninsula. Your vector 345 to join overhead CSAR helo, call sign Speargun."

My heart raced. Somebody might have survived last night's crash, and we had a chance to get him. I turned the jet toward the combat search and rescue helicopter.

"Rustler 502 copies all King, steering 345 to join overhead Speargun. Keep the vectors coming," Rivers answered.

"Will do, Rustler, Speargun currently your 347 at 20, cherubs 5," Sun King continued.

I glanced over to the mirror on Rivers' canopy bow, made sure Tony was still flying nice and tight, and started a descent through the clouds so we would be able to see the search and rescue helicopter flying at "cherubs 5," 500 feet above the water. We broke out of the clouds at 5,000 feet and promptly flew right into a thick haze, reducing visibility to about 2 miles. Well, this was going to be interesting.

"Rustler 502, Speargun is at your 350 at 11 miles," droned the Hawkeye.

Rivers did not bother to answer, but instead began to update his radar on the shoreline. "Okay, Pete, I think I see him on the radar, looks like a good vector." Our jet's downward angle allowed the ground mapping radar to pick up the low-flying helo.

"Roger that, I can't see shit out here. I'm going to level at 1,000 feet and fly right at him."

I put Tony and the deputy back into cruise formation so they could more easily adjust to the turns and gyrations it might take to find Speargun. We were only about 15 miles off the coast of Iraq, and low—not a good place to be flying a predictable pattern. I bumped the throttles up until we had 350 knots on the jet, the cornering speed at which we could effect the tightest turn. We also happened to be making lots of noise to alert the gunners waiting for us on the beach. Oh, well, what could you do?

"Sounds good; I don't see any boats on the radar," answered Rivers.

I caught sight of the small helicopter when we were almost on top of him, wrapped our jet up in a 4-G turn to the left to stay away from the coastline, and fought to keep one eye glued on Speargun.

"Rustler 502 and flight, orbit where you are; we're waiting for two F-14s to come on station. Plan on providing cover for Speargun feet dry," Sun King explained, as if it were that simple.

"Not exactly like Fallon, huh, Rivs?" I asked sarcastically. I could almost see Rivers roll his eyes under his dark visor.

"Not exactly" was all Rivers said.

During air wing training at Fallon, Nevada, we did practice CSAR, but only after an extensive brief on tactics; specific areas of responsibility; and, of course, the route to and from the probable location of the survivors. To say that we would be winging it would be an understatement—we were tasked with providing cover for a helicopter with our load of four bombs, not knowing where he would be flying or what the threat would be. There were certainly AAA sites feet dry, but what about surface-to-air missiles or boats or fighters? It wasn't the Hawkeye's fault; if they received a radio transmission from a downed aircrew there was no time to put a rescue package together by the book. By then it probably would be too late. Still, I wondered if we were not about to make matters worse.

"All right, sounds to me like the Tomcats are going to clear a path with their gun. I'm going to brief Tony to stay opposite circle from us and be ready to roll in on any threat that pops up. Sound good?" Rivers briefed me with as much knowledge as we had.

The A-6 did not have a cannon, and with no forward-firing ordnance such as rockets on board, we would need to rely on the F-14s and their 20mm guns to eliminate any troops with small arms attempting to shoot the helo down along its route of flight. It was 1300, the sun was high in the sky, and although vertical visibility was not bad, we could barely see through the haze directly in front of us. We would be highlighted perfectly to the ground gunners, and we would have a hell of a time seeing them.

"Sounds great," I said, with only a modicum of sarcasm.

Rivers broadcast the plan over the secure frequency to Tony and the deputy, and I watched their jet fall back to the opposite side of our orbit overhead the helicopter. Evidently they didn't have any better ideas.

The Tomcats reported on station, and I frantically searched the sky to try to locate them. They must have been several miles ahead of the helicopter, because suddenly the E-2 broadcast "Comex, comex"—time to "commence the exercise."

Speargun stopped his orbit and began heading for the coastline. I tightened up our overhead circle and started after him. Meanwhile, Rivers had set up the armament for our weapons load out, and had all of the switches minus the master arm flipped for a single drop of a 500-pound bomb.

We could make only four runs, even releasing a lone bomb per pass. Whoever we were looking for had better be close to the water; we didn't have the ordnance to provide the helo cover for very long.

I could barely make out the coastline of Būbiyān Island through the thick haze as it passed off to our left on our way to Al Faw. We couldn't have been more than a mile away from land, within the range of small arms, and much too close to transit before we were ready to coast in to the survivor's pickup point, wherever that might be. There were definitely guns inland of the beach; I wondered if they were shooting at us now, and we couldn't discern the tracers in the low visibility. A second later the question was answered.

"Abort, abort! Heavy AAA at the coast in. Tomcats are aborting."

Shit, I couldn't even see them. My G suit inflated as I tightened our circle over Speargun in an attempt to keep our two Intruders as far away from the beach as possible, while still providing some cover to the helo. This was going well.

"Can you see the helo?" I asked Rivers, and leveled the wings for a second to get pointed out farther into the gulf.

"Yeah, I got him, he's turning around; start your turn back in."

"Okay, I got him." I keyed the radio. "Tony, bring it in to tac wing."

Our wingman cut to the inside of our circle and flew a loose formation on our jet, freeing his eyes to look out for threats, and giving himself room to maneuver if he came under fire. I kept the G on our A-6, hoping we were making a lousy target, while I followed the helicopter's progress out over the gulf below us.

Ten minutes later Speargun was safely offshore, we were climbing to a fuel-conserving altitude, and we were all left wondering what the hell had happened. Had a survivor actually been authenticated via radio call sign, and if so, did we have a good geographic cut on where he was? Without a clear picture of the survivor's location, it was suicide to wander low over the open skies of Iraq looking for him and dueling with every AAA site along the gulf.

Back in the CVIC debrief the intel guys were not much help in filling in the blanks. It seemed that no one could say with certainty whether or not a survivor had been authenticated as legitimate, yet we had been prepared to risk five aircraft on a rescue mission to a phantom man on the ground. I was more curious than angry. What on earth had initiated the rescue? What actually happened would remain a mystery, and that was the last we heard of any radio calls from a downed crewman from Jakal 404. Shitty break.[4]

The shipboard routine quickly assimilated the role of combat operations into her daily schedule, and what had seemed a once-in-a-lifetime event only 3 days ago was now commonplace. It was still easy to maintain an edge, the feeling of being on step and in the groove during the critical portions of a strike. But the events before and after feet dry were becoming stale and dangerously predictable. Dangerous because each circumstance was anything but predictable.

The weather was a constant problem in the early days of the conflict, presenting difficulties in accurate targeting, and making a valid assessment of battle damage virtually impossible. *Ranger* sent out another strike to Umm Qasr on 19 January, but this time high above the AAA, trusting that the SAM threat had been sufficiently beaten down by this third day of the war. This lesson had been learned in the blood of all the aircrews who had been shot down and killed theaterwide in the low-level attacks of the first few days of the conflict.[5]

Some air wings had gone high from the beginning, accu-

4. The mystery of our impromptu CSAR was never revealed to us. The bodies of the Jakal crew would be recovered at the crash site after the war.
5. At least nine of the twelve Allied air losses in the first three days of the war were shot down in the low-altitude regime.

rately assessing the SAM threat as secondary to that of the AAA. But even the ones that had not were now adopting policies of minimum-altitude floors to stay above the bulk of the gunfire. The combination of exposure to SAMs while flying high and inclement weather had introduced another factor to consider—it was virtually impossible to break lock on a missile that was guiding if you could not visually acquire it and perform a last-ditch, high-G break maneuver. The danger of flying low in the AAA environment, particularly in the clouds, had been proven beyond dispute. Now it was up to the individual air wing commanders to refresh the lessons of Vietnam and not expose a vulnerability to SAMs by flying high in the clouds.

After the aborted "rescue" attempt, Rivers and I were itching for a more traditional strike, one with a clear target and criteria for success or failure. The flight we were slated for on the following night fit the bill—a high-altitude night attack into the city of Basra to bomb petroleum, oil, and lubricant (POL) tanks, and a communications facility. The strike consisted of six Intruder bombers, six Tomcats, two Prowlers, and two A-6 HARM shooters. We were in the fifth bomber, and the tactic was a simple stream raid, with each Intruder separated by a 30-second interval.

The change in tactics to high-altitude attacks after the loss of Jakal 404 the night before had caught the attention of the air wing commander. The overall lead on the Basra strike was a lieutenant commander from VA-155, but CAG decided to put his deputy in one of the Intruders to call for a weather abort if he determined it was not safe to continue. CAG had deferred to the expertise that his deputy, a B/N, possessed in the attack mission, and had made him the de facto overall mission commander for the flight. It was an unfortunate decision, as it turned out, because it was becoming the norm with the deputy's involvement in the planning process that he was ill prepared and playing catch-up from the beginning. When we finished with the planning at 2330 on the nineteenth, we were confident that between jamming and HARM shots we could make it through the three SA-2 threat envelopes and stay high enough above the AAA to get to the target and back without any losses.

We launched at 1700 on the twentieth for an 1815 time-on-target, just 35 minutes after nautical twilight, but dark enough to provide a sanctuary from the very limited AAA that could reach our run-in altitude of 25,000 feet. The plan was to "push" over the nose of the Intruders about 7 miles from the target to achieve a 20-degree dive until 15,000 feet, where we would each drop six 1,000-pound bombs. A thousand feet of altitude and 30 seconds staggered our run-ins between each bomber. The off-target maneuver was critical to avoid running into another Intruder after weapons release.

This was more like it, I thought, as the horizon darkened and clouds filled the air above and below us. We were in a clear span of sky, had plenty of visibility, and had all the players airborne and en route to the target. AAA shot up through the clouds, tracers and erratic projectile air bursts like in an old World War II movie, but most of it was well below us, and none of it appeared to be guided by radar. By the time we reached 25 miles from the target we had visually acquired four distinct SAM launches, but none of them required evasive action—the Prowlers and HARMs were doing their job. We were smack in the optimum range of all three SA-2s, and they seemed to be incapable of locking onto us. The SAM acquisition radar was painting us, but the silence from our radar warning gear's missile guidance alert was a testament to the effectiveness of the Prowler's jamming.

The Jakal lead should have been commencing his target run about 14 miles ahead of us when the beautiful radio silence was shattered:

"Iron flight, abort, abort! This is Deputy, abort!"

Rivers and I looked at each other in stunned silence for a hesitating moment. "What the hell is that about? We're at the damn target!" I looked down at the distance window by my knee—19 miles, of which four were due to our altitude. I couldn't contain my frustration and anger.

"Shit! It's an abort, let's get out of here!" Rivers was not about to disobey a direct order, and neither was I. The difference was that I had no problem complaining about it.

The thickness of the clouds had increased, and in the darkness the case could definitely be made that the weather had deteriorated below the 5,000 feet of clear sky that CAG had mandated. But we were practically in our final run to the target, and now we were going to attempt to turn six bombers around without any detailed plan to keep them from running into each other? While we were in the exact center of the threat we were trying to avoid, making us vulnerable now to both missiles and a midair collision? What was the deputy thinking? I had no other answer but to assume that he was playing catch-up with the strike plan, and was attempting to avoid the risk of having a jet shot down while the weather was below the literal interpretation of CAG's rules. But the deputy was a B/N; he had to be capable of the flexibility to realize that it was more dangerous to turn around now than to continue to the target and egress, as we had all been briefed.

The five trail bombers turned around blindly, each hoping that the others would maintain their altitude, extremely unlikely if more missiles were fired, and hoping that we would all turn simultaneously so the staggered Intruders, 1, 3, and 5 and 2, 4, and 6, who were at the same altitude, would not collide. Fortunately the lead Jakal, who had been in his target run, had the common sense to have a "selective" radio failure and continue his profile to bomb release. He destroyed the communications facility; these were the only bombs dropped on the original target that night.

The rest of us struggled to maintain separation from each other, making a mockery of radio silence and discipline, and were instructed to unload our weapons on the Mina al Bakr oil platform at the top of the gulf. Overall, a fairly intensive strike to ensure that there was no roof over the heads of the patrol boats that might wish to hide under the oil platform. It was meaningless to expose the strike to the Iraqi missile systems in Basra, only to turn around when we had completed the difficult part of the ingress, and all that remained was to drop our bombs and return to the fleet. The only saving grace in the entire evolution was Jakal lead, and their "radio failure." Far from being chastised for it, CAG recognized it for what it was—common sense—and accorded the crew of the Jakal lead with the kudos of a successful individual mission.

The trip down the ladders to the ready room was an exercise in head-shaking dismay. The Basra strike went straight to the crux of the problem with mission planning: There were many pieces to the puzzle of a strike, and if any of those pieces were missing, the mission would be certain to fail. Even if everyone was well prepared, made rational decisions, and performed flawlessly, there still remained numerous elements that were completely out of the control of the attackers.

For the past few days the weather had been the dominant stumbling block in Air Wing 2's efforts; pinpointing a target was difficult utilizing the radar only, but it was a very workable problem if the Intruders dropped their bombs from low altitude. Once the bombers were restricted to the high-altitude regime, however, the use of radar and unguided weapons became much more problematic. Winds varied tremendously in both direction and amplitude at different altitudes; on the ground, winds might be as slight as 5 knots, while at 15,000 feet they might be coming from the opposite direction at 100 knots. Unguided bombs flew a ballistic profile, one that was at the mercy of the winds throughout the fall of the weapon.

The A-6 computer and inertial navigation system could incorporate a correction to compensate for the winds at the bomb's point of release, but after that, any shift in the winds would steadily blow the bombs off target throughout their long fall to the ground. If the winds died to nothing 1,000 feet below an Intruder's release altitude of 15,000 feet, the computed correction to the bomb's release point would overcompensate for the remaining time of bomb fall. The time of fall in the dives we were conducting was about 35 seconds, long enough for strong winds to put the bombs quite possibly thousands of feet off target.

The weather in the Persian Gulf had not cooperated at all since our arrival. On our first strike, low fog had obscured the target area, making it exceedingly difficult to locate mobile targets, which could be gone in 10 minutes. After the first day the weather got worse, multiple cloud layers filled the skies, and the winds became strong and inconsistent. The slim chance of hitting the target with "dumb" bombs in a strong wind at high altitude could only be compensated for by dropping many of them. This was the only option—the cloud cover was too thick to utilize laser-guided weapons, and the risk of flying low had been deemed unacceptable. The best we could hope for were area-type targets that would be ignited into secondary explosions and fires if any portion of them was hit.

The POL facilities at Basra had been just such a target. Lead was aiming for the communications building, but that left five Intruders and a total of thirty 1,000-pound bombs to impact one of the large water-tank–like structures filled with oil and gas. The fact that the Basra strike had been such a perfect target for the deteriorated weather conditions heightened my sense of frustration. Why the hell should we bother taking the risk and doing the work if we were not allowed to drop?

My temper had settled down to a controlled simmer by the time I got to the pararigger shop to take off my gear, but the burner got turned up again as I slipped out of my torso harness with my eyes glued to the TV. Pictures of badly battered prisoners of war making halting statements to the Iraqi cameras revived my anger that we had not gotten a decent shot in tonight. The bruised faces and painfully slow construction of words by the POWs raised more questions than they answered. At first glance it would appear that the Iraqis had beaten the crap out of them.

It was clearly evident that the POWs were under extreme duress, and this alone made the substance of their statements suspect to say the least. No one was going to believe that these airmen had experienced a sudden catharsis of political understanding and were now on the side of Saddam Hussein and the Iraqi "people." No matter how the bruises had been inflicted, my heart and soul went out to the POWs; they were in the last place on earth that any navy pilot wanted to be, and that included a smoking hole in the ground. I wished them luck under my breath.

The rest of the news was not very welcome, either—more Allied aircraft had been shot down, bringing the total U.S losses to eleven, and Scud missiles were falling on Riyadh.[6] I was not scheduled for the morning, so I went to my stateroom to change and then headed to the heat and the noise of the hangar bay to work off my anger in sweat on the exercise bike.

The carrier *Roosevelt* had arrived in the gulf on 19 January, adding a third battle group to the cramped waters directly east of Bahrain. From the perspective of an ignorant aviator, the coordination between *Midway* and *Ranger* had seemed to be going fairly smoothly. The ships were staying in their designated portions of the gulf, and the planes were landing on the correct carrier, at least for the most part. Stories always abounded of errant aviators landing on the wrong ship whenever several carriers were steaming in close proximity to one another, but it was difficult to tell how much truth there was to the tales. Theoretically it would not be a terribly impossible mistake to make in daylight, visual conditions when the radios were purposely silent, but the omission of the huge painted numbers of designation on the carrier's deck from a pilot's scan was still pretty hard to explain. So far so good with our threesome, at least from what I could gather from the rumor mill.

6. Actual Allied air losses by the end of 20 January were eighteen.

I was not scheduled for a flight the following morning, and I took the opportunity to write a letter:

*20 Jan 91*

*Dear Laurie,*

*You must be worried sick. All I can say is relax, this is something I have to do and everything will be all right. I've been fine so far and am in full swing with what's going on. It's amazing how quickly you can adapt to new situations. I've launched on 4 strikes so far and have done well on them all. They are definitely getting less risky as time goes on. You've probably heard from the CO's wife that the Ranger lost an A-6. It was VA-155. We don't know what happened to the crew, we'll have to wait and see. I still haven't heard anything about the jet from Tom's squadron— please write and tell me what happened and to who. It's so hectic here I will probably never find out.*

*We have a satellite dish and get CNN. The real time news is incredible. We are walking to strikes and we can watch reporters talking from potential targets on TV. I don't know how long this is going to last, but it should be getting better. I'm doing fine and I'm happy with how I've performed under pressure.*

*We haven't gotten mail in a week, and I don't know if it's getting out or not. You are going to have to be patient and have faith. Remember—I'm perfect and nothing can happen to me. Believe me, just kidding.*

*Keep in touch with my family and share news. I think about you all the time.*

*I love you, see you soon,*
*Pete*

I decided to head for the ready room, and was drinking coffee and catching up on paperwork when Rivers and I got tagged for a last-minute tanker that had been added to the flight schedule. We flew under the morning sun to the very northern reaches of the Persian Gulf to provide fuel for the airborne fighter combat air patrol, and from our orbit up high we were afforded a comprehensive view of the gulf waters. I was surprised at the amount of oil that had permeated the gulf; from about 29 degrees and 20 minutes latitude north it was one constant oil slick. *Exxon Valdez* was definitely off the hook, I thought.

It was refreshing to bag a day hop, to be able to see some of the horizon, and the coastline we had been bombing. The situation reverted to the normal inky darkness that evening when Rivers and I launched on a night surface combat air patrol. We had gotten a late start when the ordies fell behind in their loading of the bombs for the night missions. It looked like it was going to be "one of those nights" when the yellow shirt taxied our Intruder, finally loaded and ready to go, into the cat track, accidentally blowing a tire on our A-6. The squadron troubleshooters saved the day—or night, as it was— and had us up and going again with a new tire in less than 15 minutes. The extra half an hour on the deck was whisked out of our minds with the force of the catapult as we shot into the night sky.

It was fairly clear that we could expect to be out on station for a while when we got the signal to join with the air force KC-10 tanker while en route to the north. The KC-10 was a converted DC-10 airliner, and it held a lot more gas than the older KC-135s. It had a nice, long hose with a soft basket to plug into; overall easier, safer, and a far more enjoyable tanking experience than the risk of snapping the Intruder's refueling probe off on the rigid steel rim of a KC-135. We got our gas without delay and were soon heading back north to await tasking from the surface combat patrol controller.

We didn't wait very long. We had not yet arrived on station when the off-going A-6 SUCAP announced he had dropped his bombload on several small vessels hiding under the oil platforms at the Nowrouz oil complex 30 miles from the coast of Iran. We got a vector, I rolled our Intruder over on its side in a turn to the right, and we listened to the details. The clouds were low, down to at least 1,000 feet above the water. An unknown number of small, fast boats were zipping in and out of the cover of the oil platform, very likely laying mines in a defensive barrier to a possible future amphibious assault by the coalition forces. Rivers rolled out his radar and started looking for the movers while I dropped our jet down to 2,000 feet to optimize our radar-only attack.

Rivers found several contacts out in the open, we got clearance to drop on them from the E-2 Hawkeye, and we made our first two runs, releasing a single 500-pound VT-fused bomb apiece. I pushed our jet's nose over and put us into a slight dive. Rivers refined his radar picture using the A-6's automatic moving target indicator mode to predict where the bomb would hit along the boat's speeding course line. We were both heads down throughout the target runs, flying completely on our instruments during the attack. I thought about small-arms fire but realized that these were probably all vessels under 50 feet long, and they would have a hell of a time lining up a deck gun with the boat bouncing in its race to escape.

We turned back around after our second run and saw that both blips on the radarscope were gone—probable but not certain indications that they had sunk with their loads of mines. We had two rockeyes remaining, and it didn't take long to find one last contact, larger and fast, speeding away at 30 knots. We released our rocks, and I slammed the Intruder into a 4-G turn off target to avoid any metal they were putting into the air. Next time around the pattern the radar blip was still there, but he had slowed down to about 5 knots. We were out of ordnance, so we passed what information we had to the E-2, who confirmed later that our initial two targets had indeed disappeared from his radar as well. We turned back toward *Ranger*, never having seen our targets, but fairly confident that we had sunk two and perhaps disabled one. This was the closest thing to positive confirmation that Rivers and I would receive of a kill during those first few days of the war, conditions as confused as they were by the inclement weather and high-altitude attacks.

For the next several days the air wing pressed the attack—the SUCAPs continued around the clock, nightly strikes went into Umm Qasr and Basra from high altitude, and the Iraqis gradually became more reluctant to turn on their missile-tracking radars with the constant threat of inbound HARMs. The ship and the air wing were in a groove; the launches and recoveries went flawlessly, and the jets were staying "up," thriving mechanically on the fast pace of flying that kept all their hoses and joints lubricated with their lifeblood of fuel, oil, and hydraulics.

Scud launches increased into Israel, but she kept her cool and didn't respond with the counterattack that Saddam was hoping for. On 22 January the first oil fields were ignited in fires that would eventually engulf much of Kuwait in a thick, black mantle of smoke. This frustrated response by Saddam's forces was designed to either evoke international outrage or, more likely, to provide cover for Iraqi troops on the ground.

Rivers and I were manning up our jet on one busy evening when the monotonous drone of the yellow gear was interrupted by the flight deck's 1MC:

"This is the captain: Clear the flight deck right now—missile's inbound!"

Then another urgent voice reverberated throughout the ship: "General quarters, general quarters, all hands man your battle stations!"

The general quarters Klaxon erupted, and the mass of workers on the flight deck streamed into all available exits for cover down below the carrier's steel deck plates. Enlisted troops ushered the flight crews in through the open hatches ahead of themselves, recognizing that there was a limited number of aviators on board, and thereby putting themselves at risk to ensure the safety of the carrier's war fighting commodities. This was the first real threat to *Ranger* herself, and as we assembled in our various general quarters stations in flash hoods and gloves, our gas masks strapped to our hips, the war became a lot more real for the sailors. This was more tangible than merely launching jets with bombs, only to see them return with empty racks and exhausted but hyper aviators.

The radar that had scanned *Ranger* turned out not to be from an Iraqi Exocet missile, like the one that had almost sunk the USS *Stark* several years earlier, but was from a similar radar frequency of a French F-1 flying out over the water back to its airfield. It was a healthy reminder that our floating air base was still vulnerable, and reassuring that we managed to clear the flight deck of more than a hundred men in under 3 minutes.

Iraqi aircraft began to flee their own country for the possible safety of Iran, their archnemesis only a few years earlier. On 27 January twenty to thirty Iraqi jets risked the skies and headed for the Iranian border, most making it there to sit out the war with their lives and aircraft intact, but under the firm control of the Iranians.

The *William Tell* Overture played three to four times a day with the launching of each major air wing strike. The aviators complained how sick they were of hearing it, but I doubted that there was a single one who did not get a chill up his spine with each repetitious rendition. Strikes went out, the bombs were dropped, the missiles shot, and some did not return.

The weather frustrated our understanding of the impact we were having. Battle damage assessment was virtually nil; a radar blip that disappeared, a radar site that stopped transmitting, an occasional satellite pass that caught a glimpse through the clouds of a target destroyed.

The results of our efforts were too nebulous, uncertain; we could not tell what was working and what was not. Our losses were decreasing, but we all knew that the sanctuary of high altitude would not exist forever. Once the ground war began, it would only be fair that we get back down in the thick of things to ensure that our bombs were on target while our troops were at risk. The more of the Iraqi defenses that we could destroy before then would be translated directly into the number of our soldiers on the ground who would live. The clouds and high winds hampered our effectiveness, our learning curve, and even our morale.

On 28 January the weather cleared.

# Chapter Twelve

# . . . thro' the perilous fight . . .

29 January–6 February 1991, the Persian Gulf

I peered around Rivers' shoulder at the picture of the Iraqi Osa 2 guided missile patrol boat that Bluto had given us to review. The Styx antiship missiles stood out like four giant ribbed condoms, two amidships and two aft, but despite their comic appearance the danger that the 126-foot vessel presented was very real. Each of the ship-blasting missiles had a range of 25 nautical miles. The Osa 2 was capable of a 500-nautical-mile range at its top speed of 36 knots, and there were no ships in the Persian Gulf that did not fall under its theoretical threat. The fact that the Osa was quick, and could stretch its range up to 750 nautical miles when slowed to 25 knots, alleviated its need for frequent refueling and made it elusive to our battle group's forces; that, and the lack of timely intelligence due to the overcast skies.

But the weather was CAVU (clear and visibility unrestricted) now, and all the vessels in Iraq's navy were coming to light, running out of places to hide, and unable to prosecute coalition shipping because of the constant threat to themselves. It was 2230, and our "armed surface reconnaissance," as SUCAP was now called, had been canceled to free two A-6s to target an Osa 2 that had just been imaged at the port of Ash Shu'aybah, 20 miles south of Kuwait City. We had 30 minutes to come up with a plan to coordinate the 280-mile ingress to the target, get each of our Intruders into position to drop our load of two 1,000-pound laser-guided bombs, and then return to the fleet.

A Prowler would accompany us and provide jamming for the SA-2 that guarded the coast, and we would be on our own to avoid the AAA from the port emplacements and the four sets of twin 30mm guns on the Osa. There had been reports of radar-guided AAA in the area, but we were confident that we would be in and on our way out before our bombs impacted and the Iraqi defenses became fully alerted.

The Jakal CO and Stilts were leading the ministrike from the other A-6, and once the B/Ns let us know from which direction they wanted to attack, Stilts and I got to work on a navigation route and a set of simple tactics. Rivers and Jakal 1 did their targeting thing, measuring offsets and looking for prominent geographic fixes with which to update their radars. By midnight we were in tension on catapult 1, relaxed in our ejection seats, able to see the dim night horizon for the first time in days, and eager to take advantage of the break in the weather and the fortuitous timing of the intelligence. The clear night sky created the illusion of daylight compared to the hazy cloud cover of the past week.

I fought the urge to do a clearing turn off the cat, flew straight ahead, and started our climb before we began the now well-worn habit of running through our preliminary combat checklist. I flipped the TACAN to the air-to-air mode and saw in the DME window that the Jakal CO was 5 miles ahead of us. Perfect: We had more than 45 minutes of flying time to whittle that down to 2 miles, barely 15 seconds between our jets. The Jakals would fly in 2,000 feet below our altitude to guarantee separation between our two Intruders. We would work a general timing problem to be at the target within a window of deconfliction with other Allied strikes, but we would rely primarily on the TACAN to maintain our 2 miles of separation. With only two bombers we could afford the luxury of sacrificing an exact time on target, and instead fly off of the

TACAN. If the TACAN did not work, then we would suck it up into a night formation position before we neared the coast and had to extinguish our lights. All four bombs would be guided to the target almost simultaneously, reducing the problems of smoke and debris masking the laser signals and making the bombs go stupid.

We flew up the gulf past As Shu'aybah, well to the east of it, to circle back around and attack from the northeast. The pier ran north to south, and this would give us a run down the length of the Osa, optimizing our chances of hitting it if the laser reflection guided the 1,000-pound bombs a little too long or too short. At 35 miles from the target I reefed on a level 4-G turn at our altitude of 20,000 feet and pulled the nose around to the attack heading of 235 degrees.

We rolled out of the turn, and I flipped the external lights master off with my left thumb. I checked that the tailhook was up, while Rivers turned off our transponder, put the video system to record, and turned the ALQ-126B onboard jammer to stand by. Somewhere offshore to the south of us, the Prowler pilot was aligning his jet with the SA-2 site while the two electronic countermeasures officers in the backseat did their damndest to make certain that all the SAM radar operator could see was a screen full of snow and static. I pushed the throttles to the firewall and felt the Intruder accelerate.

The lights along the coast were distinct and well defined, and the contrast of the night's clear sky with the gloom of the past week was distracting; it was as if we were flying in a completely different part of the world.

"Flir's coming out, steering's good to the target." Rivers had his head in the radar boot, and I felt the Intruder's nose yaw slightly to the side as the forward-looking infrared ball turret swiveled out of the stowed position.

"Roger, showing 23 miles to the target. How's the picture?"

"Excellent," Rivers replied. "I can make out the port from here; steering's right on where the Osa should be."

The TACAN clicked down to a mile and a half, and I

strained my eyes outside, looking for the dark form of the Jakal A-6. No way that I was going to see him with his lights off, and we were getting too close.

"Rivs, got to lose some distance from Jakal. Hold on." I looked over my shoulder and tightened my grip on the stick.

I pulled the jet 60 degrees to the left, and then immediately back slightly to the right of the target steering on my ADI. I held that course for a second until the TACAN clicked back to 2. There was no point in burning off airspeed, not when we were about to enter the SA-2 envelope. It was better to keep our knots up and create spacing between the Jakal and us with a few quick turns. I looked at our heading: 234 degrees, close enough for government work. Steering was right on.

"Nineteen miles, the whole city's lit up." I could see Kuwait City to our right—absolutely no attempt at a blackout.

"Okay, I'm starting to break out the pier on radar," Rivers replied.

I followed steering and kept a sharp lookout for any advance notice that we were coming. Evidently there was none.

"Jakal's at 2 miles, 12 miles to the target," I reported.

"All right. I'm starting to break out the pier on the flir, ACUs set, master arm to go," Rivers rattled off.

"Roger, master arms coming on," I said, fighting the urge to make a smart-ass crack about his unintentional "pier-flir" rhyme. I flipped the guarded toggle switch to the up position, "nine miles, no AAA yet." The radar early-warning gear was quiet, and there were no tracers to be seen from the approaching coastline.

"Program's coming on." Rivers reached down with his right hand and started the chaff program. Each bundle of chaff dispensed out our tail was accompanied by the now familiar click-click in my headset.

"I've got the pier, there it is, I'm on the boat, handing off." Steering moved imperceptibly as Rivers depressed the upper button on his slew stick, refined his steering, and handed off to the flir.

"Seven miles; I'm pushing over." I pushed the Intruder's nose down until I saw 20 degrees of pitch on the ADI. The TACAN DME was creeping under 2 miles, but I disregarded it. The Jakal should be in his dive over 2,000 feet below and ahead of us, and I needed to concentrate on the target and steering. We must really be a surprise, I thought—not a single tracer.

"Six is up, six is up," our guardian Prowler transmitted over the radio.

Shit. I glanced down at our radar warning gear: nothing but a blank screen. The Prowler's ultrasensitive receivers were evidently picking up indications of an SA-6 scanning the skies.

"Nothing on the warning gear, Rivs, 6 miles, I've got a hammer, committing." I squeezed the commit trigger on the control stick and held the wings level dead center on steering. With the commit trigger depressed, the computer was now free to release our weapons once it determined the exact point in time to do so.

The bomb release hammer took forever to begin its march down the ADI, but then it quickly accelerated and shot off the bottom of my screen. I raised the right wing and started a 20-degree angle-of-bank turn so we would not fly through the nadir of the flir. The nadir was the point where the rotating gimbals on the flir/laser's turret exceeded their range of motion and would freeze, causing the laser spot to come off the Osa.

"Keep it coming, c'mon," Rivers coaxed the bombs to guide down the laser spot to the target, "a little more, there! Go, get out of here!"

The instant the bombs exploded, the sky lit up around us, nothing dense, but the thin sparkle of random tracers. I felt the weight of G on the stick and kept in the angle of bank that was taking us out over the gulf. The altimeter bottomed out at 12,700 feet, and I kept the back pressure on the stick until our jet had climbed to 14,000 feet. The Jakal had even altitudes on egress, we had odd, that would give us each at least 1,000 feet of vertical to maneuver in if we needed to. Suddenly a rapid "Beep, beep" from our radar warning gear grabbed my attention.

"Shit, missiles!" I looked over my left shoulder and saw in the distance the distinctive orange glow of an SA-2.

I stuffed the Intruder's nose downward. Screw the altitudes, I thought, and the A-6 accelerated with the negative-G force. I started pumping out chaff with my left hand in quick bursts of two, or at least I hoped that's what I was doing. The program had eaten up a lot of chaff on the way in; I didn't know how much we had left.

"Okay, I've got three launches; shit, it's gotta be just about max range, Pete." Rivers craned his head over his right shoulder.

I wasn't going to take any chances. Satisfied with our airspeed, I cranked in a 4-G turn to the right, and then another back to the left. The warning gear was showing an acquisition radar but didn't indicate that any of the SAMs were tracking us. I put our tail to the target and opened the distance from the coastline. I listened acutely for the danger sign of a high-pitched warble over my headset, our indication that a missile was guiding to us; the warning gear was silent.

Two minutes later and well outside any SAM envelopes, I turned the Intruder back around toward the target for a look from 14,000 feet. We had to be nearly 30 miles away, but the fire in the port was still clearly visible.

"How'd we do, Rivs?" I asked, fairly confident with the answer.

"We nailed it. First one must not have guided, I saw it fly by long, but the second one hit it smack in the center. I think Jakal's hit the stern or the pier slightly to the left."

One thing was for certain: Concrete docks don't burn like the picture I was seeing out the side of the canopy now as I turned us back toward *Ranger*. We would find out later in the intelligence debrief that the Osa was still burning strong when the Prowler left his station 45 minutes after our time on target.

Knowing that we had accomplished our mission for the night changed the atmosphere going back to the ship dramatically—no more second-guessing, no more repeated runs on targets that might already have been destroyed but lacked the evidence to support that premise. The weather had cleared, the cover was gone, and now we would see how long the Iraqis could hold up under a devastating bombing campaign.

Even the trap back aboard ship was less difficult without the envelope of the clouds to distort the senses and confuse the eyes. We hurried to debrief and get out of our flight gear before pizza shut down in the dirty shirt. Sitting in the warmth of the brightly lit room at 0245 was a surreal experience—it had taken 13 days of bombing, but finally we were able to absolutely confirm our battle damage via VTR and our own eyes. There really was an enemy down there, not simply mystery radar returns through the clouds—and we were hitting that enemy.

The momentum had picked up considerably in the air wing. In the improved meteorological conditions, Snax and the skipper had that same night taken out a Silkworm antiship missile site, and four of four targets were destroyed in a strike to Basra; for a change the Intruders had the tangible battle damage assessments to prove their success. The combination of clear weather, crews more seasoned to the combat environment, and increased flexibility to meet late-breaking intelligence information was paying off big time. The Iraqi navy realized that their brief respite under the cover of the overcast had ended and that they were rapidly running out of places to hide.

The clouds had not departed the Kuwaiti Theater of Operations totally, however. The following night Rivers and I made our bombing runs into Umm Qasr on radar through the overcast, and once again we wondered with no absolute certainty where our 4,000 pounds of high explosives had landed. But only 30 miles to the south, out over the northern gulf, the night sky was clear, and it provided our forces the opportunity we needed to decimate the Iraqi navy as they attempted to steam for the relative security of Iranian waters.

The Iraqi navy was finding life too perilous in the confines of port with our around-the-clock strikes, and was rapidly losing the last vestiges of cover afforded them by the inclement weather and the oil platforms of the northern gulf. In a nautical version of their comrades in the Iraqi air force, the navy had decided that there was a better possibility of recovering their forces from the shores of Iran than from the silt at the bottom of the Persian Gulf. On the evening of 29 January, four Iraqi patrol boats decided to make a run for it before they were destroyed. Under what cover they could only hope for from the smoke of the oil fires, they extinguished their lights and steamed from their hiding spot somewhere between Al Faw and Būbiyān for Iranian waters.

Kato and the XO had just finished unloading their bombs in a strike to a Silkworm site on Al Faw Peninsula, and had headed to the south to look for suspicious surface contacts. The plan was increasingly to keep some of the A-6s that were engaged in less distant strikes, like those to Al Faw and Būbiyān, on station in the northern gulf to provide greater around-the-clock armed surface reconnaissance (ASR) coverage. To achieve this, Kato and the XO had been loaded with ordnance designated for the Silkworm site, and two additional 500-pound laser-guided bombs (LGBs) to utilize in attacks on Iraqi surface combatants.

The XO had worked his radar magic and found the four darkened shapes on the glassy waters almost immediately as they steamed in formation for the coast of Iran. The targets were quickly confirmed by the E-2 as hostiles, and the Rustlers set up for their second attack of the night. The XO targeted the lead vessel, hoping to create as much confusion as possible for the other three, and Kato pushed over into a shallow dive until within range. The first LGB scored a direct hit, and the three remaining Iraqi boats scattered to present a more difficult target. The XO chose another mark, Kato set up for another run, and the second patrol boat was stopped in flames dead in the water.

Out of ordnance and running perilously low on gas, but with two boats still pressing on for Iran, the XO looked to the Hawkeye for assistance. A Jakal A-6 was vectored to the vicinity of the sea battle, but soon it was learned that the Intruder's laser was not working and he could not guide his LGB. No problem: The XO quickly coordinated a plan of action over the radio, and while the vessels continued their race toward the safety of Iranian waters at more than 30 knots, the Jakal rolled in on one of the two remaining boats and dropped his laser-guided bomb, utilizing his radar for targeting. Confident that the bomb was in the "basket," that combination of altitude and distance from a target where an LGB had enough energy that it could physically be guided to the target, Kato flew close in trail, and the XO illuminated the chosen patrol boat with his laser.

Seconds later, only one of the four Iraqi boats was still under way. In an hour, Kato and the XO had prosecuted a successful attack against an Iraqi Silkworm missile site, had sunk two vessels themselves, and had been instrumental in the destruction of a third.

On board *Ranger* that evening the enthusiasm could be felt in the passageways; the days of frustration and doubt fell away. We were rapidly accomplishing *Ranger*'s initial task of destroying the Iraqi navy and its accompanying threat to the sea lines of communications and coalition shipping. In addition, *Ranger* had been actively prosecuting targets outside her area of responsibility as surface warfare commander—communications sites and fuel dumps in Basra, airfields, and bridges.

On the same night that Rivers and I bombed through the overcast at Umm Qasr, the CO and Snax executed a strike that opened up our arena of involvement farther yet. Leading

a massive night formation of twelve Intruders, they engaged
in the air wing's first bombing of the elite Iraqi Republican
Guards and their tanks and artillery. The concept of A-6s en-
gaging in B-52-style carpet bombing would soon fall to the
wayside, but the air wing would actively seek out Iraqi armor
and troop concentrations in smaller formations for the duration of Desert Storm.

But the Iraqi navy, while in disarray and floundering, was
not yet defeated. The action in the days to immediately follow
would free up more attack aircraft to destroy the Iraqi army,
and produce a credible threat of a Marine Corps amphibious
invasion that would divert thousands of Iraqi troops from the
Saudi border, where the real offensive would begin.[1]

I stretched my legs in the reclined Naugahyde of the ready
room chair, maneuvered my coffee cup around the bulge in
my SV-2 made by my knife and anti–nerve gas shot kit, and
took a sip of the lukewarm coffee. As we had been virtually
every morning since the conflict began, Rivers and I were up
after a few hours of sleep and camped out in our flight gear,
this time standing one of two alert 15 armed surface recces
for the air wing.

It was 1000, there was no shortage of empty ready room
chairs after the previous night's strikes, and I had my helmet,
nav bag, and oxygen mask spread around me in comfortable
disarray. I was wearing the remainder of my flight gear,
barely dry from our hop that had trapped at 0400, but I felt
curiously refreshed. We had just come off the flight deck to
preflight our Intruder and get the inertial navigation system's
alignment under way, and the fresh air had been invigorating.
The sun was shining, the breeze was relatively cool, and it
had been quiet as the air wing rested between cycles. The
small touch of nature had a calming influence of physical re-

1. It was estimated that six to ten divisions of the Iraqi army were eventually
diverted to the defense of the Kuwaiti coast from an amphibious assault.

newal, and it stayed with us on our trek back down into the gray steel belowdecks of *Ranger*.

We had a 4-hour alert, and with no indication of whether we would be called away on a mission, we had settled into our chairs to alternate our time between napping and doing paperwork. First, paperwork. I looked over at the only ready room chair within reach that was not covered in flight paraphernalia and worked up the courage to tackle the stack of folders, paper-clipped memos, and enlisted evaluations that reached 6 inches high. One more cup of coffee and I dragged my tired mind to the task.

By the time I reviewed, corrected, signed, and passed on or diverted each individually packaged headache, my stomach told me it was noon, no easy feat sitting beneath 60 feet of steel passageways and out of sight of the sun overhead. I grabbed my helmet, mask, and nav bag and went to the front of the ready room to break Rivers from his hypnotic navy-speak-induced trance.

"Dirty shirt?" I was too tired to say more.

Rivers looked up as if he had no idea who I was, what I had said, or why anyone would speak at all. Ever. He waited exactly 2 seconds, lowered his eyes back down to his armchair desk, and said, "Sure."

Evidently the effects of the sun had worn off completely. He struggled to his feet, with a Herculean effort moved his foot-tall stack of papers to the drawer beneath his seat, and shuffled after me, picking up steam all the way to the door. We took the escalator to the O-3 level and nourishment.

Nobody paid a second glance to the two of us in our full flight gear—everyone was long past caring. Alerts were normal on any cruise, and it seemed that each of the air wing's squadrons was standing one sort of alert or another, 24 hours a day. For each actual flight we would launch on, we briefed, got suited up, and manned our jets once or twice for either a spare or an alert. Although it was unlikely that we would launch, we needed to be prepared physically in our flight gear, and mentally ready for the possible mission.

Rivs and I didn't talk a great deal over lunch; we quickly ate our sandwiches of mystery meat, washed them down with bug juice from the dispenser cooler in the corner, and went back down below. Two more hours, and then we could count on either an hour or two of sleep, or a continuation of the paperwork shuffle without the threat of having to race to the flight deck to interfere with our concentration. But first, one more cup of coffee.

I must have closed my eyes, because when I awoke my mug was empty, there was drool on my name tag, and my watch said 1320. How come I don't feel rested? I wondered. I staggered out the door to the head down the hall and splashed some water on my face before returning to the ready room to review the SDO board for any possible changes to the schedule. No changes. I sat back down.

The ship was still in a lull in flight operations, and the quiet was pervasive. The only people in the ready room had to be there, which basically meant the SDO, Rivers, and me. All other visitors made a quick circuit by their mailbox, and cleared it out to bring to the deep shelter of their stateroom, out of the way of the line-of-sight tasking of a more senior officer. This was *Ranger*'s equivalent of the graveyard shift—we had been flying all night, every night, for the past several weeks, and our body clocks had adjusted, if you could call it that, almost exactly 12 hours out from what most would consider normal. I closed my eyes again.

"Now launch the alert 15 armed surface recce! Now launch the alert 15 armed surface recce!"

The volume of the 1MC ripped through the ship, shattering the serenity that the inactivity of the morning had cultivated. My body reacted and I grabbed my helmet, oxygen mask, and nav bag in one hand, knocked over my coffee cup, and raced for the door before the loudspeaker's message had fully registered in my mind. I could feel Rivers at my heels.

I bounced my survival vest off the open door, careened my head into the doorjamb, and put a small gash in my forehead before I regained my balance and bolted down the passageway toward the escalator. I pumped my legs over the knee knockers, slamming my flight boots down onto the steel deck and giving warning to the sailors in the way: "Make a hole!"

Those who had been in the passage between our ready room and the escalator flattened themselves against the nearest bulkhead, officer and enlisted alike, and gave us and our bulky flight gear as much room as possible to race down the corridor. Over one last knee knocker, and I pivoted to the left and punched the button to start the escalator in its upward travel. Three sailors had been walking down the dormant escalator and frantically jumped over the handrail to the 3-foot sheet metal housing on either side of the moving steps. I took the stairs two at a time and barely kept ahead of Rivers, whom I could hear starting to breathe heavily behind me. For a few brief moments we were two of the most important people on board *Ranger*.

About two-thirds into our upward travel I abruptly stopped, turned around to face Rivers in case he was heads down and still churning his legs, and let the escalator move us for a few seconds while I got my helmet and oxygen mask secured. I could feel my skullcap absorb the blood from the cut in my forehead, and I attempted to divert the trickle away from my eye with a twist of my head. Rivers finished putting his helmet on a fraction of a second before I did and looked on with aggravated impatience as I snapped the helmet strap around my chin and turned back to our run. We nearly knocked over two lackadaisical 19-year-olds at the top, brusquely pushed them aside, and took the remaining two knee knockers at a gallop.

I slammed the hatch open to the catwalk on the port bow and shot through it, leaving Rivers momentarily in the dust as he turned to secure it behind him. I didn't waste time getting to the set of steps only 20 feet away but placed my hands on the flight deck and vaulted the 3 feet up to the shiny steel plating of cat 2. Keeping my head low, I ran in a crouch under an A-6, took a quick glance in either direction for speeding yellow gear, and opened my stride to a full run to our Intruder, sitting on "L" 1 in front of the island.

I reached my boarding ladder on the far side of the jet just as Rivers stopped in front of his. He grabbed a piece of paper with the ship's present position on it from one of the squadron avionics technicians and scampered up his ladder. While I was strapping myself in I could hear the yellow huffer turn up to a high-pitched whine as starting air was hooked up to the underside of our Intruder. My eyes scanned the cockpit rapidly to ensure that all was as I had left it 3½ hours earlier, looked over at Rivers, and got a head nod while he inputted our position into the computer. I flashed my left fore and middle fingers at the plane captain in the turn-up signal.

One at a time the Intruder's engines came to life in a deafening roar. I gave Rivers the thumbs-up to close the canopy, and we armed our ejection seats and watched the stored heading alignment count its way down to being ready. The 30-year-old inertial navigation system chugged along, slowly sorting out its set of gyros and getting a picture of what was level. Ordinarily the alignment would take 15 minutes to complete. The stored heading mode was supposed to speed that up, but by how much was never a sure thing. We sat still and waited.

My eyes were pried from the instrument panel by a flurry of activity in front of the jet. I looked up and saw that the yellow shirt was waving his hands frantically in the breakdown signal, anxious to get us on our way taxiing to the catapult. I keyed the intercom: "How much longer?"

There was no reply for 3 full seconds, then Rivers said, "All right, let's take it. I'm ready."

I popped my thumbs outward above the glare shield, and the yellow shirt immediately responded with an almost violent imitation to the deck apes waiting to unchain us from the padeyes on the flight deck. Seconds later we were taxiing forward, quickly but deliberately—we were the only jet moving on the deck. The Jakal crew must be manning up on the fantail, I thought, and I took it easy with the power. I didn't want to get careless and blow some kid off the flight deck in my haste to get airborne. I stomped on the right rudder and pressed the nose wheel steering button on the control stick, and the Intruder turned in its own radius toward the cat track.

The yellow shirt handed us off to his buddy standing at the far end of the catapult, who gave us the signal to spread our wings. The second they were down and locked I lowered our flaps and slats, gave the controls a wipeout, and slowed our momentum for the critical phase of steering our nose gear catapult bar into the shuttle. We felt the familiar clunk over the shuttle of the A-6 squatting down into position, and I turned my head to an ordie in a red float coat who came out in front of us with his hands above his head. Rivers and I made our hands visible above the canopy rail, assuring the ordnance handlers that our fingers were nowhere near any of the switches on the armament control panel. Moments later the ordie gave us a thumbs-up, signifying that our laser-guided skipper bomb and two rockeyes were armed, ducked his head, and ran off to the safe line on the port side of the catapult.

The cat officer had control of us now, and without hesitation he put us into tension. The jet screamed, the throttle and stick shook in the Intruder's frustration to fly, and I gave the instruments one more scan to verify that everything was where it needed to be.

I keyed the ICS. "Ready to go, Rivers?"

Rivers gave an affirmative nod of his head and replied, "Thirteen minutes."

I turned back to the cat officer, rendered a crisp salute, and we shot off the bow of the USS *Ranger* at 150 knots, exactly thirteen minutes after the 1MC had blared its command to our sedated ears in the comfort of the ready room.

With the rapid acceleration of the jet came a light that

should not have been there—my eyes focused on it momentarily and checked our airspeed, and then I looked outside to the horizon for our daylight clearing turn off the cat.

Rivers automatically reached up with his left hand and toggled the center panel switch to MAG/VGI, allowing the standby gyro to display attitude information on the ADI.

"Shit, platform light," he let out in a frustrated tone.

That meant that our inertial nav had dumped off of the cat, leaving us with about the same navigation and attack options as a World War II bomber. "Shit" was right.

Between the abbreviated stored heading alignment and the violence of the catapult shot, the inertial system had been unable to maintain the stability of its spinning gyros. I had barely completed the clearing turn when button 7 on the number 1 radio came alive.

"Rustler 504, your vector 325 for 275, buster," transmitted *Ranger* Departure Control.

The throttles stayed at military thrust and we "bustered" at our best speed to a contact, the nature of which was still unknown to us, somewhere in the far northern reaches of the Persian Gulf.

"Dammit, did we lose it all, system's shot?" I asked, knowing full well that there was no middle point in the A-6—you either had an alignment, or you didn't.

"Yes. I can try to get us a level table, but that's about it." The anger in Rivers' voice was barely controlled. He switched the inertial system to the dead-reckoning mode, a manner of crude navigation that required frequent radar updates. "We're not going to have any flir stabilization for the skipper, no automatic deliveries for the rockeyes."

Great, I thought. The last time I had practiced a manual bombing run was in the Philippines, and I couldn't remember when before that. I checked that we were in a stable 300-knot climb and began to dig into my nav bag for my cheat sheet with the mil depression settings for our iron gunsight. I studied the chart, and wrote down the numbers on my kneeboard for a 500-knot, 10-degree dive, and a 500-knot level lay-down. Just wonderful.

"Rustler 504, strike, switch secure for your control with Sun King 602."

Rivers switched on our encoding gear and gave the E-2 a call. "King, Rustler 504 up for your control."

"Rustler 504, King, your vector is 321 for enemy surface contact," answered the E-2.

We leveled off at 20,000 and flew north at nearly 500 knots, hoping to catch the Iraqi boat before it entered Iranian waters. Rivers got the inertial to level, which meant that we had marginal attitude information, but without flir stabilization the laser could not be held on the target, and the skipper could not be guided. I dialed the mil setting for a 10-degree dive into the bulky metal gunsight that partially obstructed my forward view.

We ran through the combat checklist expeditiously, paying particular attention to ensuring that I had flares selected on my throttle switch, and Rivers had chaff dialed into the program. Flying low in the daylight opened us up to several threats that were lessened significantly by cover of darkness— heat-seeking missiles and small-arms fire. Any troop on the ground or sailor on a boat could fire a handheld, heat-seeking SAM at a low-flying jet, and the job was that much easier if the aircraft was flying a predictable flight path—say, a bombing run. It was estimated that the Iraqis had about 20,000 of the shoulder-fired missiles, able to reach well over 10,000 feet high. Most small arms, like the AK-47 assault rifle used by the Iraqis, were effective up to about 6,000 feet.

We had no choice but to attack in daylight; that was when the Iraqi had decided to make his move. I had opted for a low attack, a 10-degree dive with a 1,000-foot bomb-release altitude for one simple reason: I figured it was the optimal delivery if I was to get my bomb to hit the target. The higher the altitude we dropped from, the more time the enemy would have to maneuver his boat out of the way. Higher also meant that the rockeye would be more susceptible to wind correction inaccuracies, a particularly egregious error because we had no inertial system to tell us what winds actually existed at altitude. Last, the only manual delivery I had practiced in the preceding few months had been a low dive, and that just might make the difference in us hitting a moving target.

Rivers kept working the flir, knowing that getting it to track sufficiently for a laser spot was an extremely slim chance, but working it all the same. We approached the area where the contact had been spotted, and Rivers switched his attention to the radar as the E-2 refined his vectors. I started the Intruder down to 10,000 feet to be in a better position to identify the target visually.

"Okay, I've got the contact on radar," Rivers let me know over the intercom; then he depressed his radio foot pedal. "King, Rustler 504, radar contact, showing 323 at 23 miles."

"Roger, Rustler, that's your target. Request you identify it visually and report back."

"All right, Pete, I'm going to slew us over to the left of the boat to keep us out of handheld range. Let me know when you see it."

"Okay, steering's showing 18 miles, don't see anything yet," I answered.

The distance closed and we continued our descent down to 6,000 feet. The haze from the oil well fires dissipated in the lower altitudes, and at 12 miles I began to see a shape in the distance.

"Got something, Rivers. Shoot, it's pretty big."

Rivers lifted his head out of the radar boot when we closed to within 10 miles. "That's got to be a Polnokny class, looks like he's doing 5, maybe 10 knots, probably laying mines," Rivers said.

The Iraqis had three of the 266-foot amphibious landing ships in their inventory, each designed to land tanks and troops on a beachhead. If the Iraqis were to attempt an end run with special operations troops into Saudi Arabia or one of her neighbors, these would be the ships to transport them. At this stage of the conflict they were most likely utilizing all the vessels they possessed to put out mines in a defense of the coastline. I knew that each Polnokny carried SA-N-5 Grail missile launchers, naval variants of the SA-7 infrared missiles, which were mounted in fixed positions for greater ease when firing from a ship. They also had 30mm guns, and who knew how many handheld, heat-seeking missiles. The good news was that the ship was big and would be more difficult to maneuver out of the way of our bombs. I pulled off to the west, well out of range of anything the Polnokny could fire at us.

"King, Rustler 504, we have visual confirmation that the vessel is an Iraqi Polnokny class, appears to be laying mines. Request clearance to drop," Rivers transmitted over the radio to the E-2.

There was a brief pause; then, "Rustler 504, King, your weapons are red and free, cleared in on the target." The approval from the Hawkeye orbiting high to the south came only after consulting with the local surface warfare commander on a nearby ship.

"All right, Rivs, this is what I see. We run in on him quartering from the stern, reduce his view of us. Ten-degree dive popping out flares off target. What do you think?"

"Let's try to line him up once on the flir, from out here, see if I can stabilize for the skipper first," Rivers replied. "If I can't hold it steady, let's do the rockeye."

I pointed our Intruder at the Polnokny, now steering an erratic course east toward Iran at 20 knots, but it soon became apparent that we were not going to be able to guide our skipper. We had no other ordnance but our two rockeyes. I dropped us down to 3,000 feet and pulled the jet around until we were pointed at the Polnokny's stern while he steamed to the east. I jammed the throttles forward to the stops, fairly confident that we had been out of eyeshot long enough to keep them guessing about which direction we were going to attack from. All we needed was about 15 seconds of surprise on the run-in before we dropped our rockeye from a half a mile away.

Our A-6 accelerated to 500 knots indicated airspeed, and I triple-checked that the crosshair reticle on the gunsight was illuminated on the square piece of 4-inch glass.

Rivers verified that the switch positions on the armament panel were correct one last time and said, "ACU's set, master arm to go."

"Roger," I let out under my breath into the oxygen mask. "Almost there, here we go."

"Master arm's on." Rivers toggled the big metal switch up.

I kept my eyes glued to the Polnokny and rolled the Intruder inverted so we could establish a dive with positive G forces. Looking at the swerving ship from upside down, I pulled back on the stick until the G meter spiked at 3, released the stick pressure, and rolled the jet back to the upright position. I looked out through the gunsight—there was the Polnokny, straight ahead; that was the easy part. My dive angle was right at 10, and the pipper on the gunsight was short of the target, just where it should be. Rivers read out the airspeed: "495, 500, 505."

We crept through 500 knots, but I kept the throttles pegged to the stops—speed was life. I would pickle off the bomb just a touch early to compensate for the faster-than-planned airspeed. I traded furtive glances between the gunsight pipper, our dive angle, the Polnokny, and our altitude, trusting my airspeed would not go too far above 500. Fourteen hundred feet, 1,300 feet. I hoped they didn't see us, but I didn't dare look around to check if they were shooting; I couldn't spare the distraction from my concentration on the target. It would not have mattered at any rate—we were on government time. Like the last 7 miles in a level attack, it was now our job to fly directly at the target regardless of the defensive threats. The U.S. government owned our lives for the final run to the target.

One thousand feet, the pipper tracked across the midsection of the Polnokny.

"Pickle!" yelled Rivers into the intercom to key my attention to our altitude.

I depressed the pickle button on the control stick and felt the hesitating lopsidedness as the single 500-pound rockeye was released. I yanked back on the stick, broke our rate of descent 800 feet above the water, and snapped the Intruder into a left 6½-G turn while pumping out three sets of flares, two at a time. I unloaded the G and dumped the nose to keep our airspeed up, accelerating away from the Polnokny but turning our hot engine burner canisters straight at any heat-seeking SAMs that might be trying to target us. I pumped out another set of flares and made a 4-G jink to the right.

Back into the right-hand turn, Rivers and I both craned our necks to look for missiles and mark our hit. It seemed to take forever for the canister to open and dispense its hundreds of tiny bomblets, but finally we saw the pattern of the small explosions—the majority had gone long, harmlessly into the water, with perhaps a dozen of the tank-busting bomblets impacting the deck amidships. The Polnokny broke off from its course toward Iran to weave in an attempt to confuse future attackers.

"From the east, keep him from heading to Iran?" I asked Rivers about the next attack run.

"Yeah, let's set up over there. We're not going to stop him with a rock anyway, just slow him down," Rivers answered.

"Rustler 504, King, Jakal 403 is approaching station, he will be joining the attack with you," the E-2 interrupted our plans.

"All right, he's got a skipper. Let's see how he does," I said to myself as much as to Rivers.

Two minutes later the Polnokny was still steaming erratically, making virtually no headway toward the safety to the east. We stood off to the west to allow the Jakal plenty of room to set up for his skipper attack. We didn't have long to wait.

I could just make out the Jakal flying in low over the water directly behind the Polnokny. At several miles from the target, safely out of the range of small-arms fire, the Jakal turned abruptly, and although I couldn't see it, I could imagine the 1,000-pound bomb's rocket motor igniting as it propelled it toward the laser spot somewhere on the Polnokny. Seconds later we found out exactly where that laser spot was.

The stern of the ship, just below the superstructure, burst into the flames of a fiery explosion. A fireball as large as the superstructure itself went straight up into the air and settled back down to the water. The Polnokny burned out of control. All directional control on the ship was immediately lost, the vessel was apparently no longer under its own steerage, and the fire appeared to be a self-sustaining inferno. It was a truly impressive sight—I had never seen such destruction from so close.

I turned our jet away from the Polnokny to increase our spacing, reversed course, and headed back toward the burning ship. I flipped the master arm up for another rockeye attack, this time level from 500 feet. We would have no problem hitting the stationary Polnokny from level and low, a dangerous profile, but I was counting on all hands giving up their defensive stations and trying to fight the fire.

I was boresighted on the task at hand, my vision tunneled by the attack profile and the adrenaline pumping through my system.

Rivers spoke up: "There's lifeboats going over the side." In the distance tiny, circular orange shapes started falling over the rails.

"Roger, 5 miles, master arm's on," I replied, staring straight ahead at the burning hulk.

"Pete! I said there's lifeboats going over the side!" Rivers reached up and turned the master arm to off.

The use of my name brought me back slowly. I pulled on the stick and arced away from the burning wreckage.

"Thanks" was all I could manage to mutter. I felt cold and a little sick.

I had no time, then, for reflection. The radio began to chatter.

"Rustler 504, King, new contact, a second Polnokny currently off the south of Būbiyān Island. Your steer is 340 for 25." The E-2 was going to keep us busy. I stood the jet on its side and pulled us around to a 340-degree heading while Rivers stuck his head back down into the radar boot.

Almost instantly he was back out again. "There's steering, showing 22 miles."

I fine-tuned the course, advanced the throttles, and kept our belly pressed down to the water 500 feet below us.

"He's not very far off the shore, you can come in from this direction, just make sure we turn left off target; otherwise we might end up over land." Rivers gave me a mental image of what the radar was telling him.

"Okay. Listen, how about a laydown, better surprise, and we won't highlight ourselves to any gunners on the beach?" And I'll have a better chance of hitting the bastard as well, I thought.

"Okay. Max knots all the way."

I rechecked that the mil setting in the gunsight was for a level laydown, in the daylight, just the kind of two-dimensional-only profile they teach us not to do in flight school. Too easy a target without taking advantage of moving the jet in the vertical to confuse the gunner's targeting solution. Screw it; we were going to get this guy.

Out of the haze I made out the now-familiar form of a Polnokny amphib. The Radalt was pegged at 500 feet, our speed was 500-plus knots, and we headed at a perfect angle to string the bomblets from port bow to starboard stern. Six miles; I could see Būbiyān Island behind the Iraqi ship.

I didn't even attempt to move the jet around. My full

concentration was on keeping our flight parameters as tight as possible so my gunsight reticle would accurately depict where our bombs would impact. Man, it was a big ship. I left it to Rivers to scan outside the cockpit for any fire coming from the fast-approaching Polnokny. He was reassuringly silent.

My right thumb depressed the pickle button as the pipper crossed the target. I pumped out what had to be our last remaining flares and pulled hard to the left in a climb—off target was a good place to start working that third dimension. Craning my neck back over my shoulder, I saw the bomblets cover the center of the ship and ignite dozens of small fires.

Out of ordnance and now targets, we continued our climb and took up a heading back to *Ranger*. Ninety minutes had elapsed since the alert had been called. I struggled to keep my eyes open during the flight back to marshal.

The Battle of Būbiyān, as it was later known, ended on 30 January with the destruction of the majority of the Iraqi navy. The bulk of the enemy vessels had either been sunk or rendered inoperable, but still there were threats in the far reaches of the Persian Gulf that would not be neutralized for several more weeks. Most of these boats did not stray far from port, and ventured out only to lay mines close to the Kuwaiti shoreline, particularly off of Faylaka Island, the first step in a potential U.S. Marine amphibious assault.

The outline of how the war was to progress for *Ranger* was becoming evident, and three distinct missions began to emerge in addition to the collateral duty the *Ranger* battle group exercised as overall surface warfare commander. Each of these missions, or "phases," was inextricably linked, and it was difficult if not impossible to pinpoint a beginning or an end to any of them. Only the destruction of the Iraqi navy provided a degree of closure. The Battle of Būbiyān brought to a head the conflict on the seas, with only limited, isolated instances of hostilities on the waters to follow.

Air Wing 2 had been attacking strategic targets concurrently with attacks on enemy missile patrol boats, and this effectively comprised the first phase. Airfields, petroleum production facilities, power plants, radio/relay sites, and communication complexes were bombed virtually from the outset of the war, and *Ranger* juggled her assortment of naval and strategic targets through rigorous flight schedules that lasted 20 hours a day on average.

The second phase of Desert Storm for Air Wing 2 was ongoing from the moment I had squeezed the commit trigger and launched our first HARM against the SA-2 at Umm Qasr—the suppression of enemy air defense, or SEAD. In addition to reactive attacks through the use of HARM, bombing runs were made on SAM sites, air defense headquarters buildings, and weapons storage areas where the missiles and AAA were warehoused. SEAD missions in their various forms would continue until the conclusion of Desert Storm, gradually evolving into strikes to destroy the ammunition dumps that also were supplying the soldiers in the field who, it seemed, our ground forces must inevitably fight.

The third and final phase of our involvement in Operation Desert Storm was the most important, and consequently comprised the majority of our strikes—the preparation of the battlefield for the Allied ground offensive to come. Any action that would make the job of the Allied soldiers on the ground a little easier and less dangerous fell under the broad umbrella of battlefield preparation, but when the rubber hit the road, it came down to three things: killing Iraqi soldiers, and destroying tanks and artillery. Additionally, lines of logistic support needed to be disrupted, and supplies of ammunition and artillery had to be destroyed; it was a comprehensive effort to soften up the enemy to the maximum extent possible prior to the coalition committing to a ground offensive.

It did not take long to be confronted with the sobering realization of what our soldiers were up against. It was only a few hours since the Polnokny attacks, and I was getting geared up again to fly a night tanker to support the F-14 CAP station almost directly overhead of where the Battle of Būbiyān had been waged.

We were making our final walk through the ready room when our attention was caught by a flurry of activity as several Swordsmen burst through the door, fresh from the Intelligence Center. The Iraqis had mounted a limited offensive, possibly about fifty tanks, just south of the Kuwaiti border into the Saudi town of Khafji. The word going around was that there were ten dead Marines and ten wounded, and the air wing was scrambling to put together some spare bombers for night close air support (CAS) for the Marines.[2] We walked to our jet with the realization that the situation was beginning to change rapidly, and we were not in total control, not while there were 500,000 Iraqi soldiers in the Kuwaiti Theater of Operations.

Over the next several days the air wing made the transition from bombing boats to battlefield preparation. We had all been trained and were ready to fly close air support, missions that put an A-6's bombs so close to the friendly forces that radio contact and clearance to drop by a forward air controller (FAC) were required. But the ground forces were not actively engaged in combat yet—there were sporadic flare-ups along the battle lines, and certainly myriad special operations going on behind enemy lines, but other than Khafji there were no sustained, clearly defined engagements on the ground.

This was obviously a good thing: Why bomb the enemy close to our guys when we could bomb them from the comfort of 20 miles in front of any friendlies? And so the term "battlefield area interdiction" was introduced. The plan was simple: Radio contact would be established with whoever

2. Actual Khafji killed in action ended up being eleven Marines. We found out much later that the two Polnoknys we helped to disable may have been part of an attempt by the Iraqis at an amphibious end run to cut off Khafji to the south.

happened to be controlling a sector; it might be a Marine airborne controller, or a command post in some distant bunker where the "big picture" was undoubtedly laid out in great detail on a vast table. We would receive vectors to a convoy, or general coordinates to artillery or tank emplacements, and then it would be our job to find and destroy them with whatever our load of ordnance for the evening happened to be.

Instantly the flight schedule altered all of the ASR (armed surface recce) mission subheadings to BAI (battlefield area interdiction). The ordnance loadouts were slower to change than the schedule, and for the first few nights we were still carrying the 1,000-pound laser-guided skippers. Skippers were a tad overkill for a single tank, and difficult to launch and guide from 10,000 feet overhead the target.

For the dedicated strike aircraft, the ones that were not in a reactive mode but launched with a smattering of knowledge of where their targets might actually be and what they might look like, the weapons loadouts were becoming fairly predictable: either rockeye cluster munitions, or general-purpose bombs of the 500-to-1,000-pound variety, normally eight to twelve of each. One or two laser-guided bombs would be bolted beneath the wings if the weather was favorable, and multiple attack runs could be expected. The bombing run-ins were still from high altitude, usually releasing weapons no lower than 10,000 feet, but there was an unstated understanding that once the ground war started, all artificial limitations were off—we would do what was required to support the grunts.

Due to the round-the-clock operations and the pace of the flight schedule, the squadron duty officer shift had been reduced to 12 hours; this enabled an aviator to stand the duty and man up one or two jets in a 24-hour period. What it did not necessarily leave was a great deal of time for sleep, but the consistent release of adrenaline that most of us were experiencing seemed to overcome this, at least while we were airborne.

The standard 24-hour duty cycle had also been modified so

that an officer would be present in the ready room at all times to guard the supersecret AKAC authentication cards locked in the safe. These cards held the constantly changing code words that would verify a forward air controller's identity, and prevent an enterprising Iraqi from talking on the radios in his best Western movie voice in an attempt to get us to bomb our own troops. Pretty critical information to keep under tight wraps, but a touch overkill, I thought, when the price was the one commodity we all seemed to be running short of: sleep.

Only three people knew the combination to the safe, and it made perfect sense to have an officer immediately present when the safe was opened. But during the brief lulls in the flight schedule the SDO was "chained" to the desk just the same, despite the fact that the safe was securely locked, a petty officer stood guard, and we were surrounded by a water moat.

Good news did arrive that evening on the personal front. A squadron B/N had been into Bahrain to work various coordination issues with the folks on land, and he had been in telephone contact with the families back at Whidbey. He had received a message from Laurie that my parents had made it out of Syria and were waiting out the war in Athens. That was better, I supposed. Syria was a potential war zone at any moment, but on the other hand Athens, while beautiful, had a grand tradition in recent history of being a meeting ground for various terrorist organizations. I concluded that it was definitely a step up, and hoped that my parents had the sense to maintain a low profile, even in Greece, a country where our family had lived while I was growing up, and which in many respects we all considered a second home.

I sat back in the cushioned metal chair and tried to make the most of the duty. Word from the outside world trickled in slowly, and as the jets returned from their strikes against the Iraqi lines it became evident that yesterday's foray into Khafji was not part of a major offensive. The tanks that had ventured into Saudi Arabia were systematically wiped out after the initial element of surprise had eroded. The discipline of the coalition forces to hold in their positions had been maintained, and they had not ventured into an early ground battle of greater proportions.

Saddam and his army were being pressured into a waiting game—they could not elicit an early offensive from the coalition, and they were at a decided disadvantage if they initiated an attack themselves. The Iraqis were gradually being forced into hunkering down and trying to survive our ceaseless bombardment, fighting the war on our terms, and playing to our great advantage in airpower. With the exception of the Scud missiles they fired with great inaccuracy, they were mostly impotent in their attempts to lash out at the coalition armies.

The Scuds were by no means wholly ineffective, however. In a strategic sense their only value lay in bringing Israel into the war, and apparently that was not going to happen. But in terms of loss of human life, the Scuds could be devastating. Nightly attacks into Israel were soon joined by launches against Allied forces in Saudi Arabia, occasionally with horribly successful results. Patriot missile batteries were deployed to Israel and Saudi Arabia to intercept the Scuds, but a few managed to slip by the array of defenses.

The duty went quickly until the final 3 hours from 0500 to 0800, when the ready room emptied. It was the Jakal's turn at manning the alert bomber for the early-morning hours, and all of the Swordsmen aviators were either eating or in the rack. I reread the 2-week-old letter I had gotten from Laurie, kept my eyes glued to the ready room safe, and listened to the clock tick down the minutes. One thing is consistent in all aspects of navy life: The duty sucks.

Saturday, 2 February, was *Ranger*'s thirty-first day at sea since leaving port in the Philippines, by any measure a full month. Life on the sea evokes images of salt spray, crashing waves, ubiquitous marine life, and exotic ports. On an aircraft carrier it's slightly different. True, we could catch a moment here and there on the flight deck to watch the sea snakes, and this far south the smell of the burning oil well fires did not block out an occasional whiff of salt air from the water 60 feet below the flight deck. But overall it was more like living in a city.

Once belowdecks the ship could have been anywhere—it could have been sitting in the middle of the desert as far as the majority of *Ranger*'s five thousand personnel would have noticed. It was the lack of certain things that defined everyday life on the boat: no women, no children, no old people, no one in civilian clothes (except for the gym and the shower). There were no trees, no birds, no grass, and for the most part no sun. It was the little things we all took for granted ashore that began to weigh heavily on the soul—even in the middle of the worst city, you can look around and somewhere there is a tiny patch of green, a child, or a bum. There was no variety on the carrier, and most of all there was no beer.

There was one exception. At forty consecutive days at sea, the flight schedule permitting, all hands on board a U.S. naval vessel were awarded a "beer day." Each thirsty sailor and aviator would be entitled to two beers, possibly cold, definitely out of a can, to drink on the flight deck. Hoarding and saving the beer was not allowed; each beer was issued opened, and was to be consumed on the flight deck during a brief few hours. If you had the duty during that time you were out of luck, unless you could coerce a comrade to stay dry and stand in for you. Teetotalers were very popular people on board ship for this event; it might happen only once or twice on a cruise, and an extra ration of beer was always welcome.

Our thirty-first day in a row at sea quickly lost any luster it might have possessed when *Roosevelt* lost an A-6 off the coast of Būbiyān Island. It was a typically low-visibility day, with the haze inherent in the northern Persian Gulf competing with the billows of smoke from the Kuwaiti oil fields to make the horizon blend into the water in one continuous shade of gray. The best guesses on *Ranger* were that an SA-7 shoulder-fired missile had either picked off the Intruder or that they had inadvertently flown into the water. Bad news regardless, particularly with no word on the crew. After countless flights over and around Būbiyān it was becoming easy to get complacent, and we all did our best to reintroduce into our minds just how hazardous it was to fly in what was rapidly becoming our backyard.

That night our skipper led a strike of twelve Intruders to Iraqi artillery positions and barracks just to the south of Kuwait City. Rivers and I were number twelve in the attack, and as we witnessed our bombs wreaking havoc on the enemy troops, it became evident just how ugly this war was getting for the Iraqis. The strike dropped a total of 144 rockeyes, effectively carpeting the target area and undoubtedly killing countless Iraqi soldiers.

The sortie took almost 3 hours of flight time total for us to complete, and with a half a million Iraqi combatants in the KTO the sheer magnitude of the effort required to beat down the enemy ground forces was becoming apparent. The next day, now more secure from attack with the effectiveness of the Iraqi navy significantly diminished, the *Ranger* battle group moved 50 nautical miles farther north to cut down on the turnaround time of the strikes that would launch from her decks.

With the round-trip distance whittled down, CAG decided to rearrange the composition of the strikes to provide for a more flexible and rapid response to new intelligence. The ministrike packages would nominally consist of four Intruders with an accompanying Prowler to provide jamming and HARM support if required. The fighters would simply stay on their combat air patrol stations—the Iraqi fighter threat was now considered fairly negligible, and there was no reason to have our Tomcats play escort inside the range of the SAMs and AAA. The plan required less time for logistics, and we could now launch and recover most cycles of aircraft in 1 hour, 45 minutes, adding several attack sorties a day to the war effort.

Over the course of the next several days Rivers and I were afforded the opportunity to try out the new, smaller strike compositions, and they were a tremendous improvement. Not only was our flight time reduced, but also the hours required to plan for each strike were effectively cut in half. Only approximately a dozen aviators were needed to brief each mission now, and the plans became simple, concise, and familiar. In fact, they were becoming uncomfortably familiar.

The story that the rumor mill was generating about the *Roosevelt* A-6 was that the downed crew had been flying low, in the daylight, outside Kuwait Harbor, where there were well-established defenses in anticipation of an Allied amphibious movement around the Iraqi flank. We were developing set habit patterns in our flying and were becoming too accustomed to the northern Persian Gulf. We were beginning to grow dangerously relaxed. Complacency was quickly becoming our greatest enemy, followed shortly by the ten thousand Iraqi soldiers in each of the "kill boxes" we were bombing. I took out some extra survival gear and started to carry a .45 in my SV-2 in addition to my pistol. It probably wouldn't do a damn bit of good, but the extra weight was a physical reminder of how I did not want to become a "war criminal" in the hands of the Iraqis.

Intelligence was putting out the word that the Iraqis might be moving some of their SAM batteries farther south, to protect their troops. If the mobile SA-6s began to pop up during our BAI ministrikes, a more comprehensive response to the threats probably would become necessary, possibly requiring us to revert to the larger attack packages and their comprehensive HARM coverage.

The state of the Iraqi mobile air defenses was the great unknown. Intel had numerous suspected SAM sites charted up in CVIC, but because they were mobile, it was exceedingly difficult to tell in real time the exact location of each individual site. Sometimes we would fly into a suspected threat ring and get absolutely no indication on our early warning gear that there was radar activity in the area. At other times aircraft would receive an occasional radar spike as a SAM operator made a quick sweep of the skies and then turned off his radar in fear of a retaliatory HARM salvo. And occasionally a radar-guided missile would be fired at a bomber.

Initially we began to carry an extra HARM on one of the bombers, hoping that by having a HARM on a striker it would be close enough to fly out and destroy an active enemy radar before they could guide their missile to one of the attackers. The Iraqis were not up for a game of dueling missiles, however, and after several days it became evident that we were better off leaving the radar defense to the Prowlers and their jammers. The Prowler crews had refined their jamming to a subtle art, and the Iraqis quite often were not even aware that their radar pictures were being manipulated. The extra station freed up room for more bombs, and with the type of area targets we were prosecuting, more was definitely better.

Routine of any sort was automatically grasped by most of the aviators on board *Ranger*. There were sufficient unknowns in the air, over Kuwait and Iraq, and behind the ship, that any information that could be cubbyholed into a filed recess of the mind was welcomed. The first several weeks of February 1991 enabled us to resolve much of the uncertainty that had plagued the air wing prior to the outbreak of hostilities into a logical and somewhat predictable setting.

Air Wing 2's area of concern was fairly well defined, and for the most part the missions were more similar than they were different. *Ranger* was the night strike carrier—approximately 80 percent of our missions had been flown after sunset to take advantage of the A-6's night attack capabilities. The darkened skies of Kuwait and Iraq had been the consistency to our daily lives, and now we were adding to that a consistency of mission—the kill box. Night after night, strikes of four to twelve Intruders launched from *Ranger*'s decks, steady in the calm gulf waters, to geographic squares in the desert to seek out targets and destroy them.

The Iraqis were not terribly difficult to find—for the most part the only objects of any significance in the sandy dunes were the components of Saddam's army hunkered down and doing their best to stay alive for one more night. Each kill box was not a perfect square, but varied in shape to conform to the concentrations of enemy and friendly positions. The sides of each box ranged from 10 to 25 nautical miles, encompassing several hundred square miles of terrain.

The Iraqi defensive positions in and around Kuwait were all fair game to us, and our kill box strikes seemed to rotate in a circle around Kuwait City. Our small strike package would oftentimes split up in the kill box to attack a greater area of the dispersed artillery pieces and tanks. Many had been buried up to their turrets in a desperate attempt to hide their heat signature from our flir and their armor from our shrapnel. The pounding the Iraqis were taking had to be incredible. The bombing went on endlessly, 24 hours a day, putting not only the enemy soldiers' lives at immediate risk but also throwing their supply lines into disarray, leaving them hungry, cold, and hopefully deeply disillusioned.

# Chapter Thirteen

# . . . the battle's confusion . . .

The steady onslaught into the kill boxes was not without disruption. Sprinkled amid the uniformity of the kill box strikes were targets more in line with what the A-6 crews had traditionally trained to attack.

On the evening of 7 February *Ranger* launched three successful strikes against strategic targets, the variety of which represented the differences in the types of missions we were being tasked with. The initial strike of the evening mined the runways at Shabiah Airfield, southwest of Basra. Quick to follow was a mission to a thermal power plant in Basra, a devastating attack that virtually leveled the complex and blacked out the area indefinitely.

On the third strike of the evening, Rivers and I flew in the second of four Intruders to attack a SAM support facility and vast ammunition dump in the Kuwaiti town of Al Jahrah. Our XO was leading the strike, and he stressed the impressiveness of the target's size and dimensions in his brief. Ammunition and surface-to-air missiles were being stored in a massive, square complex dotted with numerous dug-out, circular revetments and trenches designed to protect the stores from fragmentations and bomb blasts. Each side of the square had to be a mile long, and the entire facility was fenced off with bunkered guard positions to eliminate saboteurs who might try to penetrate its perimeter.

The complex's central location, northwest of Kuwait City, placed it at a relatively safe distance from the front lines, yet close enough for the timely resupply of SAMs and depleted ammunition to the Iraqis who would be fighting in the KTO. The XO's plan was simple and deliberate: The four Intruders would fly in close trail high over the harbor of Kuwait City in land to the west. We would then turn south for a brief run to the target, drop our ordnance, and continue out to the east almost directly over Kuwait City. This would get the four A-6s feet wet in the most expeditious manner possible.

The drawback to the plan was the direct overflight of Kuwait City after the Iraqi defenses had been fully alerted by the explosions of our bombs. We could expect to encounter more substantial AAA than at the fringes of Kuwait City, but we would be out of the threat envelopes all the faster. It was a trade-off, but the advantage of pointing our jets out over the ocean as quickly as possible outweighed the potential risk of trying to scurry around the defenses in the desolation of the desert.

It had been a long day so far for Rivers and me. We had initially been slated to fly in the strike to mine the airfield at Shabiah, but our jet had a mechanical problem before we ever got to the catapult, and the strike had launched the spare in our place. That had been before sunset. Since then we had been shuttling back and forth between the ready room and the Intelligence Center as late aircrew additions to our XO's strike, which was to launch at 0030. I yawned profoundly as I taxied along the catapult track and waited for the lukewarm coffee I had guzzled 30 minutes earlier to kick in.

The rapid acceleration of the cat shot was its normal invigorating wake-up call, and with *Ranger* 50 miles farther to the north, it did not take long for the strike package to arrive at the initial point. Rivers and I took our position 30 seconds behind the XO in the lead, a deceivingly close 3 miles, and trusted in our TACAN's air-to-air mode to keep us from flying up his darkened tailpipes in the night sky.

Kuwait City was its usual bright self—no blackout, not a clue from our run-in altitude of 17,000 feet that there was a war going on. The winds must have shifted, I thought, because the sickeningly dense oil cloud was not obscuring our visibility of the shooting flames of oil well fires to the west. The fires had been raging for more than 2 weeks, and the foul, evil-looking cloud would move in and out, changing altitudes and position as if it were actually the same wretched specter, not a continuous outflow from the fires to who knew what final resting place.

We would not have to entertain the problems and possibilities that the ominous vapor presented to us on this evening. The troops back on *Ranger* would not have to waste valuable hours washing the soot and slime from our jets, whisking it off before it began to eat at the skin of our aircraft. And we would not have to fight the clouds to capture the target on our flir, wondering as we cinched our oxygen masks down tightly into their bayonet fittings just what the filthy gases were doing to our engines.

Rivers acquired the well-defined outline of the ammunition storage area before we initiated the turn to the south for our short final run in. The Iraqis' defensive positions presented an ideal sketch of exactly where to bomb—if it had been round instead of square, I would swear it was a bull's-eye. The routine of the last 7 miles to bomb release was second nature; I reefed the Intruder in a hard turn to the left and shot my left hand forward, advancing the throttles to their stops, taking whatever speed our jet's bulbous nose would allow.

The radar warning gear was quiet, and it contributed to the eerie silence that had my hackles up in a state of anxious paranoia. Where were the guns, the missiles? I had expected a concentrated defensive effort. It was exceedingly quiet. I kept looking over my shoulder in a frantic scan of the horizon and the desert floor below. I thought about it some more, and concluded that it wasn't paranoia; they were trying to kill me.

I looked out the front windscreen to the target and saw no tracers; the evening was quiet and still. The lights of Kuwait City to the left were imposing but in an odd way comforting—it felt like our small jet would easily be lost in the near-daylight goings-ons of the big city. To the right was the desert and uninterrupted darkness except for the distant oil-fed fires. I pushed the stick forward, accelerating the A-6 until we were pointed at a 20-degree angle to the ground, rushing up at us at 6,000 feet per minute. I barely heard Rivers' progress through the now-familiar litany: "I've got the target, handing off, laser's on." I kept my head on a swivel; don't fixate; keep your scan going; it's the bullet you don't see that will kill you.

I felt the bombs take turns coming off opposite sides of our jet, setting off the radar altimeter tone in our helmets when they broke its beam to the earth for a fraction of a second. I pulled back hard on the stick; try not to go any lower, not any closer to the guns on the ground, there, 10,000 feet on the barometric altimeter, now hard to the left, unpredictable. The XO's bombs lit off, carpeting the tank-killing bomblets over hundreds of yards. Almost immediately the emptiness of the night sky was disturbed by the fireflies of tracers far below—it looked like light weapons, not much that would reach up here.

"Still tracking," said Rivers. I could almost feel him willing the pattern of our bomblets to fall under the crosshairs of his flir reticle. "Got it! Still tracking." Rivers watched the bomblets light off in hundreds of individual sparkling flashes, each explosion milliseconds apart, physically separated at impact only by the position they once held tightly clustered together in their 500-pound canister.

"Secondaries!" The news that a pilot wants to hear—anything that blows up has to have been of use to the enemy.

The early-warning gear let off a beep, and I looked down at a lone SA-2, no threat for now. We were speeding toward the safety of the water at more than 400 knots, but we were lower than I wanted to be. Ten thousand feet is still within the range of a lot of guns. Climbing meant we would bleed down our airspeed, though, and that meant longer to the water and less ability to maneuver and pull G's if the need arose. I stayed at 10,000 feet and kept the Intruder moving in a gentle weave to present an unpredictable target to any ground gunners who might see us.

"There's four's bombs. . . . Oh, man, oh, man! The last Jakal got something! There's a shock wave covering half the complex! The whole place is on fire!" Rivers said over the intercom with his head still buried in the boot, looking at the flir.

I couldn't resist it. I snapped the Intruder up onto its left wing and strained my neck back over my shoulder—even a rapid glance from 10,000 feet up and 8 miles ahead made it clear that the strike had done some major damage. I stopped my sight-seeing with an icy pang of guilt—if we got shot down now it would be my own damn fault, spotting the target when I should be spinning my head, looking for threats. I didn't look back to the target again until we were well beyond the bright buildings of Kuwait City, but when I did, I was glad I had not missed it.

Despite the flood of city lights, the destruction our attack had wrought was obvious. The grid of the target area flashed and flickered in the random pattern of a blaze out of control. Whatever had been stored in the facility had lit off in an explosion that detonated everything in the complex, effectively eradicating the dug-out square with its trenches and revetments from the terrain.

I looked at our fuel: 6,800 pounds, just enough to get back to the ship, shoot an approach, and have about 3,200 pounds of fuel when we called the ball. A bit too tight for a peacetime night trap, but fairly comfortable given the high-tempo pace of operations we had grown accustomed to.

We caught a wire on our first pass, fortunately, because otherwise it would be an automatic trip to the tanker and the transformation of a smooth and nearly effortless recovery into a nerve-racking hell of a reason to be late for midrats. The intelligence debrief in CVIC was even more of an eye-opener than our short sight-seeing turns over the gulf trying to gauge the effectiveness of our strike. The Hawkeye, 70 miles from the target in an orbit out over the gulf, could still see the flames from the ammunition dump burning nearly an hour after the attack. That was a lot of missiles that could not be fired at us, and a hell of a lot of bullets and shells that could not be used against our soldiers and Marines when the inevitable fight on the ground began.

I thought back to the sparkles of tracers coming up from the compound—there had to be at least several dozen Iraqis down there shooting at us. The tracers were still airborne when the secondaries from the rockeye decimated the target area, unquestionably killing all within the complex. I didn't feel remorse in the true sense, rather an uneasy and more vivid perception of the scope of our actions—they were trying to kill us and protect weapons that would harm our troops on the ground. We were trying to kill them.

It bothered me that I could not see them, that I was forced to conjure up an invented visual image to fully accept what we were doing. The only proof of their existence was the projectiles from the weapons that had been in their hands. I felt a sense of detached wonder and curiosity: What exactly had happened to those men in their last few seconds, their final moments on Earth? What did they look like? What were their names? Were they cold and hungry? In some bizarre fashion was it a relief to them to be "removed" from the war? It took imagination to begin to understand the impact of our strikes, and there was an infinitely fine line between comprehension and selfish rationalization. I reminded myself that this was not a video game, the windscreen was not a TV, and that people were going to continue to die on every strike. For now, however, the important thing was to not let that dead person be Rivs or me.

*9 Feb 91*

*Dear Mom and Dad,*

*Everything is just fine, we're even settled into a routine of sorts. If it comes to a ground war things will undoubtedly intensify for us quite a bit, but we have all adapted to the basics of war and it shouldn't be any great hurdle.*

*I was flying pretty hard initially, but now we fly on average about once a day. It was real busy for the first two weeks, but now it's just a pain in the ass getting the administrative BS done that we blew off for that period. None of the more humdrum aspects of the job go away in war, still lots of busy work managing the troops.*

*Now that we have some perspective I can tell you that things were pretty exciting the first week or so (the first night in particular), but they have calmed down considerably. Once again the biggest danger is now complacency, but I'm not going to concern myself with it (get it?). I've got some good stories, but they will have to wait. Let's just say I never thought my eyes could get as big as they did the first night. I'm keeping a log of all that's happened so don't worry (too much) about my memory. I'm hearing from all sorts of people, many I haven't heard from in years.*

*It sounds like the public is being supportive of the effort. That really means a lot, but so does keeping perspective on what this was, is, all about so that we don't lose sight of goals in the long haul. Half an answer is no answer.*

*Hard to believe that I've only been gone 2 months (as of today). On the other hand . . . it's been 5 weeks since I've seen an old person, a baby, a female, or touched dirt (or seen an insect for that matter). We are definitely making a big difference here and I'm very pleased with the overall strategy of the war. Some of the smaller things on a lower level I question, but Bush is definitely doing this right, and Schwarzkopf is acting as he should—a shrewd military man, not a politician. It's only a matter of time.*

*We can get into philosophy at a later date, but I feel*
*honest and correct in what I am doing. Make no mistake—*
*I don't enjoy killing people, and that's what war is, but*
*true integrity may have to be judged by how one actually*
*backs up what his professed convictions are. Anyway, all's*
*well. None of your letters have made it to the boat yet,*
*should get them all at once.*
    *Love,*
    *Pete*

The red instrumentation in the cockpit let off an eerie glow.
I looked around Rivers' head before starting the turn to the
right. Satisfied that the air immediately off our wing was
clear, I snapped on 4 G's and pulled us around to the target
heading of 335 degrees. Somewhere close behind, our wingman was following in our flight path 1,000 feet above us. The
night had been quiet, and we had crossed the harbor north of
Kuwait City without a murmur of opposition. I was barely
aware of the eight rockeyes hanging under our wings until I
was reminded by the slightly sluggish response of the controls to the onset of G.

The four Intruders on the kill box strike had launched from
*Ranger* at 2015 into the dark gulf skies of 10 February. Jakal
led and his wingman were attacking a concentration of Republican Guard vehicles and artillery in the southern portion
of the kill box, and our two Rustler jets were hitting a similar
site to the north.[1] Our target was 50 miles northwest of
Kuwait City, just beyond the intersection of where two of the
sporadic desert roads met. I slammed the throttles forward to
the stops and started pointing our jet down from our perch
18,000 feet above the sandy floor.

"Pushing over Rivers, nothing but quiet and dark out here,"

1. The Republican Guard divisions were positioned to the north of the battle
lines, ostensibly to be used as an elite source of reinforcements. Their alternate purpose, or perhaps their primary, we were to find out later, was to ensure that the Iraqi army regulars could not retreat through them into Iraq.

I said into the oxygen mask, not bothering to look over to my B/N for a response. "Twelve miles."

"All right," came the voice magically from the face stuck in the radar boot. "I've got some revetments, looks like something's in 'em. Can't tell what."

I took advantage of the peaceful progress of our dive and put the forward-looking infrared display onto my ADI for a moment. Despite the somewhat degraded picture, I could make out the horseshoe-shaped revetments scattered around a series of trails etched in the dirt. "Master arm's coming on, waiting for the attack," I hinted to Rivers.

"All right, laser's on, I'm tracking, in attack."

"Eight miles, nothing out there." I stared straight ahead, forcing myself to occasionally glance out each side just in case some enterprising SAM operator had picked us up on his radar. I had the cockpit lights turned down as low as I could stand it, trying to keep my eyes as dark-adapted as possible so I would immediately pick up the slightest flash coming from outside the Intruder.

The radar altimeter cycled and I felt the familiar lopsidedness give way to that welcomed responsiveness in the flight controls. The rockeyes were in their vertical travel toward the unsuspecting Saddam loyalists below. The canisters dropped in a staggered group of eight, and then opened at their pretimed setting and dispersed their bomblets in a wide pattern of destruction. I pulled back on the stick deliberately but smoothly, so Rivers would not lose the flir picture that would mark our hits, and swung our A-6 back into a climbing turn to a 110-degree heading.

"Okay there! Good hits, secondaries." Rivers was back with me, looking outside just in time for the first flickers of gunfire to stab the night sky in their futile search for us.

"How'd we do?" I asked, with an almost complete disregard for the twinkle of bullets below us. Our warning gear was silent, and without radar to guide it the light AAA from the target area was almost completely ineffectual.

"Bull's-eye. Covered the revetments, still couldn't tell what exactly was in 'em. Could have been trucks, artillery, maybe even half-buried tanks." Rivers was clearly satisfied with the outcome of the strike.

By the time our wingman had pulled off target we were steady on a heading back to the coast at the relatively safe altitude of 18,000 feet. Somebody must not have liked what we had done, however, because by the time that we were going feet wet the coastal AAA had come alive and was shooting guns of sufficient caliber to reach up and touch us, even at 18,000 feet. Naw, I thought, there's far too much going on around here to raise much concern over a strike to a kill box 50 miles away. We must have just stumbled into the tail end of someone else's strike. We were inadvertent participants in the escape of another group of bombers from the riled hornet's nest.

That same night we heard in the ready room gossip that the Allies were attempting to take advantage of the pounding with psychological warfare. Evidently Arabic leaflets had been air-dropped earlier in the day with a simple but profoundly important message: "We will bomb you tonight— flee or die." I could imagine the soldier on the ground, grimy with sweat, reading the note in the waning daylight, probably with great confusion and thinking, "You mean that you are not bombing us now?"

Later that night a C-130 pushed two 15,000-pound "Daisy Cutter" bombs out their cargo door into the desert where the leaflets had been dropped; not exactly a precision bombing run, but that was not the intent.

For comparison, the largest weapon the A-6 could carry was a 2,000-pound bomb, which would blast a crater roughly 80 feet in diameter. A total of 30,000 pounds of high explosives impacting in the same spot would create in the mind of anyone who might survive it a previously unimagined understanding of destruction. The Iraqi soldier who had survived years of brutal warfare with Iran would now be forced to face the reality that he was opposing an adversary the likes of which he could not completely comprehend, or hope to prevail against.

The next day more leaflets were dropped: "We told you we would bomb you. We did. Put down your arms and flee or die."

I think I knew what my answer most likely would have been, given the choices. I had to remind myself not to fall into the ethnocentric trap of assigning my logic and priorities to the Iraqis, people of a different culture, heritage, and experience in dealing with the facts of war. Screw it. Force of arms was an unfortunately universal language; they had their choice, let them make it. All they had to do was put down their weapons and walk out of Kuwait.

Inclement weather again became a factor in our attacks in mid-February. Faylaka was Kuwait's only island of appreciable size, and it served as an effective barrier to a coalition amphibious attack north of Kuwait City. Faylaka also had the unfortunate trait, for those Iraqis dug into defensive positions there, of being an easily accessible target set off from the more concentrated defenses on the mainland. The thick clouds that migrated over Kuwait in mid-February did not bode well for the Iraqi contingent manning their weapons on Faylaka Island.

Faylaka's primary advantage in its defense was that it was indeed an island, but the natural barrier the water presented to the contingency planning of our Marines proved a logistical problem to the Iraqis as well. Resupply had to come by boat, and most of the boats in the Iraqi navy were sitting on the bottom of the Persian Gulf. Most, but not all. There still existed myriad small tugs and assorted vessels that could be used as ferries between the northern harbor of Kuwait City and Faylaka. They also could be used to lay a perimeter of mines, adding to the defense of the coastline. The coalition response was to attempt to isolate the island as much as possible by maintaining aircraft on station in the northern gulf to attack the small go-fast vessels before they reached Faylaka.

One of *Roosevelt's* Intruders had the duty in the darkening skies of 11 February. He was standing watch for any boats attempting to make the run out to Faylaka when his protective orbit was disrupted by a surprise concentration of gunfire from the island. The A-6 crew knew they had been hit; how badly they were not certain. They quickly put some space between themselves and the obviously accurate gunners on the island below them. A wingman joined on them to survey the damage. With half of their wing blown away, it was determined that lowering their flaps would be a very bad idea, and, in fact, trying to land on the carrier at all was not such a great plan. The crew diverted to the island nation of Bahrain and safely landed at the Sheik Isa military airfield.

Until this point attacks against Faylaka Island had been fairly isolated. Part of the reason for this may have been sensitivity to the fact that there were ancient ruins from the time of Alexander the Great on the western portion of the Kuwaiti island. A more likely factor, however, was that Faylaka did not pose an immediate threat to the coalition battle lines, and our strike forces could be better utilized in the kill boxes on the mainland. The end result was that the enemy troops on Faylaka had been left relatively alone thus far, and had likely grown accustomed to firing at our patrolling jets with little fear of reprisal. In a well-timed irony, the cloud cover that had moved in on the same day that the *Roosevelt* A-6 had been hit dictated the airborne abort of no less than five individual strike packages, and a reroute to their alternate target of— Faylaka Island. Mere hours after the Iraqis had staged their successful antiaircraft defense, more than twenty Intruders dropped their full ordnance loads on their artillery positions, a fact that would be quite difficult to dispel to the Iraqis on Faylaka as the pure coincidence it was.

Over the course of the next week Rivers and I would drop bombs on and around Faylaka Island on five separate missions, two as weather contingency alternates and three as pre-planned attacks to beat back the island's defenses. The ships of the various battle groups stationed in the Persian Gulf worked northward, moving forward the threat of a Marine amphibious invasion force, and pressuring the Iraqi generals to honor the possible offensive from their eastern flank.

The air wing alternated among the steady onslaught into the kill boxes, the backup strikes to Faylaka Island and their resupply boats, and the occasional strategic strike to a bridge or facility of importance farther north of Kuwait City. Rivers was an air wing strike lead, one of the senior lieutenant commanders who had passed an approved syllabus and were qualified to plan, brief, and lead major air wing attacks, and he had been anxious to work his own strike from start to finish. On 14 February he got the opportunity to run the show, and I had the opportunity to view it from the front-row seat in the planning evolution. It was not the sort of Valentine's Day gift I had been counting on.

The mission itself was fairly simple, but the timing and composition of the strike did have a few minor twists to them. It would be a dusk raid, with the sun still high enough in the sky to make our A-6s vulnerable to shoulder-fired, heat-seeking SAMs in addition to the omnipresent AAA. It was not the environment we either trained for or were most effective flying in. The target was a large ammunition dump in Kuwait City. Six Intruders would be required to participate to achieve an acceptable probability of destroying the entire complex. We would each drop 500- and 1,000-pound bombs, iron bombs without the benefit of laser guidance. By dropping dumb bombs we would not be slaves to the predictable flight path required to hold the laser spot on the target.

Utilizing laser-guided bombs would not have allowed for the requisite amount of high explosives to reach the target area. After the impacts of the first bombs we could expect the target to be obscured by smoke and debris, possibly denying a viable laser track for as long as 15 minutes. We did not have that long to wait for each subsequent Intruder to make its bombing run, and the target area was too closely spaced to allow for multiple simultaneous attacks on it. We opted for iron bombs with a kick, the larger 1,000-pound variety for half the Intruders, and a loadout of twelve 500-pounders for the other half. The mix would kick up some good frag, carpeting the entire complex of the ammo dump with flying metal.

The challenge that arose was that the spacing among six aircraft would be too long, all surprise would be lost, and a potentially severe hazard would be posed to those flying the last three jets over Kuwait City. Daylight stream raids, as they were called, were extremely dangerous to the final Intruders making their attack runs. The enemy was fully alerted and aware of the general direction the strike was coming from, and the bombers could be acquired visually and made convenient targets to handheld SAMs in their turn back toward the water. Without the element of surprise and the cover of darkness we needed to compensate for our vulnerability.

The logical solution was to split the strike package into two groups of three Intruders each. Rivers devised a plan to let the first three bombers get to the target while the remaining three Intruders loitered offshore, well away from the action. After a 5-minute lull, we hoped that the Iraqis would relax their guard, thinking the strike was over, just as the second group of Intruders started their dive downward from 20,000 feet overhead. To complicate the defenders' job further, we decided to stagger the direction that the two individual strike packages would attack from by 60 degrees of heading. The first group, coming from the south and then turning west toward land, would come off target to the left out over the water, and the second package would make their return to safety to the right. We would all follow a rigid timeline to ensure that our flight paths did not conflict with one another's, and allow the Prowler out over the gulf to turn his jammers on and off in conjunction with the arrival of each group.

In an ordinary war this might not have been such a great plan. Five minutes was not a great deal of time for the enemy to relax their guard, and under most circumstances I would have expected them to keep their eyes and guns trained skyward for a much longer period. But we were counting on the regimentation of routine that the Iraqis were developing in response to our attacks. They were used to our strikes hitting rapidly and departing just as quickly, leaving their defenses largely impotent and frustrated. The sheer magnitude in numbers of daily bombing sorties should have desensitized them to a degree, and we were counting on them being eager to relax from their alerted postures quickly so they could rest for the next Allied attack.

Rivers decided that we would fly in the second strike package. This way he could keep watch over the entire mission, and be at the lead of the more perilous second group if his plan did not turn out to be such a hot idea and last-second alterations were required. This thrilled me enormously, and I was eager to be the first to see just how well this new tactic would turn out (heavy sarcasm).

We didn't have long to wait; about 4 hours after the target had been assigned to us up in intelligence we were advancing the throttles and going into tension on cat 1. Our A-6 wallowed slightly in the clearing turn under the increased drag of the six large bombs hanging on the ejector racks under each wing, then recovered quickly, and accelerated. Once we had climbed to altitude I slowed us down to 270 knots for our transit to the rendezvous stack 40 miles from *Ranger*. There was no rush; our Intruder had been the first airborne, and we would need to wait for the others to play catch-up. I saw our two wingmen from across the circle moments after we had established our counterclockwise orbit at 22,000 feet, and I waited patiently for them to gain sight of each other and close with us.

Dash 2 got aboard quickly, not wasting time with finesse but racing straight in at a good clip until he had to pop his speed brakes to slide under our fuselage into position. Dash 3 was slightly more cautious and did not have to use his speed brakes, and in less than 3 minutes we were on our way north, on a 308-degree heading. Five miles to the west and 2,000 feet lower the south group had joined up in a mirror image of our procedure, and had set a course of 300 degrees as they adjusted their speed to adhere to their timeline.

Our three jets plodded along at a fuel-conserving 330 knots, flying comfortably in the bright afternoon sky. This was a different war than that of the past several weeks, flying a formation in the daylight on our way to the target. I had to kick myself to fight off the complacency that the warm glow of sunshine was seducing me into; being able to sightsee was fine, but shooting at us would be the goal of any sight-seeing gunners in Kuwait City this afternoon. Better to keep my mind on the business at hand.

"All right, Rivs, air-to-air mode is all set in the TACAN; these guys are too close to see if it's working yet." I hunched my chin forward and spoke into my dangling oxygen mask.

"Okay if I put them into cruise?" I nodded my head, and Rivers made a hitchhiking signal over his shoulder.

We had 30 minutes to get our timing in order while we flew the remaining 150 miles to the initial point, where we would accelerate and turn west toward the target. I began to make out the coastline of Kuwait. There was not very much smoke south of the city, and the beach far in the distance looked like it could have been any sandy resort strip. From 30 miles away you could not see the barbed wire and barricades to amphibious landing craft, much less the buried mines and gun emplacements. Definitely not a vacation resort, I reminded myself.

Rivers ran through the mission check-in on the secure strike frequency, satisfied himself that all the players were airborne and in position, and made a determined effort to stay off the radios until the last A-6 was feet wet. Valuable lessons had been learned during the first few days of the conflict, and one of them had been that the Iraqis had radios, too. In addition to hiding under the oil platforms and spotting incoming strike aircraft, the Iraqis had been scanning frequencies on their radios as well. English-speakers were not difficult to come by, and it was a safe bet that the enemy would compromise anything broadcast without encoding. Of course, we would have been foolish to say anything in the clear, but the realization was slow in coming as to the extent to which radio activity was tipping off the Iraqi defenses.

I did not know if they used simple triangulation or the strength of the signals transmitted from our aircraft, but the few times we did break radio silence approaching a target we were usually met with AAA in the air before we ever got feet dry. It was a simple reinforcement of a lesson we had all learned in training—keep your mouth shut and maintain radio silence. The enemy doesn't necessarily need to know what you are saying; the fact that transmissions are being made is enough to clue them in to the fact that bombers are airborne, and might possibly even point them in your direction of flight.

The distance window clicked down to 18 miles. Out the left side of the canopy, Kuwait City looked peaceful. The distant haze masked the smoke from the oil fires to the west, and no activity broke the picture of distant tranquillity. At eleven miles to the IP that all changed.

The bombs from the first Intruder in the south group exploded well past the beach, somewhere in the vicinity of the target area, but we were too far away to gauge their effectiveness. I couldn't make out the tiny shapes of the A-6s in their 500-knot dives 25 miles away, but I could see that I was not the only one looking for them. Tracers, much more difficult to see in the bright skies than at night, broke the skyline. The gunfire shot up over the city, the shells reaching 16,000 feet in the air before running out of poop and falling back to earth.

In the lingo we had become accustomed to, I would characterize it as moderate AAA—enough crap in the sky that positive action was required to avoid running into it. Every few seconds a slightly larger light would shoot upward, corkscrewing its fiery tail in a bizarre yet somewhat predictable pattern, top out around 15,000 feet, and then I would lose sight of it when the handheld SAM's rocket motor ran out of fuel.

Five miles from the initial point I gave the hand signal to push our wingmen out into their prearranged staggered formation of a mile in trail. Once going down the chute in our target runs, the three Intruders would have enough room to maneuver to avoid threats from the ground without worrying about running into one another. The singular advantage of daylight that we enjoyed was the ability to suck it up into a relatively tight attack formation. My left hand moved the pair of throttles to their position of intensity, against the firewall, the setting saved for the critical moments, such as the catapult shot and the final run to the target. The cockpit filled with the noise of screaming jet engines, and I felt the forward tug on my seat as the thrust caught up with the throttles and our Intruder was propelled forward.

"Jakal 33, lemon." Stilt's familiar voice broke the radio silence, followed in quick succession by "Jakal 34, lemon," and "Jakal 35, lemon." Everything transmitted over the radio was via code word now. "Lemon" simply meant "feet wet." Three for three.

"Coming left, Rivs. Here we go." I stood our A-6 up on its port wing and eased in 3 to 4 G's, keeping my pull loose enough around the corner of the initial point so our wingmen could hang with us. I steadied up when the heading came through 260 degrees.

"There's steering to the target," Rivers said, taking his head out of the radar boot long enough to look outside at Kuwait City, 20 miles in front of us. "Stuff's still coming up," he observed, then put his head back down to refine his radar picture.

I rocked the Intruder's wings to the right in the newfound freedom of daylight, swinging gently back and forth to get a good look at our two wingmen strung out behind us. They were glued in position; I pulled back on the throttles to give them some airspeed to play with.

"Fourteen miles," I said, actually enjoying the sensation of looking out over the glare shield and seeing the land meet the water, a vivid contrast from what we were accustomed to viewing—a dark sky interrupted only by tracers. "All set with the program?"

"Ready to go. I've got the target on flir, pretty damn big buildings," Rivers answered. The munitions were supposed to be stored in the large, barrackslike structures. "Let me know when we're at 7 miles and I'll hit the chaff program."

The sun was almost directly off our nose, but our vantage point looking down from 22,000 feet kept it from shining directly into our eyes. As soon as we pushed over to our 20-degree dive the look-down angle would become more comfortable, and the sun would not blind us from seeing the bullets and missiles coming up at us. I hoped.

The AAA had completely died down, and so far it appeared that our plan was working. The Iraqis seemed to accept the previous three A-6s as the entire strike complement and had relaxed their vigil, or at least paused in their immediate response of throwing metal into the air.

No doubt about it—we were making our run in on a city, and a fairly large one at that. I scoured the buildings and streets 10 miles ahead and 4 miles below us for the target, but there was no way I was going to pick it out from this distance. I wasn't certain I would see the target at all from our perch at 22,000 feet. Fortunately, I did not need to; the magnification of the forward-looking infrared would take care of that. But I cross-checked my small photo of the target area with the outside picture anyway—if the flir went tango uniform, a visual designation might be more accurate for target acquisition than the radar alone.

"Ten miles, city's quiet, no shooting yet, warning gear's clear." The radar early-warning system didn't make a peep; not even the ubiquitous "2" appeared on the round screen. "Pushing over," I said to Rivers and tightened my grip on the controls.

I stuffed the stick forward until Rivers and I hung in our ejection seat straps with the roller coaster–like negative G, and held the nose down until the ADI steering symbol began to track downward on the dive angle marks. At 20 degrees down I relaxed the uncomfortable eyeballs-out pressure on the stick and let the Intruder stabilize in 1-G flight.

"Seven miles." I began to weave our Intruder back and forth, bracketing the turns within 5 degrees of steering while flying an unpredictable course.

"Programs running, master arms on, in attack, I've got it on the flir," Rivers let out in one quick breath. The airspeed indicator marched past 500 knots indicated. "Tracking."

I felt up to the canopy bow with my left hand and double-checked that my dispensables were preselected to flares, never taking my eyes from the gunsight in front of me. I pulled the commit trigger halfway to see where the flir was looking, and the gunsight reticle jumped down and slightly to the right. The pipper was fixed smack in the middle of five long buildings, oriented from east to west, just like they were supposed to be. Five similarly aligned rows of buildings became visible north and south of our target. The three sets of buildings farthest to the north were in flames.

"You're on the target, committing," I shot back and squeezed the trigger with my right hand to its full depression. Only in the light of day could I give my B/N a visual feedback of exactly where his pencil beam flir was looking compared to the bigger picture surrounding it. Rivers knew he was on the target, though; there was no mistaking the row of nearly identical buildings.

The altimeter wound down faster and faster; our vertical speed was pegged at a 6,000-feet-per-minute rate of descent. My right hand kept a light grip on the stick while I did my best to keep us in a 1-G steady-state dive and on steering. The release hammer slowly, slowly marched its way down the ADI.

"Fifteen thousand feet, hammer's still coming down," I let out, the tension building in my voice.

Damn, I had started our pushover too early, we were driving into the target, and our release solution for the 1,000-pound bomb's ballistic profile would not come until a lower-than-planned altitude.

"I'm tracking, keep it coming . . ." Rivers muttered under his breath into the ICS. "A little more, there! Pull up!"

The Intruder shuddered six times in rapid succession, and the controls jumped to life in my hands. I shot a glance at the altimeter: 13,000 feet.

"Uhhh . . ." I grunted under the weight of 5 G's as I fought to arrest our jet's screaming progress toward the ground. I leveled the wings to maximize the airflow beneath them and tried to get the jet back into a climb. The VSI needle hesitated at the bottom of the dial for a fraction of a second and then snapped back up to the top of the instrument. The altimeter bottomed out at 9,500 feet; I relaxed the back pressure momentarily, slung the stick to the right, and heard Rivers' helmet bang against his headrest as I put the 5-G pull back in.

Rivers went immediately back into the boot—he knew that if the Iraqis had not started shooting yet, then they did not know we were here. They would not know until our bombs exploded. This was his strike, and he wanted to see what damage had been done. The moment our bombs hit he bolted upright and scanned the starboard side of the A-6 for threats.

"Here it comes! Looks like mostly small stuff," I said over the intercom. I watched the tiny balls of fire come up around the canopy. "What've you got over there, Rivs?" I kept my thumb poised over the expendables button on the throttle quadrant, not wanting to highlight ourselves unnecessarily, but ready to pump out the ultrahot flares if we needed them. I felt absolutely blind cutting starboard through the air, sitting high up on the outside of the turn with the wing blocking my view of the ground immediately below us.

Hesitation. I kept the turn in to the right and the coastline. "Rivs?"

"Missile, missile! Break left, break left!" Rivers had been monitoring the progress of the corkscrewing yellow glow for a second, waiting to see for certain before we committed ourselves.

My stomach dropped. Where the hell was it? I snapped the wings violently to the left in a slight overbank to avoid bleeding off any more air speed, wrapped the jet up into a 5-G break in the opposite direction, and pumped out two flares in rapid succession.

"You still got it? Where the hell is it?" I yelled into the intercom.

"Pete!" Rivers flinched visibly, and then just as quickly he noticeably relaxed. "Did you just put out some flares?" he asked.

"Yes. Where's the SAM? Can I come back around to the right?"

"Yeah, we broke lock, keep the pull-in to the right, 1-2-0 outbound," he answered.

The A-6's nose worked its way around until we were pointed out over the gulf. We were doing 330 knots and 12,300 feet, too low and slow. I bunted the nose with a touch of negative G to get us accelerating away from the tracers still coming up around us. You didn't get too many second chances to dodge a missile in an A-6; its high-drag fuselage simply bled off energy too quickly in the 4-to-6-G turn required to break a SAM's lock. I decided to sacrifice some of the sanctuary of altitude for life-preserving airspeed.

Moments later Rivers made his "lemon" call, and it was

echoed almost immediately by our two wingmen. I relaxed slightly after Rivers checked in with Red Crown and we were on profile to fly back to the ship.

"What happened back there with the missile, Rivers? Wha'd you see?" I asked.

"Oh, shoot. Just as you put your turn in I lost sight of the SAM, and then the next thing I saw was a bright flash from our tail. Damn, I thought the thing went up our tailpipe! The flare scared the shit out of me!"

"Yeah, I noticed, I thought I was going to have to wear my mask all the way back to the ship!" I said. "You sure that seat cushion is all right?" Rivers just shook his head.

"How'd we do with the target? It looked like the south group nailed the buildings to the west, couldn't see ours," I asked Rivers.

"We strung ours smack in the middle, hit at least four of the buildings. Pretty good secondaries; we pulled the flir off the target before I could see the impacts from dash 2 and 3."

Between the attack from the south group and the impacts of our bombs we had hit at least four of the six rows of buildings. The aim point for our wingmen was the remaining set of structures on the southerly edge of the complex. It was beginning to look like the strike was a total success.

Rivers checked out the battle damage assessment with the remainder of the strike's players, and it turned out to be a clean sweep. Our two wingmen had dropped their total of twenty-four 500-pound bombs on the southerly edge of the target and had confirmed that all six rows of buildings in the compound were ablaze. Rivers passed the information over the encrypted strike frequency to *Ranger*, and we flew at a leisurely pace to be back in our Case 3 marshal position for the 1900 recovery.

We may have had the novel benefit of a daylight sortie during the mission, but when the sun dropped below the horizon, darkness came quickly, even at 20,000 feet. These were the most difficult night landings to adjust to—our eyes had been adapted to the bright sunlight for hours, and when we pushed out of marshal toward *Ranger*'s stern there were traces of light still coming over the distant horizon. I knew from experience that the comfort of flying with a discernible horizon would evaporate quickly when we passed through the scud layer of clouds at 5,000 feet. The approach would be exclusively on instruments from that point on, with the last vestiges of daylight disappearing abruptly and forcing our eyes to adjust to the stark contrast of utter darkness in the few brief minutes before our Intruder attempted to trap.

For the second time that afternoon my heart began to race, and I shrugged off the building tension. We approached three-quarters of a mile behind *Ranger*'s fantail. I concentrated on maintaining wings level, making small course corrections to stay on centerline, all the while stealing peeks outside at the brightly lit carrier deck. Early evenings like these were particularly conducive to vertigo, and I put my absolute faith in our flight instruments. I struggled with lineup and established a reasonably stable rate of descent for the glide path. But the only part of the approach that came easily was the angle of attack—the amber doughnut was locked in place, never showing a flash of green or red while I worked the throttles at a steady and seemingly random rhythm.

Two lineup calls from the landing signal officers told me before the hook had engaged the three wire that I had blown an okay pass. I momentarily slumped my shoulders forward, took a deep breath, and refocused my concentration on following the signals from the yellow shirt directing us toward the bow. I almost lost sight of the yellow shirt as he taxied our right tire inches from the slick deck edge, attempting to spin our jet around. My hands shook, I mashed the nose wheel steering button, and we entrusted our lives to the taxi director. Only after we had shut down and popped the canopy did the salt breeze slowly bring me back to a semblance of calm.

I let Rivers go through the intelligence debriefing solo, and

I went below to shed my flight gear and relieve the SDO. It was going to be a long 12 hours chained to the duty desk, but at least I had a stack of second-class evals to entertain me.

The nights blended together in a frenzied schedule, and the air wing increased its state of readiness to perpetual 5-minute alerts. Aircrews now sat in their jets ready to start engines at a moment's notice, prepared to launch in response to short-order tasking with little to no warning. The marginal semblance of a sleep cycle for the air wing was disrupted further. I was tired.

The prospect of the ground war loomed ever closer, and we were subject to daily rumor mill revisions of when we could expect the battle to begin. *Ranger* steamed farther north to get closer to the action, and it became dramatically apparent that other coalition naval combatants were advancing toward the shoreline of Kuwait as well.

In the early-morning hours of 18 February the USS *Tripoli* hit a mine while cruising 20 miles south of Faylaka Island. *Tripoli* was a Marine Corps amphibious landing ship, and the first conclusion I leaped to was that the invasion of Faylaka was imminent. *Tripoli* had off-loaded her amphibious landing force of Marines, however, and was acting as a support ship to launch helicopters in mine-clearing operations in anticipation of a Kuwaiti beach landing or feint. At approximately 0700 that same morning, the USS *Princeton*, an Aegis missile cruiser, detonated a second mine and sustained serious but reparable damage.

The knowledge that our forces were operating directly off the coast of Kuwait pumped renewed vitality into our weary ranks, but the news was followed quickly by a sobering incident. A stealth fighter attacked a command and control center the Iraqis had been using as a civilian bomb shelter. The Baghdad civilians who had been killed highlighted with pinpoint accuracy the genuine tragedy of war: Scores of civilians, innocent women and children, were dead in the blink of an eye. The Iraqi premise that the bombing was in any way an intentional act was far overshadowed by the fact that it did the Allies no tactical good, and of course hurt us politically.

What it did emphasize with medieval brutality was that civilians will be killed in war. It could not be avoided—it was a truism I am certain that all who have dropped a bomb in anger carry with them forever in a deep recess of their minds. But it was at best an unproductive thought to have while risking our lives nightly, and at worse, if allowed, it could become debilitating.

I secretly hoped for the ground war to begin sooner than later; prolonged war is the greatest gift possible to the evil in man's soul. I was incapable of discerning what was going through the mind of the average Iraqi soldier, but in mid-February it did not seem at all likely that Saddam and his army would capitulate from a bombing campaign alone.

The evening that *Tripoli* and *Princeton* hit mines in the far northern reaches of the Persian Gulf, Rivers and I flew a kill box mission southwest of Kuwait City. It was a typical strike—we dropped our ordnance during the first attack run on revetted vehicles, then made a second pass to target a tank with a laser-guided bomb.

What caught my attention was the visual picture of the Saudi-Kuwaiti border from the air. My first thoughts were of the apocalypse; fire and smoke inundated the division between coalition and Iraqi forces, the battle lines surrounded by the absolute desolation of the sandy desert. The ground war had not yet started, and the terrain looked ravaged and deadly; it was spiritually haunting. In old Babylon fires had been lit as a long-range early warning of impending battle. What I was observing from my God's-eye view, the air consumed by smoke and flickering flame, was a larger-scale version of similar circumstances thousands of years ago. I could only wonder with quiet trepidation how the next several weeks would unfold; I had no doubt that we would win the war. But at what cost to our soldiers and Marines?

Following the initial days of the air campaign the intensity of the fear of the unknown and the personal and professional uncertainty had largely subsided. The routine of the mission that had grown familiar replaced the oblivion of the future. It had become difficult to distinguish between proficiency and complacency. That all began to change mid-February. In our own individual ways the men of Air Wing 2 started to realize that the ground war portended to bring back both the sentiments and the realities of the first few days of the conflict, perhaps with even greater intensity. Tensions rose gradually, usually masked by confident, even overconfident, professionalism and surety of purpose. But we all knew the tension was there. Something new was on the horizon.

The daily politics of the war rebounded off our tired minds, occasionally penetrating and sparking a glimmer of emotion, but ordinarily inciting nothing more than a detached feeling of isolation. Which war were the folks back home talking about? Was it the CNN reporting of Baghdad, with nightly cruise missiles and round-the-clock coverage, or did it revolve around obscure Russian envoys shuttling back and forth in increasingly futile attempts to reconcile our "differences"? Flying high over the battlefield, or sitting in the depths of the ship, made it difficult to even relate to the images of destruction and carnage following a Scud missile attack into Saudi Arabia. Aircraft carriers were designed to operate independently and solely with their own assets, and although *Ranger* was integrated into the larger battle plan in ways we could only imagine, it was transparent to us. The nonfliers onboard could have been anywhere in the world; they could not see the sandy dunes 50 miles away, only an occasional glimpse of the water. The meager physical evidence

they possessed of our nightly bombings was the empty ordnance safety pins hanging on our Intruder's multiple ejector
racks when we trapped back aboard the ship.

We aviators were only marginally more in the know. True,
we saw the targets through the artificial TV representation of
the forward-looking infrared, and even occasionally in daylight. The bullets and surface-to-air missiles certainly appeared to be real enough, but they would only transcend that
final level of understanding to physical reality if we were unlucky enough to be hit by one. We rarely saw individual Iraqis,
soldiers on the ground who were objects of our destruction.
The evidence we witnessed of their demise was in the form of
melting armor and fiery explosions from 5 miles' distance.

The experience of releasing bombs one hour and eating
pizza the next in an artificially lit steel cafeteria was unnerving in its lack of apparent consistency. How could both
be real? We all took it in stride, like we took everything that
happened on cruise in stride. It was a source of pride to present an unflappable image, but the image was more than skin
deep; it was an effective defense against questions that could
not be answered, and answers that should not be questioned.
The time for that was before—and ultimately after—a war
began.

The limited exposure we did have to the individual Iraqi on
the ground was more often than not the CNN view of the
world: coverage in Baghdad, or a limited clip that had passed
the censors in Allied headquarters. Censorship in war is
life—information has to be denied to the enemy, and if the
media were to put sensitive information directly into Iraqi
hands, it would make the media the enemy. And as tempting
as it may have been, we were under strict orders not to bomb
our media.

Perhaps the most popular video clip released to the general
public during the war was that of the "Luckiest Iraqi Alive."
The flir image of an attacking jet's gun camera showed a picture of a bridge with the crosshairs set squarely on the center

span. A truck comes into view, and then drives under the flir's reticle and safely out of range seconds before the bomb impacts, utterly decimating the bridge. Great PR footage, a near-sanitary war; even the soldiers don't seem to get killed.

Air Wing 2, like most of the combatant outfits in the theater, I am sure, had similar video, with a slightly different end to the story. The video is there, with the crosshairs tracking a group of trucks as they race down a road. The guys in the trucks obviously know that someone is after them, because soon into the footage the trucks abruptly pull over to the side and stop, and their occupants get out and begin running for a nearby ditch. Here is where things change. The flir reticle moves off of the stationary trucks, and the crosshairs are now superimposed over the ditch where the Iraqis are trying to hide. Seconds later the ditch blows up, undoubtedly killing all of its cowering inhabitants. "The Most Unlucky Iraqi."

What was a more important target, the Iraqi soldiers or the trucks? I don't really know, but maybe the B/N responsible for the attack and the footage had a more honest assessment of what we were engaged in than the rest of us. It was easier to "play" the war as a video game, a win-lose set of individual circumstances with no further-reaching ramifications, no ultimate truths wrought from the destruction. What was sincerely disquieting was when I would catch myself "playing the game," and not feeling the disturbing, profound unpleasantness of what we were actually doing. The video was a reality check, a tangible reminder that there was a face to each of the casualties we produced with our attacks. The clip oddly enough never made it to the media for general consumption.

*Ranger* was launching four strikes a day, each with four to eight bombers to prosecute the target, and this did not take into consideration the tankers, alerts, maintenance check flights, and ad hoc missions added on in reaction to real-time intelligence. In spite of the frenzied pace, attempts were made to record the lessons learned thus far from the conflict and to maximize any training opportunities. The air wing leadership had the foresight to recognize that, fortunately, the navy collectively might only engage in sustained hostilities once every 5 to 10 years. Now was the time to take note of what was working, what was not, and to begin to prepare the next generation of leaders in the strike community.

The existing air wing strike leads had all been at the forefront of at least one combat mission, and it was time to bring the more junior officers into positions of responsibility leading the attack. The experience we would gain now would hopefully translate into more effective leadership years down the line, when we were COs and XOs.

My opportunity to lead an Air Wing 2 strike came in the early-morning hours of 20 February. In typical fashion, the strike lead and planning team assignments had been posted on the dry marker board outside the Intelligence Center 4 hours before the mission was due to brief, more than enough time to prepare with the prepackaged routine of strikes we had been flying.

Rivers and I had flown a maintenance check flight a few hours earlier, a required sortie to ensure that all a jet's systems were functioning correctly after a fairly major repair. I was feeling refreshed from the relatively relaxing daylight sortie over the safety of the gulf, and my faithful B/N and I trekked up to CVIC to see what we had to work with. To place me ostensibly in charge was not that far a stretch—Rivers would be sitting next to me, he was an air wing strike lead, and naturally he would have the authority to overrule any decision I would make. Hell, we had been working strikes together for the past month, and it seemed to be nothing more than a formality.

Our kill box was in central Kuwait, on the western side of the city, and getting there was the first issue at hand. No point in flying over enemy territory longer than we had to, I thought, and drew out a rough course on the topographical chart just south of the Allied ground forces along the Kuwaiti border. With some help from a Jakal crew we soon had the basic outline of the strike put together, and I sat down to deal with the only part of a kill box strike that truly required precise coordination: the target area tactics.

We had six Intruders at our disposal, each loaded with six 1,000-pound bombs. Concentrations of troops and artillery were scattered throughout our assigned zone, and it was easy to pick out three distinct targets on the map to divide our forces in their attack.

The lead of each section of two A-6s would strike their respective aim-points simultaneously, followed half a minute in trail by a wingman. We would have a total of 30 seconds of "government time" exposure over the target before all the bombers were on their egress and heading south for the safety of the Saudi border.

A Prowler and a section of fighters would loiter by the Allied lines, ready to act if the threats dictated it. The only augmentation to the standard defensive pair of AAA and handheld SAMs was the possibility of a radar-guided AAA battery that intel had reported might be in the area. The planning was fast, the brief was quicker, and the clock was striking midnight when our Intruder catapulted off the pointy end.

The flight along the Kuwaiti-Saudi border was as instructive as the strike itself. Rivers could see lines of hard radar returns south of the fortified positions; Allied tanks and artillery amassed in position for the ground offensive to come. The Iraqis had lit fire trenches along the border, and the oil wells continued to emit their ominous clouds. The smoke in southern Kuwait rivaled that of the oil well fires to the north, and it was abundantly clear that this was where the action would be. From our ingress altitude of 15,000 feet I could almost feel the tension along the haze-obscured battle lines, the random trails of fire piercing the night sporadically through small holes of unobstructed visibility. I saw a vague picture of confused energy: flames, fighting machines, and soldiers hunkered down in fortified positions. It was abundantly clear that the amassed power of potential energy was too great; it could not dissipate, but had to climax in the violence of battle.

Following our turn north toward our targets an unfamiliar call sign interrupted the radio silence—the "purple" net, the highly sensitive airborne radar listening station, had picked up evidence of an active radar-guided AAA site directly on the exit route we were planning to use. No sense in taking chances, I thought. I directed our wingman to change the turn off-target and egress to a new point still at a safe separation distance from the other four Intruders returning from their bombing runs.

We ran our string of bombs through the middle of seven revetted artillery pieces, causing explosions to highlight the target area briefly for our wingman before he released his ordnance and began the right turn back to the south. The strike had been painless to plan and frighteningly predictable to execute. I marveled at how circumstances had changed so dramatically in the previous month, and how we had adapted mentally at such an astonishing rate.

We knew that the ground war was inching closer by the minute, we knew it by the pace of the flying. After a few hours of sleep we were planning again for an evening attack to yet another kill box. But first we had the obligatory spare aircraft to man and, of course, it launched. We followed the skipper's lead to bomb tanks through the overcast on Būbiyān Island, maintaining the pressure on the Iraqis to honor the threat of an amphibious assault from the east. No time to debrief on our return; we immediately struck out for the ready room to listen to the plan for our originally scheduled kill box strike.

Our flight gear had not yet had time to cool down to that uncomfortably soggy, sweat-stained wetness when we were putting it back on. The plan, the brief, the flight were as canned as a Fallon training sortie, only without the stress of trying to do it in the "approved" method. Our strikes may have been simplified, but they were effective. They had to be simple—there was no time to plan extraneous or fancy maneuvers.

We approached the now-familiar coastline of southern Kuwait, and our package of four Intruders pushed inland toward the geographic points assigned for destruction. We had barely flown 10 miles feet dry before it became obvious that we were going to have problems. Simultaneously the inertial navigation system dumped, our headings and ADI froze in place, and the TACAN needle started to spin aimlessly. Faced with serious navigation challenges, a press on to the target would have been difficult at best, and finding the target would have been nearly impossible. We turned around.

I stared at the wet compass flopping back and forth with each minor wing dip our Intruder made. I was pretty certain we were heading east, out over the water, and Rivers quickly confirmed it for me on radar. Getting back to *Ranger* was no simple feat without operable navigation systems on board our jet, and myriad vessels steaming in the area creating a confusing radar picture. Fortunately the radios worked just fine, and Red Crown quickly got a skin paint on their radar of our returning A-6. Evidently our radar-highlighting transponder had decided to mysteriously freeze up as well. Typical navy, I thought: Just when you begin to get comfortable with a situation, wait a few minutes, because things will change.

We eventually managed to break out *Ranger* on radar after steering the vectors given to us by Red Crown on the backup compass. I struggled to keep our wings level using our standby gyro. We jettisoned our bombs in a clear patch of water—we could not trap with the extra weight—and we orbited over the carrier, waiting for our cycle to end so we could recover.

We looked out at the clear skies over the Kuwaiti coast far in the distance. A Scud missile rocketed from one end of the horizon to another, landing somewhere in Saudi Arabia. I thought about the bizarre levels this war was being fought on. Those on the front lines who were not fighting; those behind the front lines getting hit by Scuds; and those of us living in relative safety behind our water moat and flying in and out of danger behind enemy lines. Fortunately it was soon time to "charlie," and the landing with the limited instrumentation we possessed demanded my attention more than the useless philosophizing that was bound to pull a muscle.

A series of popped circuit breakers in a paneled fuselage compartment turned out to be the culprit for the mystery malfunctions, all effected by a power surge in the electrical system. At least that was the best that maintenance control could come up with as the scenario 2 hours later as we were sitting in our flight gear in the ready room, manning the alert. It was 0300, and I was tired enough to live with the "anomaly—fluke—it just blew" answer. At least for now.

Besides, we had other issues on our minds. The word drifting down from intelligence was that the ground war was planned to begin with an 0400 "H" hour, possibly as early as today. That gave us an hour before we could expect to launch on either a close air support or BAI flight in support of the ground offensive. I wasn't holding my breath, but you never knew, and one thing was certain: If we were not prepared, the unexpected would occur.

The prospect of successful peace talks by the Soviets with their erstwhile allies was a subtle tease to the situation as we viewed it from the ship. On the one hand, anything to avoid a ground war would be welcome news strictly from the perspective of avoiding coalition casualties, but on the other, the overtures by the Iraqis appeared to be such obvious red herrings that it made no sense to reward them with our attention. Saddam would publicize on an evening radio broadcast that the Iraqis would "never surrender," and then the next day the Soviet foreign minister would publish a convoluted schedule of quid pro quos for the withdrawal of Iraqi troops. In the end neither tack was acceptable, so it made little substantive difference, but it did keep us wondering.

The integration of a normal squadron schedule and routine into the disruption the war had introduced was approaching completion. One evening I returned to my stateroom from a kill box strike to work on evals, only to be interrupted at 0530 by a call from the SDO desk. One of the young workers in my division had a grandfather who was dying, and I needed to let him know about it. I waited until shift change—might as well let him enjoy a last hour or two of sleep before he had to confront the situation. I managed to finish up these various "collateral" duties by 1000 and get some sleep; the planning meeting for the evening's strike was not until 1300.

President Bush continued to tow a hard line, and responded to the tenuous Iraqi/Soviet peace "deals" with a simple statement: "Get out by 1200 Saturday." I had to nod my head in satisfaction and comfort in the knowledge that the president recognized that we were already playing hardball, and that Saddam had nothing left to negotiate with. The choices were simple, the messages were direct, and the end result would be the same; all that might differ was the route we would take to get to the goal. The Iraqis absolutely had to clear out of Kuwait.

I felt a touch of unease as I read a Stateside newspaper that had migrated out to *Ranger*. Polls back home were indicating that a sizable portion of the American people thought Saddam was "bad" because of his disregard for the environment. Talk about a lack of perspective, I thought. Certainly smoke and oil pollution are not good, but to have the environmental impact of Saddam become the primary indicator of his detrimental role in the world was a bit much. Invading a sovereign nation, threatening to grab 40 percent of the world's oil supply, murdering thousands, and toting weapons of mass destruction while displaying an eagerness to use them seemed to me to be slightly better definitions of his "badness."

The geographic isolation of the United States and the television-induced distortions of reality we Americans possessed were beginning to be manifested in public opinion. I couldn't tell if I was overreacting to a small sideline of a story, or if the general feelings in the States were running on such a superficial level. Thousands of people were dying in the Gulf War; the majority just didn't happen to be Americans, at least for the time being. It seemed to me that it would be appropriate later to focus on the environmental after-effects of the conflict. If sympathy were warranted now, it would be better served on the dead people rather than the dead birds mired in oil.

Walking out onto the flight deck for the first strike of the evening, I realized that I had not seen the sun in almost 4 days. *Ranger* was almost exclusively in the night strike business, and there had been little time to get out on deck during daylight. Lately we had turned to bombing most of our kill box targets on radar only; the smoke was usually too thick to get a decent flir picture. Southern Kuwait was enveloped in a billowy blackness, and it appeared that perhaps barely a quarter of it was from the round-the-clock attacks of the Allies. The Iraqi forces had purposely created the remainder by exploding the Kuwaiti oil wells and lighting fire trenches in defense of their front lines. The result was that Saddam was somewhat successful in reducing our ability to more accurately target his army, but only marginally so. The sheer numbers of troops and artillery in the field, coupled with the relative ease of acquiring them on radar in the flat desert, still left them vulnerable.

We trapped aboard after the evening's strike with our laser-guided bomb still attached under our wing, unable to utilize it on a second attack run due to the reduced visibility. When the last plane had landed that night, *Ranger* broke away from the circles she had been steaming in her designated "carrier box" in the Persian Gulf, and began to cruise to the south for three consecutive no-fly days to conduct maintenance and give everyone a break. For the first time since we had left the Philippines, *Ranger* would not be pushing water beneath her keel while we swung on the anchor off the coast of Bahrain.

The last time most of us had touched dry land was 50 days ago. While we would still be denied this luxury in the days to follow, at least we might catch a glimpse of the coastline, or enjoy a quiet walk on the flight deck without the concern of being sucked down a jet engine intake. We were planning on three days to catch up with the work around us; we got one.

# Chapter Fourteen

# . . . the war's desolation . . .

23–28 February 1991, the Ground War

The metal-on-metal tapping reverberated throughout the steel frame of *Ranger* as hundreds of chain links streamed out the fo'c'sle and followed the anchor to the silt bottom of the Persian Gulf. Each individual link was almost 2 feet long, and the acceleration of the ratcheting tons of steel from the anchor locker in the bow could be felt throughout the ship. It was a physical reminder of her vast bulk, and the enormous difficulties of maintaining her immense form in a set position while at sea.

It was not uncommon to drop the 30-ton anchor while deployed. At many ports of call, anchoring was the only method of disembarking without the availability of a deepwater harbor, or a pier large enough for a carrier to dock. A water barrier was also the most effective first defense against a possible terrorist attack when cruising off shores that might not necessarily be deemed secure. In rare instances flight operations could even be conducted with the anchor down, but they required perfect winds and a great deal of room for aircraft to maneuver around the ship. Without a substantial headwind, the stress on a jet's tailhook during a trap could be dangerously excessive. "Flanker ops," as they were called, were usually acceptable only under ideal conditions and when there was a degree of urgency to getting aircraft airborne.

No such urgency existed for *Ranger* as she languished east of Bahrain on the morning of 23 February. The point of stepping away from the conflict to the north was to conduct the required maintenance that could not be accomplished with the round-the-clock flight operations of the past 39 days, and to give *Ranger*'s crew and Air Wing 2 some needed rest. *Ranger* also had passed that magical milestone of 40 consecutive days at sea, and the prospect of a lukewarm beer on the sun-drenched flight deck was hard to resist. We had barely adjusted to the idea that the catapults would be silent for several days when the plan began to change.

I was the SDO for the 12-hour night shift, and with no aircrew preparing to fly, and the AKAC authentication code word cards safely locked away in the Intelligence Center, I was fast asleep in the relative comfort of my rack when the phone rang. I looked at my watch: 0413. Not much chance that anyone would be calling for Snax or Tony this early, I thought, and pulled my legs out of the metal bunk frame and stumbled over to the phone. The petty officer in the ready room on the other end of the line sounded excited, and understandably so—CAG's office had called each squadron to let them know that 13 minutes prior, the ground war had started. The flight deck Budweiser would have to wait. I flipped on the lights and turned on CNN, hoping to wake up Snax and Tony with some "breaking news."

After the initial bout of swearing, I managed to capture my roommates' attention long enough to fill them in on the reason for their rude awakening. They looked at me skeptically, particularly because by the time I had pulled on my khaki uniform, CNN was still mute on the subject. It was another small indication of the professionalism of the team that President Bush had assembled to orchestrate the war, that this new and profoundly important phase of the conflict had maintained the element of complete surprise to the media. President Bush was clearly a man of his word, and was not about to fritter around the edges with his message to Saddam Hussein.

President Bush had accurately called the commencement of the air war, and now he had done the same with the ground war. His deadline of 1200, Washington, D.C., time, for Iraq to withdraw its forces from Kuwait had been rigidly adhered to. It was reassuring that the commander in chief was standing behind his words with quick and effective action. I grew more confident that our forces in the gulf would not be left hanging out to dry with a mission objective that deteriorated into political expediency and pandering.

By the time I reached the ready room, the squadron heavies had already been informed of the escalation of the conflict. There was a brief flurry of activity as the department heads cycled in and out, feeling obligated to take action but having no tasking to accomplish. CAG's office phoned again and told us to expect the ship to weigh anchor at 1200 and to be ready for flight operations by 2100 that evening. Once the initial burst of squadron energy had dissipated, the ready room began to calm down, and the anxious aircrew migrated up to the Intelligence Center to track the progress of our troops.

There was little need to make the trek up to the intelligence spaces, because the boys in CVIC had a production all ready for broadcast on the individual squadron ready room TVs that would answer the brunt of our initial questions. The videotape had obviously been made at least a day or two earlier, and had been sent out to the aircraft carriers to educate and motivate the attack aviators once the ground war had started. In a televised brief that alternated between a sterile outline of the battle plan and an impassioned plea for effective air cover, a Marine Corps major walked the aviators through the challenges and the risks that were about to be encountered.

The navy and Marine aircrew could expect to conduct round-the-clock close air support (CAS): the Hornets and Harriers during the daylight, and the A-6s once darkness fell. The plan was to get the maximum number of jets airborne possible, and circle them in a holding pattern to be vectored into the fight in twos. The targets were Iraqi artillery and tanks. We probably would have to fly low below the clouds and smoke for better target acquisition, and we would need to exercise maximum flexibility to adjust to the changing circumstances as our forces advanced (hopefully), and as the strongholds of the defenders were better defined.

The video continued to roll, and the Marine Corps major's tone took on a gravity that was matched by the fervor of his eyes and the beseeching gestures of his hands. The Marines, his comrades in arms, would be making two breaches through the fortified positions the Iraqis had erected along their lines. Once beyond the barriers of fire, mines, trenches, and earthen mounds, the two Marine divisions would be facing up to sixteen divisions of Iraqi soldiers—hardly the numerical balance the attacking force would ordinarily choose. The army would be operating to the west, in a flanking maneuver; the Saudis and their Arab allies would advance up the Kuwaiti coast.

No one was certain of the degree of destruction that the previous weeks of bombing had inflicted on Saddam's armies, and there was no way of knowing how strong a defense would be encountered. The possible responses could not be completely anticipated; it was going to be uncharted waters for two full divisions of U.S. Marines, and the only advantage they clearly possessed was airpower. The major concluded his presentation with the blunt and unambiguous message that if we did not do our job, a lot of Marines would die. If there had been doubt in anyone's mind as to whether we would be getting back into the low-flying business, it had just been dispelled.

The day progressed slowly, and we waited impatiently for *Ranger*'s anchor to come up so we could begin to steam north. Subtle frustration mounted as the anxious bomber crews alternated between CNN and CVIC in an attempt to get the latest information. Word was circulating that thousands of Kuwaitis were being rounded up and executed. At 0744,

CNN reported that Faylaka Island had been taken, and between 500 and 1,000 POWs had been captured.[1] I tried to remember how many times I had gotten shot at while bombing Faylaka Island, and now it was ours. I had difficulty processing the image of Faylaka in coalition hands; 5 weeks had instilled a picture and understanding of the area that was rapidly changing.

Finally *Ranger*'s props began spinning, pushing her massive form back into the fight. Once under way, the TVs were turned down, and the aircrews focused their attention on the missions we would fly that evening. CVIC churned out new briefing packages, replete with hundreds of additional radio frequencies, and dozens of new geographic fixes to be utilized by the forward air controllers (FACs) who would be directing our bombers to their targets. The intelligence officers in CVIC were in constant motion in their attempts to update locations of the battle lines.

Eleven hours into the ground war, intelligence reported that the offensive was 15 hours ahead of schedule. Shoot, I thought, that had to be good. Thousands of Iraqis were surrendering, and our army was encountering enormous success in cutting off the retreating Iraqi armies to the north and west. There were isolated reports of chemical weapons use; some Marines had tripped a mine while breaking through the initial defenses, but they had been completely outfitted in their protective gear and were not injured. *Ranger* went to a higher level of preparedness against chemical attacks as a precaution—we were back to carrying around our gas masks on our hips full-time.

The Intruders were excruciatingly silent, loaded with 500-pound bombs and rockeyes, resting dormant on the flight deck while *Ranger* narrowed the distance to the "box" where

1. The news of Faylaka's capture had been leaked to the media as part of an Allied disinformation campaign. Attacks were conducted on and around Faylaka to lend credibility to the threat of an amphibious assault, but no actual landing in force was ever undertaken.

our carrier would operate. The sun had set hours earlier when we finally experienced the anxious relief of launching to help out the grunts on the ground. Rivers and I catapulted with five other Intruders as part of what we hoped would be a constant stream of attack resources available to the FACs. We initially broke off into sections, two jets apiece at various assigned loiter points, as we waited for our specific mission tasking. Each section eventually would separate, and each Intruder would then be called in to the target individually.

We moved our A-6 from one holding point to the next, careful not to deviate from the instructions of the ground controllers who would eventually hand us off to the forward air controllers. CAS was a complicated evolution, even when it had been modified to bomb a distance farther from our lines than normal. The multitude of acronyms made close air support to an aviator what "normal" navy-speak was to a civilian. Our troops were advancing too quickly for us to get too close; the last thing we wanted to do was drop on friendly forces. With the constant flow of jets to and from the front lines, coordination was critical if midair collisions were to be avoided. After orbiting for what seemed like days, we were finally given a frequency change to the FAC, and were instructed to start our run-in to the initial point. The IP would be the last geographic fix prior to the FAC assigning us our target a few short minutes before we dropped our bombs.

Our FAC was airborne, working out of the two-seat Marine Corps variant of the F/A-18 Hornet. The pilot flew in erratic circles over the target while the backseater described the aim point, and then vectored in the bombers from the assigned fix where they had been stacked up and waiting. Rivers cycled the A-6s steering to the initial point, and it was immediately obvious that there was going to be a problem. From the chatter on the forward air controller's radio frequency it was apparent that the previous Intruder had not left the initial point and that we could expect to be delayed on our attack run.

Normally this would not have been a big deal, but the IP where we would be holding was directly over the southern portion of Kuwait City. I thought back to the strikes we had conducted in and around the same general area, and the threats we had encountered—SA-2s, SA-8s, AAA, and hand-held SAMs. The good news was that the ground offensive was so far ahead of schedule that the air defenses had probably retreated, were abandoned, or were in disarray. We hoped.

The Intruder ahead of us finally left for his bombing run, and we entered our orbit overhead Kuwait City low enough below the clouds to ensure that we could maintain visual sight of the ground and any projectiles that might come up from it. We had started our third turn overhead and were both getting just a bit antsy, flying such a predictable profile in the brightly lit city skies. I looked down as we turned back in from the coastline to the west, and got my first unobstructed view of the city streets. I held my breath. Block after city block was in complete flames, each fire in a perfect line, not a building left untouched in each row. This was not from bombs, artillery, or tanks—the Iraqis were systematically destroying the southern portion of the city, torching the buildings one after the other, block by block.

For the first time during the war I got truly angry—not with the artificial anger generated by frustration or fear, but with a seething fury at the bastard Iraqis who had deliberately and with great planning decided to decimate the city. There was no defensive advantage I could discern in doing it, nothing more than a vindictive rage and lust for revenge at the Kuwaitis. I had a very bad feeling at what might be found in Kuwait City after its liberation.

The picture of the devastation below was mesmerizing, and it held my attention in a rapture of fascination. It was one of those rare moments as a bomber pilot when I felt that I was a part of the panorama; I could witness the effects of the battle below, almost feel the heat of the flames. Then the detached frustration we had all grown accustomed to returned with a vengeance; I thought, ironically, how despite the thousands of pounds of destructive force strapped beneath our wings, we were powerless to hinder the mayhem at our feet. We were not members of the world below; we were merely hostile visitors, raining down fire and blast in what we could only hope were precisely angled attacks, pinpricks that somehow might limit the ultimate cost of the conflict.

My turn over the city had become a lazy arc, bereft of the cut of G or an unloaded acceleration. I leveled the wings, and we flew back to the west, in line with the perfect succession of fires. I couldn't pull my eyes from the scene.

"They're torching the whole damn city," I seethed into my oxygen mask: "Block by block, they're destroying the fuckin' place, Rivers."

The anger flowed out of me easily and with comfort. I don't know why this was the first time that the pathetic waste struck me, why the realization came over me in an epiphany of understanding that there was nothing good to come out of this. Maybe it had to be done: I guess I knew it was "right" that we didn't let the animal Saddam go any further. But the situation in its entirety didn't feel "right"; it felt empty and cold. Man, I was pissed. All of the killing and suffering that had been inflicted over the past weeks and the sight of burning buildings were getting to me.

Rivers' reply was in a calm, quiet voice: "We've got a missile coming up." I could barely hear him, wasn't certain of what he said.

"Pardon me?" I asked, sure that his comment had been in reference to the devastation on the ground.

Rivers' voice came back at me over the intercom, this time strong and loud: "Missile, missile! Break right! Break right!"

Oh, shit. I snapped the stick to the right, panicked in the knowledge that I had let my focus wander. Where was it? I was blind to the right; I pulled hard until I felt the wings start to wag in an accelerated stall. I forced myself to relax the G, keep the turn on, don't depart the jet from controlled flight. The airspeed indicator needle was going down through 340. Dammit, I remembered that I had chaff selected on my canopy bow; the warning gear was silent; it had to be a heat-seeker. I groped up the canopy bow with my left hand and toggled the dispensables selector switch to the "flares" position. My hand slammed back down to where the throttles were against their stops, and I hit the flare button as quickly as I could. It was all taking too long.

"Where is it, Rivers?" I yelled into the intercom.

Quiet, Rivers stared intently out the side of the canopy. We had been in the right turn for maybe 2 seconds. I started to roll us back to the left as I pushed down on the nose to pick up airspeed.

"Keep the turn in to the right! Break right!" Rivers had figured out whatever the picture was he had been taking in.

I slammed the stick back to the right and overbanked to get the nose down—we needed more speed. I pumped out two more flares in rapid succession.

"Okay, okay, its gone, we're all right." Rivers' voice had returned to its normal flying monotone.

I instantly leveled the wings and pushed forward on the stick until the A-6 was accelerating in 0-G flight. The airspeed indicator arrested its downward progress and began to inch around the dial in a clockwise fashion: 330, 340; at 350 knots I pulled back on the stick and got us climbing back up to a safer altitude.

"Shit, Rivers, relaxed is one thing, but put a little inflection in your voice, would you? I thought you were screwing with me." Between my complacency and Rivers' staid attitude we had almost gotten ourselves shot down in the brightly lit skies. Shit, that was stupid.

No time for self-recriminations: The radio came alive.

"Rustler 3, Combat 401, your target 265 for 18, coordinates north 2-9-1-2-4-5, east 4-7-4-4-8-5. Artillery in the field. Egress south. Call leaving the IP." Rivers frantically wrote down the latitude and longitude of the target as the Marine airborne forward air controller spat it out.

"Combat 401 Rustler 3 copies all. Authenticate 'Ghost,' " Rivers transmitted back, depressing the mike pedal with his left foot while typing coordinates into the A-6's computer.

There was a slight hesitation and then the airborne FAC answered, "Authenticated 'Whiskey.' "

Rivers looked down at the AKAC cards the SDOs had so diligently been guarding for the past five weeks and read across from "Ghost" in the matrix. The next word was "Whiskey." It was a legitimate target.

I made a wing dip to the left, and we steadied on a 265 heading. Our Intruder had accelerated to 400 knots, and I kept the throttles firewalled. Kuwait City began to disappear behind us.

"All right, there's the target," Rivers breathed out slowly. Steering showed 5 degrees to the right, and I corrected for it. "I show us on top of the IP."

Rivers keyed the radio again: "Rustler 3 IP inbound."

"Roger Rustler 3, cleared in hot, call off target," replied the Marine Corps airborne FAC.

It got very dark as we left the lights of the city behind us and ventured out into the Kuwaiti desert. Somewhere in the vicinity of the assigned coordinates were Iraqi artillery emplacements that posed a threat to the advancing Allied lines still several miles to the south. The smoke began to thicken and I stopped looking outside. We were in a solid mass of darkness. Rivers' face was pressed deep into the cushioned radar boot, searching for the tiny radar blips in the desert.

"I'm going to start down and try to find some clear air, okay?" I asked while simultaneously pushing forward on the stick.

"Yeah, sure," Rivers answered, as if he could care less, his attention riveted to the radarscope.

The good news about going down was that it was easy to pick up more airspeed, and when it came to speed, more was definitely better. The needle had circled to 500 knots by the time we passed through 5,000 feet, still in the oily smog.

"I don't think we're going to break out of this," I spoke into the intercom. "I'm going to ease back for the run. Anything on radar?" I pulled back on the stick and slowed our descent into the blackness. The mileage to the target clicked down to 8 miles.

"I've got some contacts on radar, right general area, nothing else around them."

The steering on my ADI moved slightly to the right, and Rivers reached up for the master arm switch. The attack light on my ADI illuminated a second later, and I squeezed the commit trigger.

The eight bombs shuddered off their racks, and I pulled back on the stick and arced our jet to the left for our egress. South was good; it was closer to the friendly side of the battle lines. We checked out with Combat 401 and kept climbing, looking for a patch of clear sky to give our engines a break from the sooty air they had been forced to consume. We were not successful until we reached 10,000 feet, only 10 miles from the coastline. There was a literal fog of war over the country of Kuwait, only it was a foul-burning smog of oil and grit.

Back on the ship it was becoming obvious that the media-directed mood of the public was beginning to shift. CNN was highlighting the concept of "overkill" and "proportionality." I wondered just what the hell they thought this was all about; it was war, and as tempting as it might be to think of it as such, it was not a game. "Good sportsmanship" had no place here; nothing did that would make the circumstances easier to endure for the Iraqi combatants. The premise of war was to make it as ugly as possible, within the guidelines of international law, to bring it to a quick, final conclusion and perhaps even deter a like-minded tyrant in the future. The Vietnam mentality of half measures was beginning to rear its head, to portray Desert Storm as a sanitary war, a "good" one where none of the good and few of the bad were killed. It simply didn't work that way.

The ground war was days ahead of schedule; our troops were advancing at a pace we had dared not hope for. The fact that the battle lines were changing so swiftly brought with it the welcome problem of not being able to rely on information even an hour old—we would not know exactly where our forces were until airborne. Circumstances were changing that swiftly.

By 0200 on the twenty-fifth, Iraqi radio reported that Saddam's army would withdraw. The litany of lies Saddam Hussein had routinely espoused did not enhance the credibility of his statement, but evidence was mounting that the Iraqis were heading north. The difference between a withdrawal and a tactical retreat was a fine line to draw, however, and at this late a stage in the conflict, words alone were far too little, too late. I applauded President Bush's resolve in not caving in to an early cessation of hostilities. We had come too far to stop short of an actual surrender.

I was overwhelmed with the responsibility and pride of providing direct support to our troops, of helping to shape events, and of witnessing the actual results with each advance of our forces. This was why we were here—to drive Iraq out of Kuwait and to irrevocably decimate Saddam's offensive war-fighting capability. Our patriotic feelings of absolute commitment to mission and country were reborn to the intensity of when we had first sworn our oaths. I was proud to be an American fighting man.

A Scud missile attack fueled the anger I had felt simmering from the image of Kuwait City burning. Twenty-eight U.S. soldiers were killed in their Dhahran barracks when debris from a missile decimated the structure. The air wing pilots were flying twice a day and wanted more. We were obliged quickly.

Whether it was a preplanned retreat or a rout, Iraqi forces were definitely moving out of Kuwait City. The highway that ran directly north and across the Kuwaiti-Iraqi border to Basra was filling with an odd assortment of vehicles. Military equipment and vehicles of all description were rolling up the highway, providing us with ample targets highlighted against the desert on either side. Just before midnight on the twenty-fifth we launched on a strike to the road only 12 miles north of the ammunition dump at Al Jarah that we had destroyed more than 2 weeks earlier. The combination of bad weather and oil fires obscured the ground down to 1,000 feet, and we made two runs, the first on revetted artillery pieces and the second on moving targets racing north. The inclement weather precluded us from utilizing our forward-looking infrared, but we got low enough to ensure that we hit the radar-reflective targets.

The minor frustration of not being able to confirm our kills was outweighed by the success the ground campaign was encountering. Iraqis were surrendering in droves. Resistance still was being offered, however, and the run for the border that many of the troops were making did not fit the coalition criteria for victory. The Iraqis who opted not to surrender, but instead attempted to flee Kuwait, posed the threat of remaining armed to fight another day. They also happened to be the occupying force of Kuwait City for the past 7 months. The atrocities that had been committed were their responsibility, and perhaps this was why they, unlike so many of their comrades in the desert, were reluctant to raise the white flag.

On the morning of 26 February we got to see just how desperate the fleeing army was becoming. Eight Ranger Intruders launched to arrive at the southern shore of Būbiyān Island at 0830. We split up into groups of two, running in for our shallow dives at 3,000 to 4,000 feet, taking turns tracking along the roads. We each made two attack runs, releasing a string of six rockeyes in our 20-degree dives. There was little point in defining a specific vehicle to target—the road was clogged with traffic, most of it commandeered civilian cars filled to capacity with escaping Iraqi soldiers.

This was the ideal type of attack for a pilot delivery, one where I could pull our Intruder around the sky with abandon, keeping both sets of eyes outside the cockpit to watch for ground fire in the brightly lit morning. I snapped the A-6 into a tight alignment with the coastal highway that ran north of Kuwait Harbor, picked a spot on the asphalt road, turned our jet on its back, and pulled down to the dirt.

The daylight picture of the road in the desert was remarkably similar to the black-and-white flir image—the sharp contrast of the asphalt with the uniformity of the desert's subtle color and texture defined the highway. The air was quiet; few of the retreating soldiers were slowing down long enough to fire up at us, too consumed with trying to escape their fate. The muddy waters between Būbiyān and the mainland blended in with the desert coast. An occasional missile corkscrewed upward. We closed with Būbiyān Island to the east, and the AAA batteries still in place fired erratically at our jets.

I kept the throttles at the firewall and we screamed downward to the ribbon in the desert at 500-plus knots. I felt incredibly vulnerable in the bright morning sun. Shit, I didn't want to die, not this close to the end. The altimeter raced past 2,000 feet, and I squeezed the commit trigger and felt our bombs release from their stations. I got the G back on the jet quickly, and we were already in a hard port turn when the altimeter bottomed out at 1,500 feet. I watched the wide pattern of the six cluster bombs kick up over a thousand individual plumes of smoke and sand, bracketing the vehicles on the road and the Iraqis on foot attempting to escape. Out of the corner of my eye I caught a glimpse of an F/A-18. I reversed my pull to the left, rocked our wings back to the right, and started a climb for our second run. It was getting crowded out here, one highway and half the U.S. Navy bombing it.

We continued along the road to the north in accordance with the strike plan and did a mirror repeat of our previous run. A rapid snap back to the right and we were climbing over Būbiyān Island, out of bombs and heading south back to *Ranger* for a rare day trap. It had been easy; necessary, but easy.

Abruptly, a loud "beep-beep" wrested my gaze from outside to our radar warning gear—a Roland surface-to-air missile radar was painting our jet: Republican Guards. I jammed the throttles forward and yanked our Intruder around the Būbiyān shoreline until the Roland indication was off of our wingtip. Just as quickly as it had appeared, it was gone. We cautiously resumed our climb, carefully leaving a wide berth around the direction from which the SAM threat had emanated. The short-range missile's search radar did not appear again. We returned to the ship.

I opened the stateroom door to the blare of the never-ending cycle of broadcast news. I had not taken more than a step when a familiar voice came out of the TV perched behind my right shoulder. With mild curiosity I turned, my flight suit hanging on my shoulders still wet with sweat from the last sortie, to see what Uncle Tom had to say.

This was not the first time I had seen our ambassador to the United Nations on TV, but something he said that I did not quite catch piqued my interest. The image on the screen shifted to something frighteningly familiar—I was confronted with the same ribbon of road I had just returned from bombing, littered with vehicles and burned-out wreckage. Tom was briefing the media, I was not certain about what, perhaps explaining what was happening to the Iraqis on the road to Basra. Or maybe the station had inserted the video clip with no direct relation to the briefing topic at hand, but simply for dramatic effect.

Seeing the road and hearing Tom tied together loose threads

I had been unable to completely comprehend previously. For the first time I could clearly visualize the triangle of circumstances that connected my family. Uncle Tom at the highest level, directly impacting big-picture policy; my parents the bystander refugees, evacuated from a potential war zone; and myself, intimately involved in the most basic unfolding of the conflict. At home, thousands of miles away, the rest of my family and Laurie bore witness to the strange role we each were playing in reality theater.

Rivers and I would bomb what was quickly becoming known as the "highway of death," with its burned-out wreckage and charred carnage, one more time that evening. An unsettling mixture of detached emotion and self-preserving instinct disturbed my thoughts after bombing the fleeing Iraqis. Elation at the success of our soldiers and Marines, relief at not having to face a determined defense so late in the war and so low to the ground, surprise that after the mental buildup, events were unfolding so rapidly and in our favor. Feelings of revenge against the occupying soldiers, weighed down by their looted booty as they raced for the border that they had disregarded months prior. But most of all came the understanding that we did not want to be forced to do this again.

The Iraqis had the opportunity to surrender, but instead they chose to run with their weapons back to the starting point of their misadventure. As history would unfold, we would have to return to Iraq to fight again, but at least we did not leave Saddam with any of his tools of mayhem that we could destroy.

Discussion of the morality of continuing to bomb the Iraqis as they drove north to Basra soon filled the airwaves and papers. This was followed later with lamentations that we did not drive far enough into Iraq, that we had left Saddam in power to reemerge as a threat to civilization. Both views, of course, are as equally correct as they are erroneous. War is never clear-cut; perhaps war by definition is immoral—an unfortunate necessity at times, but immoral. To focus on the specifics of the "highway of death" without the overall circumstances and objectives as consistently outlined by the commander in chief was to ignore reality. President Bush had concisely delineated the objectives of our actions and the terms required for peace well before we dropped our first bomb. To deviate from them now would negate the authority that the world community and the United Nations had placed in the hands of the coalition forces.

Some has been written about the reaction of our forces to the bombing of the "highway to death." The criticism revolves around the lack of apparent remorse or guilt, and perhaps even bloodlust, at bombing the relatively easy targets. Everybody reacts to the stress of war and life and death decisions differently, and to narrow the image one would construct of an individual to his reaction immediately following the events of any battle is superficial and simplistic.

Naval aviators are a strange mix of people—utterly homogeneous in certain respects, particularly to the casual observer, and radically different in their core and substance. Very few naval aviators show honest emotion easily; they're not supposed to fracture the military bearing that has been instilled in them through years of training and detached experience under the stress of carrier aviation.

Anger is the easiest emotion to display because it is the natural, instinctual outlet for stress and fear. But even expressions of anger might be as diverse in their reaction to a common event as physical violence or the mere raising of a voice. Most emotion comes out at the officers' club, or on liberty in a foreign port, where the beer either softens or heightens aviators' feelings to the edges of their flexibility, which often is not very far.

Virtually all naval aviators are college graduates—some from state colleges, some from the Naval Academy, even a few Ivy Leaguers. This is their greatest obvious commonality—

a college degree and mutual survival of the weeding-out
process to get where they are in the navy. Many are religious,
many are not, and the greatest of the values shared by the men
is a trust in their comrades, a dedication to their country, and
an absolute focus on their mission.

It is exceedingly difficult most times for an outsider to reg-
ister where a naval aviator is "coming from." The uniform,
the haircut, and the navy-speak contribute enormously to the
building of a stereotype. So do the mannerisms of each individual; some express the control of emotion in reserved sto-
icism, others in an outburst of emotional release through
inappropriate laughter or anger. Still others never express
emotion at all. But the emotion is there, it has to be; despite
years of training and desensitizing to hide the race of the
heart and the sickening chill in the stomach, anyone who has
landed on an aircraft carrier, never mind fought in a war,
knows what fear and exhilarating intensity are.

We trapped after our final bombing mission to the roads
out of Kuwait City in the early morning, still several hours
before dawn. The pace of the Allied ground offensive accelerated, and so did our flying. We had barely gotten out of our
flight gear when it was time to race up to the Jakal ready room
for the next brief.

I looked at the wall chart and followed the progress of the
Euphrates River eastward, found where it intercepted the
Tigris, and then backed off to the west 9 miles. The tiny town
on the map sat adjacent to where the Euphrates made a final
loop downward before running directly east, about 30 miles
north of Basra. Our assignment was to mine the approach to a
small bridge that crossed a tributary north of the Euphrates
with time-delayed explosives that would detonate randomly
in the hours to follow.

Why not destroy the bridge? I thought. Did our forces in-
tend to trek this far north and need the bridge in place for
their advance? The next closest westerly-running road north

of the Euphrates was more than 50 miles away. If our offensive was going to extend beyond the Euphrates, then we were going to be fighting longer than I had thought. We hurried through the brief and struck out for our jets and the dawn launch.

Our small strike package of four Intruders staggered itself in 30-second intervals above the clouds after going feet dry. Two of the bombers would seed the road on either side of the bridge with twelve 500-pound destructor mines, effectively cutting off its use to all but the suicidal for the next 24 hours. Once the first of the time-delayed weapons detonated, the road would be sufficiently cratered to slow the progress of any vehicles indefinitely, while leaving the bridge completely intact.

The brightness of the sky around us was deceiving. We flew north between the puffy cloud layers, the stark whiteness reflecting the ambient light back and forth in a dazzling brilliance. We had no reference to the ground, or view of the sun. My eyes squinted in the glare; we flew completely by our instruments and followed the inertial navigation coordinates to the target. I could barely see our wingman behind us. I flipped our Intruder onto its back momentarily as the jet turned, and craned my neck over my shoulder; there he was. Up ahead, the second of the Jakal A-6s was a blackened speck against the white backdrop.

Each Intruder in our strike was essentially on its own; we had our assigned aim points and times to be there. In a strange way it was lonely, almost 100 miles from the now-familiar coastline of Kuwait, deep into Iraq, miles from the nearest member of our strike. I had no clue with which to maintain physical perspective other than the small mileage readout by my right knee and the altimeter. The three dimensions of our existence defied our senses, and were defined by two simple numbers: 30 and 15: 30 miles from the target beneath the cottony barrier below, and 15,000 feet above the ground.

I pushed the nose of the Intruder over in the stony radio silence that contributed to the unreality of the picture. Rivers was quiet as he refined his radar video, searching for his hastily researched offset so he could guide the steering cursors to the eastern approach of the tiny bridge, to our target. I had purposely initiated our descent early, hoping we would pop out of the clouds and acquire the bridge visually, using our eyes to guide us instead of the radar's computed aim point. The target itself was not radar-significant in the clutter of the dikes and trenches, and the chances of picking it up without the flir were pretty slim.

"Do you see it, Rivers?" I asked, glancing out the front windscreen and seeing nothing but the small gaps between the cloud layers as we passed through 9,000 feet.

"I'm on the offset; nothing stands out in the target area, might be offset only," Rivers replied. If we bombed utilizing strictly the offset, our accuracy would be at the whim of the charts and the database of latitude and longitude coordinates for the area. That was a lot of variables thrown into the pot.

"I'm going to press on down, try to find some clear air. You okay with that?" We needed to bring our eyes and the flir into the game plan.

"Go for it; let me know when we break out." Rivers' head was stuck in the boot.

We didn't have any reliable weather information for the lower cloud cover in the area, and I experienced more than a little relief when our Intruder punched into clear air passing through 6,000 feet. I struggled to regain my balance with the instantaneous shift from zero visibility to an unrestricted view of the panorama surrounding us. We were about 10 miles from where the inertial navigation thought the target was, and my mind reeled trying to process the picture in front of me, trying to correlate it to the sketchy satellite photograph we had been issued 3 hours earlier.

"We're in the clear, Rivs; I don't see it yet."

I trusted the jet to maintain the flight profile I had trimmed it for, and spent 100 percent of my time scanning outside, looking for the landmarks in the photograph. The Euphrates extended as far as the eye could see, wider and more developed than I had been expecting. The size of the town caught me completely off guard—south of the river it appeared to be quite large, row upon row of dwellings and streets, sleepy and dormant.

"All right, I've got the flir out. Shit, don't see the bridge," breathed Rivers.

The target was small enough that if it was not directly in the forward-looking infrared's field of view it would be almost impossible to find. Trying to search for it exclusively with the narrow beam of the flir was terrible technique for a B/N, called "flir fishing," a maneuver that was rarely successful.

I read out the distance: "Seven miles."

My mind was catching up and I was getting my bearings as our A-6 shot toward the ground. I glanced rapidly at the photograph clipped to my kneeboard. Okay, there was the bend in the Euphrates; follow it to where it begins to turn to the west. There! A stream of water, tiny at 4,000 feet, but running north. Where was the bridge? It had to be close to the Euphrates. I saw a sharply defined cut in the desert, going east and west. Was that a road? I followed it to the stream. No, dammit—it was a dike of some sort. I scrutinized the small stretch of water between the dike and the Euphrates, and there it was—a tiny bridge, but it had to be the target.

"I've got it, Rivers, coming right." Rivers immediately stopped his radar search and reached for the master arm.

"Okay, Pete, you've got it, master arm's on, 3,000 feet," Rivers said without hesitation, handing the attack over to me.

I glanced down at our dive angle, 13 degrees; no problem. This was not a manual-bombing run; this time the computer would be providing me with the targeting solution. I pushed the throttles up against their stops, painfully aware that we had not been maneuvering since we had broken out of the clouds. I depressed the pilot attack button on the control stick with my right pinky and watched the gunsight pipper come alive with the computed impact point of our bombs.

"In attack, 2,500 feet, getting the program." Rivers reached over to his right side to activate the chaff program as he monitored our altitude.

"All right, coming back to the left a bit, lined up." I smoothly dipped the wings and tried to align the projected path of the small dot of light on the gunsight with the bridge in front of us. The computer kept the gunsight pipper steady as I gingerly moved the aircraft, careful to maintain 1 G and a steady flight path. The pipper marched up to the bridge in our diving race toward the town below. I estimated where 100 yards short of the bridge would be on the ground; I saw nothing but dirt. The pipper crossed my estimated aim point, and I punched the pickle button on the control stick.

The A-6 rocked imperceptibly from side to side with the release of the twelve mines. I snapped the jet up to the left while punching out flares. Two thousand feet. I made a quick scan of the horizon; nothing but a peaceful town, no gunfire. I overbanked rapidly so I could get a view of the bridge while the A-6 was inverted—the computer had done its job; the dust trails of the twelve impacts appeared to be fairly evenly spaced across the road. I brought my hand back to the right to swing the Intruder sunny side up and then pulled back hard to get us above the range of any gunners on the ground. Seconds later we shot back into the clouds and transitioned to instrument flying, once again completely devoid of reference to time or space. It had been just like a Fallon training strike.

Our return to *Ranger* was uneventful, a mirror image of the flight north, a surreal world of white infinity among the clouds. I couldn't help but continue to wonder why we had not blown up the bridge. Were we really going to march our troops this far into Iraq? I did not like the idea of dropping bombs that did not explode on impact, mines with their staggered delay fuses. I would not have time to consider the possibilities until events settled down in the weeks to follow, but a nagging uncertainty finally caught up with me that would stay with me, perhaps for life. That was a hell of a large town, lots of kids. I just hoped to God that none of them was allowed to play by the bridge for the 24 hours after the strike. Of course, I would never know. We trapped aboard *Ranger* in a silence of fatigue.

It was difficult to conceive that the overall ground offensive could have been more successful. All of the Allied forces were advancing faster than anyone could have hoped, and the casualties were quite limited compared to what we had been led to expect—that is, assuming you were not one of the casualties. In that case, of course, numbers are meaningless. It could not last more than a few days, not if we were to stick to our original plan and avoid a drive into Iraq on a quest for the head of Saddam Hussein.

The frantic pace continued, but we all realized that the end of the conflict was imminent. It was a rout. The Iraqis had no negotiating points; we had won. Kuwait had been liberated, the threat to the Middle Eastern oil fields had been negated, and the viability of a threat from Saddam's weapons of mass destruction had been delayed for years. The details were yet to be ironed out, but the end result was a foregone conclusion: Iraq had lost.

*Ranger* catapulted Rivers and me into combat one more time, in the early-morning hours of 28 February. We hauled our load of ten rockeyes 50 miles north of Basra on a predawn road reconnaissance, attempting to destroy the last vestiges of the Iraqi army still within range heading north. We tracked directly alongside the highway 2,000 feet below us, looking for the sharp radar reflections of tanks and towed artillery. We approached the Iraqi city of Al Amarah, found the distinct radar returns on Rivers' scope, and released the last bombs either of us would ever drop with the intent to kill.

I pulled off target, and the sky became brilliant in one final, spectacular light show. Red ropes streamed across the horizon west of us, taking one last stab into the night air in an attempt to bring us down. We had not witnessed the improbably beautiful red arcs from a common altitude since our foray into Iraq the first night of the war, and as they passed several miles to the left of us it was difficult not to become mesmerized.

This was our forty-fifth combat mission, and we knew it would be our last strike of the war. A subtle collection of images haunted my mind. I knew that the culmination of the events of the past 43 days and nights would more than likely take with them the dizzying intensity that was growing addictive. I began to gain an inkling of an understanding of how easy it could be to succumb to man's baser instincts. I could start to comprehend the attraction felt by mercenaries to their "trade," their effort to sustain an adrenaline-soaked habit of intensity without concern for the restrictions and boundaries of social condemnation. I felt empty and at a loss for the waste and the human suffering. But I also began to understand the limits we put on the human mind, some limits that should be there, some that should not. The sheer power of experience we had been privy to would be difficult to replicate in the "real" world, and I wondered whether it was a concentration of emotion that might better be left alone.

The Swordsmen delivered more than 2 million pounds of ordnance and flew 1,358.8 flight hours during Operation Desert Storm. VA-145 was officially credited with destroying or severely damaging 33 tanks, 48 artillery pieces, 41 naval vessels, 25 missile components, 23 conventional and chemical munitions bunkers, 13 oil facilities, 7 communications sites, 5 hangars, 8 piers, 2 barracks, a bridge, a power plant, and a rail yard. Additionally, the squadron mined 4 critical lines of communication.

The only number that was conspicuously missing was the one we would never know—how many people we had killed.

The VA-145 Swordsmen would receive the Rear Admiral C. Wade McClusky Award as the premier attack squadron in the U.S. Navy for 1991.

My few short months in the Persian Gulf would have an

understandably disproportionate impact on my life; I would never view the world in quite the same way. For most Americans, war gives a fleeting glimpse from the loose confines of warm liberties of how much, perhaps most, of the world live their daily lives—in absolute uncertainty, physical peril, and fear.

Our A-6 snagged the three wire on *Ranger*'s angled deck at 0630 on 28 February 1991. At 0800 the cease-fire went into effect. The war was over.

> *T. R. Pickering*
> *The Representative*
> *of the*
> *United States of America*
> *to the*
> *United Nations*

*March 10, 1991*

*Dear Pete,*

*Your letter came yesterday and Alice and I were pleased to get it. We have been thinking a lot about you over the past months, hoping Saddam would move before you had to move him. No doubt, the air portion of the campaign had a great deal to do with that. Early in the strike phase we saw your squadron was working over an Iraqi T-43 for a while. Meg also said she sent you from Europe an article in the* Stars and Stripes *which appeared here in the* Washington Post *on strike operations from the* Ranger.

*In the meantime, since the 27th of February, we have been at work on how best to wind it up. The first step was last Saturday when we set up the conditions for a permanent ceasefire. When Baker gets back from his trip, and the Iraqis comply, we'll start the next phase—some level of UN force on the ground.*

*I have had some interesting times here, but not as pressing as your own. Right after the President spoke on* the 27th I opened up contacts with the Iraqis here to help set up the "victory" talks of Safwan and to get the phase on returning the POW's under way. They have been remarkably flexible, no doubt due to some of the activities in which you have been engaged.

The next steps are going to be more difficult, particularly if Saddam hangs on. If not, who replaces him and what that leads to are also going to be unusual.

The UN has done pretty well by us so far and it has been fun working this side of the issue. None of us would have given a very big bet in August that it would have stayed together so well and for so long. In part we can thank Saddam for that. You don't get opponents like that, either in size or inflexibility all the time. Those he didn't scare, he made mad.

Sorry to hear Kuwait City looks so bad. I was there in June. The destruction on TV from the Iraqi occupation looks bad. The oil wells will take a long time to put out.

I agree with you that we need to do all we can to avoid having to go back for a second trip. So far, the way you have handled your end has discouraged others from trying. Now a good bit of what we do next is up to us. So far the political leaders here have done a good job. We'll continue to try to ensure it keeps on that way.

Hope all your missions now will be less exciting. Thanks for writing. We look forward to seeing you in July. I spoke with Marcia on the phone yesterday and all is fine here. Alice sends her best.

Tom

# Epilogue

# . . . the twilight's last gleaming? . . .

Four Years Later

The gray overcast obscured the magnificent view of Mount Rainier that should have confronted us off our nose, leaving us with nothing to absorb in our last moments airborne in an A-6 except the barren, concrete runway spanning before us. Rivers was curiously idle in the right seat. All of his B/N's tools had been cannibalized for use in another Intruder, the radar, flir, and inertial unceremoniously yanked out to alleviate the shortage of spare parts that the A-6 community constantly endured. The Washington sky took no pity and began to let flow a random trickle of drizzle that saturated the tarmac and beaded off our freshly polished wings.

I adjusted the throttles slightly to keep us on the broad and forgiving glide path of a civilian airfield, keeping my eyes outside for a reference to the horizon—many of my flight instruments, too, had been rendered inoperable prior to the final touchdown of our venerable Intruder.

"Rider 501, Boeing tower, request a low pass, downwind's left." The radios still worked, and the controller at Boeing Field evidently wanted to give the small crowd assembled a side view of our Intruder before it was parked forever beside the other "vintage" aircraft at the Museum of Flight.

Rivers eagerly keyed the mike, anxious for any activity

348

that would distract momentarily from the melancholy approach: "Roger, tower, left downwind."

The Intruder's main mounts were barely 10 feet from touchdown on the runway when I added full power, maintained our angle of attack, and let the unmistakable roar of our J-52 engines push our A-6 straight ahead. I took my time before turning back to the north, cherishing the responsiveness of the throttles as I pulled them back to level at our downwind altitude. We left the landing gear down, one last opportunity to make noise. The Seattle skyline filled our canopy windscreen, and I leveled the wings to fly back to the approach end of runway 13.

*It had been four years almost to the day since Rivers and I had dropped our last weapons on Iraq. Ranger had remained on station in the Persian Gulf until 17 April 1991, but we had been fortunate enough to break up our time at sea with a 3-day port visit to the United Arab Emirate city of Abu Dhabi on 23 March. We arrived just in time for the Islamic holy days of Ramadan. The infusion of 5,000 Ranger sailors into the Muslim port after 79 consecutive days at sea (one short of a second beer day) wreaked minor havoc on the city. Fortunately, and wisely arranged, the only available alcohol was in the somewhat isolated Western hotels, and in a cordoned-off section of the pier where the carrier was docked. The air wing let off steam at a rapid pace, but our ostracism from the local populace insulated most of them from our various antics. I doubted that any of the locals could hear the salvoed good-willed cheers of "Happy Ramadan" as naked aviators belly flopped off the diving board into the midnight swimming pool.*

Rivers pulled his kneeboard off his G suit and put the kneeboard away in his nav bag. I wondered if he would ever have occasion to remove it again. The rain came down harder, pelting our Intruder flying 1,000 feet above the ground. Interstate 5 disappeared beneath our nose on the downwind flight path, and I took a good look around—I didn't know when or what I might be flying next. Whatever it was, it would be in the civilian world; I was due to get out of the navy in less than 2 months. I inched back the throttles, and our Intruder began a slow descent to Boeing Field.

*The Iraqis had initially stuck to their deal of a cease-fire, and our post–Desert Storm flights over land were boring exercises of guard duty for the most part. Our only major excitement came 4 days after the end of the conflict, when our A-6 experienced another set of mystery-popped circuit breakers. We were left without radios or a transponder to identify us as a friend to the Aegis missile cruiser that defended the northern approach to the battle group against air attack. We flew back cautiously through the night sky as Rivers struggled to raise someone on the survival radio in his SV-2, the irony not lost on us for a second that our greatest enemy at the moment was an anxious American missile operator on the picket ship below.*

*The fates were merely toying with us, and much to our surprise and relief, the survival radio worked as advertised. Rivers directed me back to the ship with vectors provided to us via his tiny radio earpiece.* Ranger *steered a Prowler to our vicinity, and I watched the flashlight signals from the right side of the EA-6B cockpit to match our configuration changes as we dropped our landing gear and flaps in tight formation on final approach. The Prowler broke away and I swung my head forward to transition to the dim lights of the flight deck and the meatball, silently thankful to the EA-6B for their guidance back to the night carrier.*

Ranger*'s return to San Diego had been far more festive than her departure. The battle group made port calls to Pattaya Beach, Thailand; Hong Kong; the Philippines; and Hawaii before the final stretch home. The air wing flew off the carrier* to their respective bases on 6 June 1991, almost 6 months to the day since we had departed. The cruise back east had moments of enjoyment from the perspective of the ports visited, but as with most deployments, everyone just wanted to get home. The 3 months plus of letdown following the end of the conflict were more than enough of a decompression; in fact, it became frustratingly boring. The routine of paperwork and a lessened flight schedule kicked in with a vengeance, and it was easy to temporarily forget that we had actually engaged in the carrier's primary mission of combat.

Living on the boat, isolated from the rest of the world, had made me skeptical that there would be anyone who remembered the Persian Gulf War upon our return, whether all of the parades and celebrations would have dried up. My fears were groundless; our reception was spectacular, but it still seemed quite odd and out of place that such excitement could be generated from events that had transpired months earlier. What I had not factored into the equation was the desperate desire of the American people that our military "work." After the post-Vietnam drawdown of the 1970s our military had, across the board, become a hollow force, a showpiece lacking the training and depth to act in a truly effective manner.

The defense buildup of the 1980s was supposed to change that, and while the positive effect on morale was immediately evident, the proof would have to wait for our collective performance in combat. Desert Storm had provided us with the opportunity to show what the all-volunteer military could accomplish if armed with the requisite commodities of morale, training, and weapons, in that order. These three requirements for a capable fighting force are mutually interdependent, but morale is singularly the most important. Without it effective training cannot be accomplished, and it is problematic at best to induce people to risk their lives to kill others. As a group we had lived up to the cautious expectations of the

*American public, and for a few short months the U.S. military was on the firmest footing that it had enjoyed in years.*

Rivers looked for several long seconds out the right side of the canopy, lost in thought. Our A-6's angle-of-attack indexers flickered green momentarily, then reverted to an amber doughnut as I added power. Elliott Bay and Puget Sound were coming into view slightly to the left. We flew the long downwind. I turned my helmet forward and silently concentrated on getting our Intruder on the ground.

*The military's euphoria was fleeting, partially self-induced by debacles such as "Tailhook," inexcusable behavior that nonetheless was blown out of proportion. The reaction of the navy's most senior leadership to run and hide in reaction to the Tailhook scandal was a prelude to the direction the service was going to take. When the rank and file start to question the loyalty of their superiors, the organization begins to rot from within.*

*With the demise of the Soviet Union as a unified adversary, the American military experienced a period of justifiable drawdown. But instead of arresting the reduction in forces at a level that would sustain morale and the cadre of experienced personnel in the services, defense spending became the easy answer to a budget that needed to be reduced and balanced. The difficulty lay in the fact that while the Soviet Union no longer existed, myriad others had supplanted the "evil empire's" role as a real or perceived threat to U.S. interests. The combination of reduced budgets and burgeoning hot spots around the globe effectively and substantially increased the commitments of each U.S. Navy squadron, and led to more frequent deployments. The* William Tell *Overture played one last time, and* Ranger *was decommissioned and parked forever at the Bremerton, Washington, Naval Shipyard. There were fewer resources with which to train and prepare, and the time away from families increased.*

*After leaving VA-145 I became an instructor at the A-6 training squadron at Whidbey Island. I had been there for about a year when it was announced that there would be no follow-on attack aircraft to take the place of the A-12 as the replacement for the Intruder. To make matters worse, there would be no further technological upgrades to the A-6 once the ongoing rewinging program was complete. The installation of new wings had already been paid for to the tune of several hundred million dollars, and we eventually began to park our A-6s in the desert "boneyard" of Davis Monthan Air Force Base in Tucson as quickly as they could be rewinged. Every aviator in the Intruder community would need to either transition to another navy aircraft type or exit the service. I eventually decided to leave.*

I dipped our wings to the left and began the turn to the civilian square base leg of the approach, an uncomfortably unfamiliar extension of the compressed carrier pattern we were used to flying. Rivers stared out the right side of the jet, looking one last time at the ground from the B/N's seat. I verbalized the landing checklist again, touching each of the listed items with my left hand. When I got to the tailhook I shifted the control stick to my left hand, reached up with my right, and punched the retract button. The tailhook would be stowed in the up position for 501's final landing. I leaned to the left for a better view of the field as we began our turn to final approach.

*Before the final disappearance of the A-6 community, Rivers' dedication and superior performance managed to secure him a last flying position in the most enviable billet in naval aviation: squadron command. It would be a short tour, its length cut by the decommissioning of the squadron and the parking of her jets forever, but it did give Rivers the opportunity to be the man in charge of an A-6 command at sea. It was his last chance to fly the Intruder deployed, and I didn't feel right about letting him do it alone, so in January 1994 I left my shore duty early and signed up for 15 months of workups and cruise with the VA-52 Knightriders. Rivers and I flew together for the 6-month deployment, this time off the coast of Korea, attempting to deter or possibly react to the aggressions of what was rapidly becoming a laundry list of potential adversaries who would just not go away.*

*Intangibles had been changing in the navy as well as the dollar signs. Women were thrust into combat roles with little to no organized planning or preparation. As a result of Tailhook, and the rapid and haphazard assimilation of women into extended at-sea operations, the navy altered the focus from where it should be on combat preparation, to obtuse issues of force-fed values and feelings that served to divide and distract the aviators. Fear from repercussions of difficult-to-define interpersonal issues such as sexual harassment gradually began to supplant the fear of letting down one's comrades. Eventually the incentive of increased cash bonuses for aviators was used in an attempt to replace the previous reward of camaraderie, which had kept fliers in the navy. More money was great, but I never met anyone who based his decision to stay in the navy on a payoff from Uncle Sam. It was insulting to be thought of as hired killers.*

*The last straw in my bail of frustration with the navy turned out to be the time-honored and understood fact of life of deployment: family separation. Laurie and I had gotten married, and our daughter was born less than a week before I left for our cruise to the western Pacific and Korea. I would not see them again for 6 months. I kicked myself for my insensitivity to the married guys on my previous two deployments; it was tough. I marveled at how Rivers had managed it—he was involved in the lives of his four boys, yet he was rarely home. It took a Herculean effort to balance it all, yet he, and many like him, did it. It was one thing to make such an enormous sacrifice in one's family life when the navy was still an adventure, and the importance of the frequent deployments could be understood as a vital national interest. Now it was just a job. The writing was on the wall, and I wanted to make a clean break while my memories of comrades in arms and the accomplishments of the navy were still fresh and untarnished. I submitted my resignation papers.*

The rain had stopped, but there was little hope of the sun breaking through the overcast. I added power to catch the glide path as I felt the jet begin to settle, made a quick wing dip for lineup, and held an amber doughnut in the center of the angle-of-attack indexer. Our Intruder slammed onto the tarmac in a flareless landing to runway 13. The A-6 had been repainted for its final rest on a slab of concrete, and the shiny blue-and-white squadron logo was the focal point of the small reception of onlookers and family standing outside the museum. I shut the engines down, hesitated in the ejection seat for a moment, and turned to the right to shake Rivers' outstretched hand. I got out.

# Glossary

**AAA**  Antiaircraft artillery.

**ACU**  Armament control unit (bombing panel with all associated switches).

**ADI**  Attitude direction indicator (pilot's primary attitude instrument—a TV display).

**AI**  Aviation intelligence officer.

**AOA**  Angle of attack.

**ASR**  Armed surface reconnaissance.

**BAI**  Battlefield area interdiction.

**BDA**  Battle damage assessment.

**blue on blue**  Conflict with one's own forces, friendly fire.

**B/N**  Bombardier/navigator (term used exclusively in A-6s).

**bolter**  An inadvertent touch-and-go landing after the tailhook misses the arresting wire.

**CAG**  Commander, air group ("Air group" has been changed to "air wing." CAG is still the common acronym, however.).

**CAP**  Combat air patrol.

**CAS**  Close air support (bombing extremely close to friendly lines).

**CATCC**  Carrier air traffic control center.

**CBs**  Circuit breakers.

**chaff**  Metal confetti designed to draw a radar-guided missile away from a targeted jet. The small bundles are "shot" out the back end of the jet's fuselage.

**CO**  Commanding officer.

**CQ**  Carrier qualification (ship landing refreshers).

**CSAR**  Combat search and rescue.

**cursors**   B/N's radar and flir crosshairs. Operated via a small slew stick on a pedestal between the B/N's legs.

**CVIC**   Carrier Intelligence Center.

**dispensables**   Chaff and flares.

**DME**   Distance-measuring equipment on the TACAN gauge. Measures the distance in nautical miles to a transmitting ship, ground station, or another similarly equipped and tuned aircraft while in the "air to air" mode.

**FAC**   Forward air controller for close air support.

**feet dry**   Crossing the enemy beach inland on the way to the target.

**feet wet**   Crossing the enemy beach on the way back to the carrier.

**flares**   Ultrahot flares are dispensed out the back of the fuselage to draw off an infrared, heat-seeking missile. Does for a heat-seeking missile what chaff does for a radar-guided missile.

**flir**   Forward-looking infrared. Uses contrasts in relative heat to produce a black-and-white TV image of the ground.

**FOD**   Foreign-object damage (to jet engines).

**goat rope**   Ever try to rope a goat? Chaotic exercise.

**GQ**   General quarters (battle stations on a U.S. naval vessel).

**HARM**   High-speed antiradiation missile (shot at enemy radars).

**Head**   Bathroom.

**IFF**   Identification, friend or foe. Radar-highlighting transponder to assist friendly fighters and air traffic controllers in identifying aircraft on their radar screens.

**INS**   Inertial navigation system. Uses a system of spinning gyros to determine position without relying on any external navigational transmitters.

**IP**   Initial point. Final point of navigation prior to the target.

**Iron**   Air Wing 2 radio call sign.

**IR SAM**   Infrared SAM. Usually shoulder-fired; a heat-seeking surface-to-air missile.

**Jakal**   Squadron radio call sign—VA-155.

**kill box**   Geographic rectangle with 10–25-mile sides where strikes would be assigned to attack Iraqi artillery, armor, and troops.

**KTO**   Kuwaiti Theater of Operations.

**laydown**   Straight-and-level attack run. A two-dimensional-only profile.

**LGB**   Laser-guided bomb.

**"L" 1, "L" 2**   Aircraft elevators 1 and 2 on a carrier.

**LSO**   Landing signal officer.

**marshal**   The designated orbit point for an aircraft prior to commencing an approach to the ship. The carrier's radar controller for this holding phase of flight is also referred to as "marshal."

**midrats**   Midnight rations.

**pickle**   Bomb release button on the pilot's control stick; also, the act of a pilot releasing a bomb.

**rack**   Bed, sleep.

**Radalt**   Radar altimeter (God).

**Republican Guards**   Divisions of elite Iraqi soldiers, originally part of Saddam Hussein's personal bodyguard. Best-equipped and -trained, and the most loyal to Saddam of the Iraqi forces.

**rockeye**   Five-hundred-pound cluster bomb. Each rockeye canister holds several hundred individual bomblets designed to penetrate a tank's armor.

**round down**   Rounded stern of the carrier's landing area. It is rounded so a dangerously low aircraft's hook will "slap" off of it and hopefully not tear loose.

**Rustler**   Squadron radio call sign—VA-145 Swordsmen.

**SAM**   Surface-to-air missile (generally the enemy's).

**SAR**   Search and rescue.

**SDO**   Squadron duty officer.

**skipper**   Commanding officer; also, 1,000-pound laser-guided bomb with a rocket motor attached to it for firing at the target outside the horizontal range of small arms.

**SRTC**   Search radar terrain clearance. Computer-generated radar symbology on the pilot's ADI to look forward and avoid terrain during low levels at night and in bad weather.

**SUCAP**   Surface combat area patrol.

**SV-2**   Survival vest.

**TACAN**   Tactical air navigation.

**tango uniform**   Tits up—as in flat on your back, dead. An inoperable instrument.

**TC**   Terrain clearance (short for SRTC).

**VA**   Fixed-wing attack (i.e., not a helicopter).

**VSI**   Vertical-speed indicator.

**VT fuse**   Fuse designed to detonate a bomb prior to impacting the ground in order to spread shrapnel a greater distance.

**VTR**   Video and audio mission recorder; 1960s vintage. Tapes what the flir or radar is "looking" at.

**XO**   Executive officer (second in command after the CO).


*Note:* Conversion of 24-hour clock to U.S. civilian time: Subtract 12 if hour is past 12. For example, "1320" minus 12 equals 1:20 P.M.; 1130 equals 11:30 A.M.

# Index

*Don't miss these thrilling books of American courage under fire*

# THE GUTS TO TRY
## The Untold Story of the Iran Hostage Rescue Mission

### by Colonel James H. Kyle, USAF (Ret.)
### with John Robert Eidson

Colonel James H. Kyle, the Desert-1 site Commander, was involved in every stage of the Iran hostage rescue operation. Now he spares no one, including himself, in this riveting account that takes readers from the initial brainstorming sessions and training camps to the desert rehearsals, the forward staging areas in Egypt and Oman, and finally to the desert refueling site, where he decided to abort. *The Guts to Try* is a thrilling true-life adventure—exploring America's ability to react quickly, forcefully, and effectively to acts of terrorism.

"Fascinating. . .Sometimes you want to cheer, sometimes you want to tear out your hair; but you never stop reading."
—Arthur T. Hadley
Author of *The Straw Giant*

"A BIG, BEAUTIFUL BOOK. . .
Tart and Keefe give us unprecedented glimpses
into the world of aerial reconnaissance and
into the lives of American airmen. . . .
An excellent history of a Cold War event."
—*Air Force Times*

# THE PRICE OF VIGILANCE
## Attacks on American Surveillance Flights

### by Larry Tart and Robert Keefe

Reconnaissance—intelligence gathering—
has always been one of the most highly secretive
operations in the military. *The Price of Vigilance*
brings to life the harrowing ordeals that were faced
by the steel-nerved crews, the diplomatic furor that
erupted after shootdowns, and the grief and frustration of the families waiting at home. Larry Tart and
Robert Keefe have written a real-life thriller of the
deadly cat-and-mouse game of intelligence gathering in the air and across enemy borders.

Published by Ballantine Books.
Available wherever books are sold.

*This gut-wrenching firsthand account of the war
is a classic in the annals of Vietnam literature*

# GUNS UP!

## by Johnnie M. Clark

"*Guns up!*" was the battle cry that sent machine
gunners racing forward with their M60s to mow
down the enemy, hoping that this wasn't the day
they would meet their deaths. Marine Johnnie Clark
was only eighteen when he arrived in Vietnam at the
height of the bloody Tet Offensive at Hue. The
Marines who fought and died were ordinary men,
but the selfless bravery they showed in a nightmarish jungle war made them true heroes. This book's
continuing success is a tribute to the raw courage
and sacrifice of the United States Marines.

**"A fast read that brings you inside the mind
and heart of a highly dedicated 18-year-old
Marine serving in one of Vietnam's
worst combat zones."
—James Webb
Author of *Fields of Fire***

Published by Ballantine Books.
Available wherever books are sold.

*And coming in October 2002*

# U.S. NAVY SEAWOLVES
## The Elite Hal-3 Helicopter Squadron in Vietnam

### by Daniel E. Kelly

*These warriors were in a class by themselves—
the last line of defense before certain death.*

In the Viet Cong-infested Mekong Delta, where
small SEAL teams were always outgunned and
outnumbered, discovery brought swift, deadly consequences—and a radio call for backup from the
United States Navy's very best: the Seawolves.
Dan Kelly describes the origins of this extraordi-
nary outfit. Put through a training program unlike
any other, these men emerged to perform unparal-
leled feats of courage. The stories of these elite
warriors capture America's real heroes in all their
guts and glory, and demonstrate why the
Seawolves are known as the most decorated
unit in the Vietnam War.

Published by Ballantine Books.
Available wherever books are sold.